# TROPICAL STANDARD

# TROPICAL STANDARD

## COCKTAIL TECHNIQUES & REINVENTED RECIPES

**GARRET RICHARD & BEN SCHAFFER**

PHOTOGRAPHS BY **NICO SCHINCO** • ILLUSTRATIONS BY **PEARL SHEN**

**Countryman Press**

*An Imprint of W. W. Norton & Company*
*Celebrating a Century of Independent Publishing*

# CONTENTS

# FOREWORD

## Dave Arnold

You are holding the first-ever synthesis of modern bar techniques and tropical drinks. On one hand, it strikes me as odd that it has taken so long for a book like *Tropical Standard* to be written, because tropical drinks—even classic ones—are ripe for experimentation with modern techniques. It is much easier today to create fresh ingredients, clear syrups, and to balance the acidity and dilution of a drink than it was in the days of Trader Vic. Modern bar techniques have been around for a while now; most are outlined in my 2014 book, *Liquid Intelligence,* and have been used in many bars, including both of my New York City bars Booker and Dax and Existing Conditions.

On the other hand, it makes perfect sense that this book had to wait for Garret Richard and Ben Schaffer to write it. Why? Because the tropical drink culture is so suffused with history—so bound to the past—that many of the great practitioners have a difficult time looking to the future. But this book proves you can do both and have it all. More than any other bartender I've worked with, Garret can weave the modern with the past. He is never beholden to history, but he does revel in it. He also never takes up new techniques just for the sake of doing so—Garret detests a gimmick—but is always in pursuit of the delicious.

I'd always hoped Garret would write a book like this, but he first needed to find the perfect partner, someone who knew his world and also had a sensibility for complexity and nuance. Ben is that perfect partner. When Ben co-wrote *The Dead Rabbit Drinks Manual* in 2015 he accomplished a monumental task: telling the story of the biggest smash-hit bar story in recent memory—a story that wasn't only about drinks but also about a caper that spanned continents, years, and was the product of multiple exceedingly talented drink makers. And Ben is the founder and editor of an online journal dedicated to the culture of rum, *The Rum Reader,* to boot! While Ben and Garret love all spirits, rum plays an appropriately prominent role.

I first met Garret in 2018 when he came to work at Existing Conditions. Immediately, I knew I was dealing with a special kind of bartender. I had never met someone who was so immersed in the world of tropical drinks, and yet also so at home in my world of liquid nitrogen, centrifuges, and carbonation. Over time I realized that Garret has an impeccable palate. I can say without hesitation that if Garret thinks a recipe is good, it is. And I say that about only a very few people. He is one of the most thoughtful bartenders I know, with every drink approached like an essay: researched, revised, re-revised, and edited for clarity of concept and taste. Someday you should be so lucky as to be across the stick from him. As a bar raconteur, he is that rare person who is immensely knowledgeable without being a blowhard. I have seen many spirits nerds attempt to stump him with questions over the years, but I've never seen them succeed.

Regarding nerding out on ingredients and techniques, Ben and Garret have decided to pull no punches in this book, and I think you should be grateful for that. Some people might not appreciate how detailed and specific the ingredient choices are, but those unappreciative folk are looking at the situation all wrong. If you make a recipe from this book, you'll know exactly where your practice deviates from theirs. I don't think the authors expect you to source the same ingredients they do, nor do they expect you to use all the techniques they use. Rather, they are giving you a window into a particular process. Giving you that window is the most generous way possible to help you on your own journey. Reading this book, even if you don't make all the recipes, will help you hone your palate and continue to build your mental repertoire of flavors. I know it has for me.

# ABOUT THIS BOOK

What follows is a course in cocktails, a cocktail history, a compendium of new and refreshed recipes, and a rare look inside the creative and analytic processes of how drinks are developed.

The genesis of it all is the searching mind of bartender Garret Richard. He brings a detailed knowledge of cocktail craft to his fascination with the rich tradition of tropical drinks. This book comprises recipes he has developed over his career: creations and re-creations of drinks in the supremely exhilarating tropical style.

Behind these recipes are simple but powerful bartending techniques. Some are foundational techniques from the tropical canon that deserve greater attention, like flash blending and ice molds. Some are cutting-edge techniques developed by culinary innovators that open new vistas for the tropical genre, like acid adjusting, sugar adjusting, and clarifying juice. Learning these techniques unlocks not just the recipes in this book, but also affords you valuable tools for creating menus of your own.

Along the way we incorporate lessons from many of Garret's mentors and icons of the craft cocktail and tropical cocktail revivals. This cast of characters is introduced in the capsule history of cocktails that begins on the next page. The basic principles and equipment needs follow that (in Foundations on page 22). But if you're ready to jump right in to recipes, start with Preparations (on page 34).

Please follow along with updates, videos, and event announcements at our website, **tropicalstandard.com**.

## TROPICAL DRINKS:

# The First Eight Million Years

A tall, bedewed glass of ruddy gold elixir, nestled among gems of frost, studied and soaked up in the swaying shade near the susurration of the sea. The tropical drink conjures up its own optimal scene in which it occupies center stage. But the tropical drink is not just a prop in a tropical setting. It's a celebration of the bounty and flavors of tropical produce and a contemplation of the history of tropical populations.

The surface of the Earth nearest its equator, the region known as the tropics, receives more direct sunlight throughout the year than areas closer to the poles. This higher energy input has allowed tropical vegetation to grow faster and to produce offspring more rapidly, thereby accelerating the evolution of new species. Accordingly, the tropics have the richest biodiversity of any region on the planet.

The Earth's tropical and subtropical regions have given rise to a huge number of globally important food crops: sugarcane, citrus, coffee, tea, cacao, banana, pineapple, coconut, tomato, chile pepper, bell pepper. Also found in the regions are mango, papaya, avocado, guava, pomegranate, kiwi, dates, passionfruit, soursop, lychee, rambutan, mangosteen, tamarind, akee, jackfruit, durian, breadfruit, cashew, macadamia. And spices we've come to depend on, like black pepper, vanilla, cinnamon, ginger, turmeric, allspice, clove, nutmeg, mace, cardamom, kola nut. And staples now consumed globally, such as rice, potato, corn, yam, taro.

Tropical flora is the bedrock of the world's culinary menu—and of its cocktail menu. Whether as juice, sweetener, spice, or distilled into a spirit, tropical produce brought forth tropical drinks: a broad category encompassing recipes with a strong Caribbean heritage as well as waves of American imitations and innovations of drinks of that heritage. Tropical drinks wind together the traditions of the American cocktail, Indo-European punch, and multifarious strands of Caribbean coolers.

Recent DNA studies have traced the common ancestor of citrus species to the monsoon region of Southeast Asia about eight million years ago. As citrus is at the core of our conception of tropical drinks, that's where the story must begin. Fruit is destined to be eaten, its juices absorbed, and its seeds moved down the line. Many creatures took caloric advantage of this citrus progenitor, perhaps even after noble yeast had arrived on a dropped fruit in a frenzy of fermentation, thereby creating the world's first juice and alcohol medley. But humans were not among the revelers, as their debut was still a few million years in the future.

## Cocktail Crossroads

Fermentation, the origin of all alcohol, is a spontaneous, natural process caused by microscopic fungi that pervade the air, known as yeast. Yeast targets organic matter containing sugar, consuming the sugar and generating alcohol. Starchy vegetation also works for their purposes, as the starch can first be converted to sugar by other fungi. Most human societies noticed this occurrence and leveraged it to enjoy a range of mildly alcoholic beverages, such as chicha, pulque, mead, beer, and wine from rice, palm, grapes, and other fruits.

Distillation, the concentration of alcohol made possible by the different evaporation temperatures of water and alcohol, is not a natural process. It requires intent, understanding, and apparatus. Our ancient forebears made these discoveries early in the development of civilization. Archaeological excavations have found seven-thousand-year-old Mesopotamian ceramic equipment resembling basic stills, and similar finds in India have been dated to at least two thousand years ago. Distillation was later discovered independently by the Greeks and Arabs. From Arab scholars, the knowledge reached Europe around the twelfth century. The eighteenth-century French epicure Jean Anthelme Brillat-Savarin marveled at the universal "thirst for a kind of liquid which nature has sheathed in veils, this extraordinary need which acts on every race of mankind."

When European colonists arrived in the tropics, they missed their homegrown hooch. In India, there were no grapes to be made into wine for the Portuguese or barley to become beer for the English. Instead, colonists adapted to the drinks available locally, which included sugarcane distillate flavored with locally available citrus and spices. By the 1650s, this mixture would achieve fame as punch, which dominated Eurocentric drinking culture for more than a century.

The botanic bounty of the tropics, as exemplified in the ingredients of punch, awed the Europeans. This was the real payday they sought overseas: Once gold was pulled from the ground it was gone, but the wealth from crops could be regenerated over lifetimes. And what new crops they found: fascinating, richly flavored flora that effortlessly eclipsed the cabbage back home.

Crops could also be expanded to additional fertile lands. The colonizers made imported Asian sugarcane the primary moneymaker of their Caribbean territories. To run their enormous plantations, they first enslaved native populations, then brought millions of Africans and South Asians across the seas in bondage.

Metaphorically, both a crossroads and a cocktail are where disparate elements come together. In the Caribbean, the mixing of African, Asian, and European cultures and cultivars, though for rapacious purposes unconcerned with the horrendous effects on human life, brought together the necessary conditions for new classes of cuisine, including the cocktail itself.

## Cocktail Commencement

In eighteenth-century North America, Caribbean rum, European wines, and punches concocted therefrom continued to form the foundation of drinking. By the time of the establishment of the United States, domestically produced whiskey was on the rise. It was rough stuff to help rough characters get through their days of toil.

When whiskey was mixed with sugar and bitters, the cocktail was born. As William Grimes observed in his history of American drinking, *Straight Up or On the Rocks,* "The prevailing virtues of warmth and nourishment were giving way to refreshment and stimulation; the communal atmosphere of the tavern and hostelry to the less settled patterns of the barroom; and the punch bowl to the individual drink, often idiosyncratic, crafted individually for each customer." Drinking as a pure leisure activity, rather than as a medicinal or caloric concern, reached wider audiences.

The industrialization of ice, beginning in 1806, added a crucial component to the cocktail's catalog of ingredients, and the American drinking scene never looked back (excluding a few recent headline-seekers who have pretended room-temperature cocktails are delicious). In 1862, veteran barman Jerry Thomas published *How to Mix Drinks, or the Bon-Vivant's Companion,* the first bar recipe manual, which was absolutely full of ice: shaved, cracked, and lump (all of which would have been produced per drink by bartenders, hewn from large blocks with icepicks). Thomas laid out the categories of mixed drinks as they were practiced: punches, sours, flips, toddies, cobblers, juleps, slings, and cocktails. These classic forms would become the bar pantheon.

H. L. Mencken later dubbed this era the Golden Age of American Drinking (circa 1865–1900), when barkeeps reigned supreme and new concoctions were constantly under development. American mixed drinks spread far and wide, with London, Paris, Vienna, and other European capitals introducing "American Bars" to their stately hotels.

In the Caribbean, Cuba became the standard-bearer for cocktails, with its bars flourishing alongside the Bacardí rum business that fueled them. Its influence is personified by one man, Constantino Ribalaigua Vert, born near Barcelona in 1888 and raised in Havana. He followed his father into the bar trade at age sixteen, later joining the staff at the Café Restaurant la Florida, fondly known as El Floridita. He turned out many perfectly inflected Daiquiris while expanding their ranks with variations in ingredients and technique. He bought the place in 1935 and remained a calm, industrious presence there until his death in 1952. Along the way, El Floridita became perhaps the first "destination" bar on an international scale. Prohibition in America encouraged its citizens to seek drink on foreign shores, but it was the skill of the local bartenders that made those bars a success.

Another method of taking cocktails global was employed by writer Charles H. Baker Jr.: go everywhere and make cocktails there. His extensive travels, often to tropical climes, often in the company of other expats, and often involving a yacht, were chronicled in his articles for leading culinary magazines, but most importantly in *The Gentleman's Companion* of 1939, a work full of surprising examples of food and drink picked up or invented on his voyages and couched in his dryly witty prose. His convivial tinkering was inspired and comprehensive enough so that, no matter which new drink you're working on, you're liable to find that he explored it first. Baker was a proponent of "world cuisine" at a time when meat and potatoes were standard fare for most Americans, though his interaction with other cultures was always at the remove of his privileged status as a wealthy adventurer.

## Polynesian Pretenders

The islands of the South Pacific, in American and European imaginations, have been ascribed Edenic significance that says more about the imaginers than the imagined. True, Polynesia is remote from Europe and North America, which is an important first step for those who wish to escape those places. In the islands of their yearnings, one merely plucks nature's bounty as it droops from overburdened fruit trees, rather than scratching sustenance from played-out fields—or, even worse, an office desktop. The fabled tropics were a notional place where easy living welcomed all, and dreamers like Robert Louis Stevenson, Paul Gauguin, Herman Melville, and Frederick O'Brien made a living selling those dreams to other dreamers. O'Brien in particular had great influence, though he is little remembered today. His series of romanticized travelogues on the Marquesas Islands, Tahiti, and Samoa captivated readers throughout the 1920s with its promise of these destinations as deliverance from quotidian woe.

"Damn O'Brien!" is the first line of Caroline Guild's memoir of moving to Tahiti in 1923 with her husband and young daughter, when it was clear from the start that the island had no particular monopoly on effortless bliss, and that furthermore no one there was waiting to welcome her family as living gods. She later employed the term "O'Briens" to refer to foolish dreams, but settled into an appreciation of the realities, rather than the expatriate romanticizing, of Tahiti.

Another traveler found what initially eluded the Guilds in Tahiti. As a boy, Texas native Ernest Raymond Beaumont Gantt sailed on his grandfather's yacht from New Orleans to Port Antonio, Jamaica, and as a young man, he took to the sea again. He berthed in ports of call in Tahiti, India, China, Singapore, Hong Kong, Brunei, Borneo, Japan, and various points in Africa, the Caribbean, and Central and South America. But he found his O'Brien paradise in Hawai'i.

Gantt later wrote of a 1929 voyage, his third to the Hawaiian Islands, "The Captain took a leisurely course to the southwest so the crew could take in the beauty of Oahu, and the lovely cloud covered, mist enshrouded Ko'olau Mountains. . . . Rounding Diamond Head Crater, we sailed quite close to the shore towards the port of Honolulu. . . . I experienced the fragrance and aromas of the pungent earthy scent of the tropics. It was like a wet blanket soaked in a floral perfume. . . . The scene always comes back to me in living color any time I smell frangipani, tuberose or ginger."

After visiting his brother who was working as an extra in Hollywood, Gantt settled in Los Angeles and began a bootlegging enterprise. With the end of Prohibition, Los Angeles no longer lacked booze, but it still lacked the fragrance of the frangipani off Diamond Head. Combining Caribbean rum, Cantonese cuisine, and Polynesian fantasy, Gantt opened Don's Beachcomber Café, which transformed into the phenomenon of Don the Beachcomber even as he himself took on a new life as Donn Beach. (Why the difference in spelling? Part of the manufacturing of a mystique, we suppose.)

"Even the most cursory survey of the native customs of the town could not ignore the original Beach Comber Bar, located in the premises of a not too chic hotel in the vicinage of Hollywood Boulevard, just around the corner from Grauman's Chinese Theater," journalist Lucius Beebe wrote in 1936. "This tropic oasis, maintained by an authentic sort of card known simply as Don the Beachcomber, already has fourteen imitators in California alone. It seats no more than sixty at a pinch; serves the biggest Daiquiri cocktails ever seen (about the size of a fire bucket), and is jammed to the guards with hard-cash customers as long as its doors are open." Tropical drinks seized Americans on their own soil, no steamship trip required, and they didn't even have to crack a Frederick O'Brien book.

The Planter's Punch is a cocktail descended from the Indo-European punch tradition of rum, lime, sugar, and spice but in an individual serving. It was a staple in Jamaica, where Donn may have learned of it on his first trip to Port Antonio. His own creations drew heavily on the Planter's Punch structure, but multiplied its ingredients with sophisticated, nuanced layerings of flavors not before seen in tropical drinks. One of Donn's strategies for developing flavor combinations was a technique that a century later would be familiar to bartenders as the "Potato Head" approach: swapping elements in and out from existing recipes. Instead of lime, how about a medley of citrus? Instead of sugar, how about flavored syrups? Donn placed special emphasis on spice, bringing tropical flavors like cinnamon and vanilla into his drinks. The format served him well; Donn went on to invent scores of cocktails in this vein, which he called his "rhum rhapsodies."

Victor Bergeron Jr. operated Hinky Dinks, a rustic barbecue joint in Oakland, California. His visit to Don the Beachcomber in Hollywood in 1937 left him as impressed as the rest of the guests, but unlike the rest, he negotiated with Donn for the purchase of some Polynesian artifacts and began the transformation of Hinky Dinks into Trader Vic's. Like Donn, he set out for the Caribbean, to Havana via New Orleans, for cocktail inspiration to revamp his drink menu.

Vic's drinks, like Donn's, grew from the places where he learned his cocktail history. El Floridita in Havana was his Yale College and his Harvard. In *Trader Vic's Book of Food and Drink* of 1946, Constantino Ribalaigua Vert is identified as "the greatest master of rum mixing," and Vic followed Constantino in expanding human knowledge of Daiquiri variations.

After their Tahitian sojourn, Caroline Guild and her family, originally from Boston, eventually found their way to San Francisco—and into tropical drink legend—when an encounter with a prototype beverage created by Trader Vic prompted Guild to offer the Tahitian praise "*maita'i*," or "good." Thus, the Mai Tai, with its Caribbean rum and curaçao, French orgeat, and Asian lime and sugar—an amplification of the Daiquiri concept—received its Polynesian benediction from an old money Yankee.

Donn, Vic, and their rapidly increasing bevy of imitators went on to open bar-restaurants throughout the world with the potent combination Donn had concocted: Caribbean punches, Asian cuisine, and *ambiance* borrowed from the short story "Rain" by W. Somerset Maugham. Establishments serving tropical drinks flourished from the 1930s through the 1960s.

But while some originals hung on into the

1980s (with a select few still flash blending today), as with cocktail culture as a whole, classic purveyors and the tropical drinks they offered entered dark days. Carefully crafted cocktails were spurned by a new generation, who preferred uncomplicated "disco drinks" or sought their kicks with other substances entirely. During this nadir, surviving tropical bars preserved the practice of tropical drinks and, through their time-capsule menus, cocktails in general. Cocktails would persist, just out of view, until they were so thoroughly forgotten that their recovery could become a cause.

## Resurgence

The feeble state of cocktails in the 1980s drew the attention of those who knew it didn't have to be that way. Joe Baum, the veteran restaurateur behind landmark projects such as the Four Seasons, La Fonda del Sol, Tavern on the Green, and Windows on the World, planned to return the Rainbow Room atop Rockefeller Center to the art deco glory of its 1930s heyday. Evoking that era would necessarily mean getting the drinks right, a task mainstream bars had abandoned for some time. But Baum possessed an uncommon knowledge of hospitality arcana, so he sent his bar manager, Dale DeGroff, to pick up Jerry Thomas's classic book—without mentioning that even its most recent edition had been out of print for several decades.

In Thomas's *How to Mix Drinks,* the exuberance of the secret fraternity of conviviality bursts from the pages. Consider the description of punch, the first recipe delineated in the book: "To make punch of any sort in perfection, the ambrosial essence of the lemon must be extracted by rubbing lumps of sugar on the rind, which breaks the delicate little vessels that contain the essence, and at the same time absorbs it. This, and making the mixture sweet and strong, using tea instead of water, and thoroughly amalgamating all the compounds, so that the taste of neither the bitter, the sweet, the spirit, nor the element, shall be perceptible one over the other, is the grand secret, only to be acquired by practice."

A "grand secret," and several ancillary secrets, are revealed, resulting in an "ambrosial essence." It's a long way from pushing beers and shots. Dale was caught up in the inspirations he found in *How to Mix Drinks,* following the trail to later cocktail tomes, especially those recording midcentury bacchanalia such as Ted Saucier's *Bottoms Up.* The Rainbow Room's Promenade Bar became a showplace for drinks that hadn't passed over a bar top in a generation.

On his opening menu of December 1987, Dale revived classic drinks like the Algonquin, Americano, Between the Sheets, Bronx, Florodora, Jack Rose, Planter's Punch, Sazerac, Sidecar, Stork Club, and 20th Century—and the Manhattan, Martini, Negroni, and Old Fashioned.

But the revival was not just about the recipes, even though they declared the return of cocktails as a culinary experience. And it was not just about the time-honored techniques that needed to be studied and mastered anew to produce those recipes. It was an opportunity to synthesize, to improvise, to recombine tricks and ingredients from old books into new but historically connected concoctions. At the Rainbow Room, Dale's drinks were historically accurate, but he nonetheless nudged them a bit into the future. Their success was heralded by a grateful public (and a busy press office). Cocktail drinking had been returned to a conduct of great merit.

A few years into the Rainbow Room's triumphant return, a bar built on antithetical propositions opened in a small, secluded space behind an unmarked door on the second floor of a Japanese restaurant in the East Village of New York. Angel's Share, opened by prolific restaurateur Tadao Yoshida in 1993 without pomp, circumstance, or public relations, and without a panoramic view of Manhattan, instead focused on the quiet contemplation of classic cocktail recipes as they were understood in the Tokyo bars that had sprung up after World War II. In addition to its exacting re-creations of standards like the Martini and Daiquiri, the menu grew to incorporate flavors from Japanese cuisine, while staying true to the formats of classic recipes—where shiso, for example, replaced mint in a julep.

Angel's Share drinks, especially after a revamping by Shinichi Ikeda starting in 1996, were unusual in the New York of that time, but its atmosphere even more so, as crowds and noise were banished with strict policies against standing, shouting, and groups larger than four. The Shiso Julep may not be on menus worldwide, but if searching for a secret door behind which serious bartenders in ties and vests crack out classics sounds familiar, that may be Angel's Share's primary legacy.

It certainly influenced Sasha Petraske, a customer who liked Angel's Share so much he sought to re-create it, eccentric regulations and all, at the even tinier Milk & Honey, which arrived on December 31, 1999, on Manhattan's Lower East Side. He reproduced the staff's formal wear and focus on the classics, but eschewed menus, preferring to remove all barriers between the minds of bartender and imbiber. One merely spoke a few words of preference, and a drink was created.

Even though, unlike the original speakeasies, Petraske's business was legal, he made gaining entrée into Milk & Honey difficult, ostensibly to avoid noisy crowds that would agitate neighbors on the bar's sleepy block. His methods ultimately influenced a "speakeasy revival" phase of hospitality in the craft cocktail movement, with imitators adopting similar practices merely for their perceived cachet, belying the original functional intent. Petraske went on to build an empire of bars throughout New York, London, Los Angeles, and Melbourne.

Somewhere on the spectrum between the unrestrained American maximalism of the Rainbow Room's Promenade Bar and the monastic seclusion and study of Angel's Share came Dale's sequel project. Blackbird, which opened in Midtown Manhattan in April 1999, would be the only bar he would co-own, and the last at which he had a permanent shift behind the stick, before undertaking decades of consulting and mentorship. Blackbird only lasted nine months, closing just before Milk & Honey opened, but in that time it pioneered many of the menu inspirations and bar techniques the craft cocktail movement has come to rely upon. At the Rainbow Room, Joe Baum required the drinks to be historical; at Blackbird, Dale could write his own history. (For a prime example, see the discussion of the Whiskey Smash in our recipe for the Silver Lake Smash, on page 74.)

Crucially, Blackbird was also where Dale brought on Audrey Saunders, a zealous cocktail experimentalist who would become the mentor to a whole generation of bartenders. After Blackbird, she went on to open a series of well-received, innovative bars, culminating in the Pegu Club of 2005. Named after a Victorian-era British officers' club, the Pegu

Club was a redoubled commitment to the cocktail mission, promoting the heritage of gin and nuanced bitter-sour combinations to an audience raised on syrupy vodka and canned juice contrivances—and winning them over in droves. Many of the Pegu Club's talented staff went on to found bars of their own, where they continued to promulgate Audrey and Dale's rigorous, historically grounded approach to drinks.

While New York was clawing its way back to cocktail civilization, a screenwriter in Los Angeles was scrambling to save recipes from rapidly disappearing tropical bars. As a child, Jeff Berry had admired colorful drinks in fanciful glassware as waiters lofted them through the elaborately decorated Chinese restaurants he attended with his family. When he reached drinking age, the Tiki-Ti, a tropical oasis on Sunset Boulevard, became his living room.

But by the 1980s, landmark tropical palaces like Ah Fong's, the Islander, the Luau, and the Don the Beachcomber flagship in Hollywood had shuttered. Jeff determined that because he wanted to quaff these cocktails forever, and the bars that served them might not be around in that timeframe, he'd have to learn how to do the job himself. The first problem was the recipes' secrecy. Jeff began haunting the remaining bars and befriending their longest-serving bartenders, as well as trawling secondhand bookstores for Trader Vic's out-of-print oeuvre. He reaped a prolific harvest, with his painstaking research informing a series of recipe books, including *Grog Log* (1998), *Intoxica!* (2003), *Taboo Table* (2005), and *Sippin' Safari* (2007), issued under the scholarly title of Jeff "Beachbum" Berry.

## Confluence

As Dale had brought the works of nineteenth-century bar artists like Jerry Thomas back into the hands of bartenders and their guests once again, so Jeff did with the lost masterpieces of Donn, Vic, and their contemporaries. Based on these combined efforts, craft cocktail bars and tropical bars steeped in a craft cocktail sensibility began their efflorescence across the globe. The drinks were being made and enjoyed once more, and in more and more places.

Of course, not every flowering bud traces its roots to Dale DeGroff and the Rainbow Room; the contemporaneous and just as influential Dick Bradsell worked most every reputable and disreputable bar in London, and our movement has many more heroes besides. But America was in an especially precarious situation, having to dig itself out from the hole formed by Prohibition, rediscovering knowledge that was lost completely while other locations merely dealt with changing fashions.

By the twenty-first century, clever bar creators made efforts to merge the craft cocktail and tropical strands. Honolulu-born Julie Reiner brought tropical ingredients to classic but nontropical cocktail formats in New York projects like the Flatiron Lounge and the lanai-inspired Lani Kai. Painkiller (later known as PKNY) from Giuseppe González and Richard Boccato proudly put blenders back into service, unleashing their power on the tropical canon of the midcentury masters.

At "modern speakeasy" PDT, Jim Meehan, a Pegu Club alumnus, brought a shrewd eye to adjusting the classical canon into a panoply of new drinks (later cataloged in the *PDT Cocktail*

*Book*), while Don Lee, a former IT administrator who drank at Pegu Club before graduating to working shifts at PDT, popularized an influential cocktail genre with fat-washed spirits.

Dave Arnold, head of the first-of-its-kind culinary technology department at the French Culinary Institute in New York, built a bar in the back of Momofuku Ssäm Bar in the East Village, naming it after his children Booker and Dax. It was soon full of technology such as centrifuges, liquid nitrogen canisters, and rotary evaporators, with every machine in the service of making delicious drinks that couldn't be made without them.

Perhaps it was inevitable that these two technical adventurers, Don and Dave, would join forces on their next bar project, Existing Conditions. Among its achievements, it showed that the employment of unusual practices to achieve heightened flavors did not mean sacrificing the bar's casual, civilized, neighborhood feeling.

## The Next Wave

From the books of Jeff "Beachbum" Berry and Dale DeGroff, from observing the talents displayed by Jim Meehan, and from on-the-job training by Julie Reiner and Jim Kearns, Garret Richard began to build his own store of bar knowledge. It first came together as a series of pop-up evenings, known as Exotica, held seasonally in New York starting in 2017. Each event featured its own menu of renovated classics from the tropical canon, retooled with modern strategies and ingredients.

From its start at Jim Kearns's Slowly Shirley, the evenings moved to Meaghan Dorman's Raines Law Room in the William Hotel, where head bartender Jimmy Colon joined proceedings as an enthusiastic collaborator. The central concept behind Exotica, that tropical drinks were classics worth rediscovering through the lens of new techniques, subsequently inspired the development of this book.

Garret also studied under Dave and Don at Existing Conditions, serving in its merry band of nitrogen dispensers from 2018 until its closing in 2020—like many great bars, a casualty of the coronavirus pandemic. It was there that the mechanics of acid adjusting and sugar adjusting were revealed to Garret, powerful techniques that could break through the most sizable challenges in the adaptation of tropical drinks.

In 2021, Garret joined St. John Frizell and Stephen Bielawski on a new bar project, the Sunken Harbor Club in Brooklyn, which shared many of Exotica's goals. It became an established haven for the enjoyment of tropical classics and the first showcase of several of the drinks designed for this volume.

As part of these refounded traditions, this book is designed as a guide for bartenders intending to explore the possibilities of innovative techniques while also touring the rich trove of tropical drink history. These are the elements, assembled by adept hands, that will advance the next phase in the development of tropical drinks. We behold that next wave, just over the horizon.

# FOUNDATIONS

The recipes in this book are based on certain “rules of the road.” Some rules are known in bars throughout the world and some have been designed for the recipes that follow. If something sounds odd later on, check back here. A list of equipment needed for the recipes can be found at the end of this section, under Tools, starting on page 29.

While we believe anyone can follow and reproduce the recipes in this book, it’s not meant to be an introductory text on the art of making cocktails. For those setting out on their first bartending adventure, an elegant entrée to bar skills like juicing, shaking, and garnishing, along with classic recipes, can be found in the pages of *The Bar Book: Elements of Cocktail Technique*, by Jeffrey Morgenthaler and Martha Holmberg. Dale DeGroff’s *New Craft of the Cocktail* and Jim Meehan’s *PDT Cocktail Book* will widen and deepen your recipe and history knowledge.

When it comes to the realm of the tropics, there is one true source, the mentor of us all: Jeff “Beachbum” Berry. His *Sippin’ Safari* is a significant investigation of tropical drinking at its midcentury height, and the scope of the tale expands in *Potions of the Caribbean* to take in the grandeur of the genre’s geographic sweep. He is our master storyteller.

The envelope-pushing technical experimentation that inspired many of the recipes in this book comes via Dave Arnold, who outlines his inimitable mad scientist theories in the fascinating *Liquid Intelligence*. When you want to know everything about nitro-muddling, vacuum-infused garnishes, and making a toddy with a red-hot poker, Dave delivers.

But perhaps the best way to learn about cocktails is by closely observing the work of talented bartenders at your favorite bar. They may even entertain polite questions in moments of their brief repose, though much can be learned merely from watching the movements of their distinctive shakes and stirs.

## Ingredients

To portray the flavor of each drink with precision, particular brands are specified in the recipes. We also occasionally suggest alternatives, and note their impact on the drink's characteristics.

Depending on the availability of ingredients in your area or your own preferences, you may choose to make substitutions to explore these recipes in your own way. We're happy for you to use the recipes as guidelines or as gospel, as long as the results work for you.

Note that drink recipes use traditional measurements (ounces, teaspoons, and so forth), whereas recipes for ingredients, such as syrups and tinctures, are given in metric units. These recipes require precise amounts, which is much easier to achieve measuring in grams and milliliters, especially as spirits are already sold in metric sizes in the United States. The weight of ice in frozen drinks is also given in grams, as it's important to measure ice by weight and not volume; that the traditional measurements of both are called ounces often leads to confusion.

The ingredients for each recipe are given according to a common approach in craft cocktail bars: first bitters and tinctures, then granulated sugar, then juices, then syrups and cordials, and then spirits. (Soda water or sparkling wine, if applicable, comes at the end.) Within each category, ingredients are listed from smallest to largest amount used. The strategy is to keep the most voluminous and expensive ingredients until the end, in case of error or accident.

## Ice

Let's take a moment to praise ice in all its mixological forms. While often taken for granted, ice is central to almost all mixed drinks.

### DILUTION

It's probably not foremost on your mind as you sip a drink, but dilution is a huge part of what you're experiencing. Dilution is simply how much water, usually in the form of melted ice, is in the final drink. We usually think of ice in a drink primarily in terms of temperature, but many bartenders are obsessed—and rightfully so—with the challenges of dilution. But the two move together. As Dave Arnold told us, "If there's a difference in dilution, there's also a difference in temperature." (You can read his detailed investigation of ice and its properties in *Liquid Intelligence*.)

Dilution is the key to every ingredient's flavor standing on its own. Water is vital to the enjoyment of the balance of sweet, sour, strong, and bitter, bridging the gaps between those disparate flavors. Tropical drinks live and die by their water content. With proper dilution, the complex flavors of complex ingredients are revealed.

The recipes in this book pay special attention to the techniques, such as flash blending and acid adjusting, that will aid your quest for ideal dilution.

## TYPES OF ICE

The size of a piece of ice is determined by what it needs to do in the drink, as is described throughout the book. In some drinks, two kinds of ice are used in order to apply the properties of each, or to interpolate between their properties.

"Size and temperature are the two most definitive factors," Richard Boccato, who expanded his bar career into Hundredweight, a service producing precision ice for bars and restaurants, told us. "Clarity, opulence, mineral purity—those are nice, and they definitely make a presentational difference when the drink goes over the bar—but size and temperature are the only things that will really make an existential difference in your cocktail. If you are able to master those two factors, then you've got a successful drink in your hand."

Clear, flaw-free ice is a result of what's known as directional freezing. As water freezes, impurities and air are pushed into the still-liquid parts. If you've got an ice cube tray in your freezer, the water is completely surrounded by cold air, so it freezes from the outside in, trapping those impurities at the center of each cube. To combat this issue, Sasha Petraske and Toby Maloney at Milk & Honey pioneered a method of freezing ice in pans, removing the cloudy layer, and cutting the remaining clear ice into variously sized cubes. Home tinkerer Camper English later developed an ingenious method of producing clear ice in an insulated cooler within a freezer (explained on his website, Alcademics).

However, directional freezing and absolute purity are chiefly presentational issues that don't affect the flavor of a drink. If the water coming out of your tap is all right, it's good enough for ice. For our purposes, silicone ice molds or trays are sufficient, in the three cube sizes described in the following section.

Note that silicone can sometimes exhibit a characteristic odor, whereas brands using thermoplastic polyurethane tend to be odor-free. Additionally, silicone molds and the ice inside them can pick up odors from foods in your freezer. To prevent this, we recommend placing the trays inside sealable bags in the freezer.

Adding ice to the shaker, mixing glass, or mixing tin should always be the final step before shaking, stirring, or blending (unless otherwise stated in a recipe's directions). You want the ice to meet the other ingredients at the last moment, starting the clock on dilution only when the drink is close to being served.

### Small Cubes

What we refer to as small ice cubes are analogous to those produced by Kold-Draft machines, the favored ice equipment of the craft cocktail revival. Kold-Draft cubes measure 1¼ inches per side, with their sturdy dimensions allowing the cubes to survive the ballistic standards of cocktail shaking while also melting more slowly in the glass.

Ice molds in an approximate size, between 1 and 1½ inches, will do the job. Automatically made refrigerator ice cubes are generally of the wrong size and density for our purposes.

### Medium Cubes

A 2-inch cube has long been the standard of many Japanese cocktail bars and was revived in the United States by craft bartenders looking to more closely emulate nineteenth-century drinks based on ice carved from blocks.

**Large Cubes**

The current style for presenting drinks "on the rocks" is to favor one big rock. The smaller ratio of surface area to volume of these cocktail icebergs minimizes their rate of dilution. The size starts at around 2½ inches.

Some high-end grocery stores now offer premade cubes and spheres of this size.

**Crushed Ice and Pebble Ice**

The opposite of the large cube, crushed ice maximizes surface area, providing many small pieces of ice. It's a stalwart of the tropical drink but also of antecedents like the julep.

In its most basic and direct form, crushed ice can be attained by putting ice cubes in a bag and hitting them with a mallet. There are also hand-cranked machines designed for the purpose, and, of course, the ice makers in many home refrigerators generate this ice automatically.

Special-purpose machines, such as the consumer-grade Opal from General Electric and the industrial-grade Scotsman, produce tiny, soft, barrel-shaped bits of ice, often called pebble, nugget, pellet, or pearl ice. It's a more regular form that can be used in place of crushed ice. If you have access to such a machine, you'll be pleased with the results.

Plastic trays are available to make tiny ice in this shape, but the number of trays needed to produce ice for even one drink is preposterously high. If available in your area, a simpler approach is to buy ice by the bag from the fast-food purveyor Sonic, which employs Scotsman ice machines.

**Cracked Ice**

Take a small ice cube and hit it with a bar spoon or muddler so that it splits into two to three pieces: you now have cracked ice. With a bit more surface area than the original cube, cracked ice dilutes more quickly but still more slowly than crushed ice. It's called for in many recipes in the book that need this median approach.

**Shaved Ice and Ice Molds**

Shaved ice, also known as snow ice because it is shaved as fine as snow, can be used directly in the glass. In this book, however, shaved ice is used to construct ice molds. Ice molds are a feature of many tropical classics—still employed today at the legendary Mai-Kai in Florida—and they are discussed in their own section, Ice Molds and Shaved Ice, on page 114.

## Carbonated Water

For our recipes, choose plain water with carbonation but without any additional salts or minerals. Plain carbonated water can be referred to as seltzer, sparkling water, or soda water. Club soda and mineral water have salts and minerals naturally or added industrially—confusingly, this type is also sometimes called soda water. But in this book the term *soda water* will always mean plain water with carbonation.

We suggest buying carbonated water in small glass bottles. Glass bottles retain carbonation much more effectively than plastic bottles and are less prone to damage than aluminum cans.

## Salt

Salt is used in cooking to heighten the flavors of ingredients. It can play the same role in cocktails—as Dave Arnold has long advocated.

It's become more common for craft bartenders to add salt to stirred drinks—especially those featuring aromatized wines—but salt goes just as well with shaken drinks containing juice, as it helps separate the sweet and sour layers of the cocktail, clarifying their flavors on the tongue.

When creating a drink, many new bartenders find it challenging to find the perfect balance of ingredients. If the sweetener is too forward, they bump up the acid, but then the acid is too forward, so they bump up the sweetener to compensate. It's a constant arms race that results in the drink being both too acidic and too sweet. This book covers several techniques designed to combat this problem, including acid adjusting and sugar adjusting.

But the simple addition of salt is a key method of bridging the sugar and acid components. Since you're not increasing liquid volume by adding more and more acid and sweetener, it also helps with controlling dilution.

Salt, in solution, has a role to play in just about every drink (unless you're incorporating something that is already salty, like olive brine or preserved lemon). Accordingly, almost every recipe in this book includes a small amount of salt solution. It's simple to make and have on hand.

### Salt Solution

*The 4:1 ratio is concentrated enough to avoid meddling in a drink's dilution, yet not so concentrated that the salt won't dissolve.*

**80 grams water**

**20 grams salt**

- Combine the ingredients, mix thoroughly, and store in a dropper bottle. The solution does not need to be refrigerated.

## Fruit and Juice

Citrus is the main family of juices in tropical drinks, and it is easily juiced with a hand press. For thoughts on which to use, see our discussion of juice extraction on page 32.

An electric masticating juicer is needed to unlock the secrets of many less commonly used fruits, as described in the following sections.

Juice should always be poured through a fine mesh strainer, removing pulp as well as seeds, before you employ it in a drink.

Ideally, juice should be used the day it's produced, but it can last for two to three days in the refrigerator. Over time its flavors dissipate, so while the older juice will be safe, it won't be as full of character.

Wash all fruit first, especially before using citrus peels or shells in a drink.

### JUICING A PINEAPPLE, WITH AND WITHOUT A JUICER

Bottled or canned pineapple juice, while convenient, lacks the flavor and texture of fresh juice.

A pineapple is ready to juice when its bottom has a fruity, rather than green and vegetal, bouquet. If you find a pineapple exhibiting

## A BRIEF HISTORY of LIME

After the two-hundred-year vogue of punch, the next step in the tropical drink category could be considered to be the Daiquiri (or perhaps its antecedent, the Canchánchara). Most subsequent tropical creations have continued in the style of the mixed drink known as the sour (base spirit, citrus juice, and sweetener). For rum-based drinks, the juice is usually lime, and when multiple juices are used, lime is almost always among them.

This book is about expanding the boundaries of what tropical drinks can be, so not all our drinks are rum-based. And there's a whole section dedicated to stirred drinks that eschew fresh juice altogether (see Stirred, page 128). Even the mighty lime has been slightly demoted with the power of acid adjusting applied to other citrus (see section on acid adjusting, page 172). But as the sour style is still paramount, let's take a moment to consider citrus's significance.

While the first citrus trees are thought to have evolved in Asia millions of years ago, limes, lemons, oranges, grapefruit, and the myriad varieties you find in the grocery store were not among them. Citrus trees easily hybridize in the wild, and this natural process has brought us such bounty as the original grapefruit. From there, farmers ran with the idea. The fruits you see in the store are hybrids, or hybrids of hybrids, or hybrids of hybrids of hybrids—citrus as we know it is a fruit of human ingenuity.

The original species from which our grocery produce descend are the citron (*Citrus medica*), the mandarin (*Citrus reticulata*), the pomelo (*Citrus maxima*), the kumquat (*Citrus japonica*), and the small-flowered papeda (*Citrus micrantha*).

The lemon is a cross between the citron and the sour orange, which is itself a cross between the mandarin and the pomelo. The Key lime is a cross between the citron and the small-flowered papeda, whereas the Persian lime, the type you're most likely to find in American supermarkets, is a cross between the Key lime and the lemon. The sweet oranges we enjoy today are derived from hybrids of sweeter mandarins and pomelos, and the grapefruit is a further hybrid of the sweet orange and the pomelo.

The ancient species are still around. Even the relatively obscure papeda plays a role in the bar arts. Among its subfamily is the makrut lime (which appears throughout this book in tincture form; see the herb tincture on page 121) and the yuzu, a hybrid with the mandarin that has gained much culinary and cocktail acclaim.

But farmers have gone further, continually experimenting with hybrids to chase flavor variations, and, most importantly for their commercial goals, sugar content. The authoritative University of California Riverside Citrus Variety Collection database lists over 1,700 varieties!

The citrus varieties generally available today are quite different from—and usually much sweeter than—what was available when many classic cocktails were first devised. One of the objectives of this book is to return citrus to the bartender's control. In the following pages, we suggest methods of rebalancing sugar and acid in juice to recreate older flavors and invent new ones (see the sections on sugar adjusting, page 185, and acid adjusting, page 172), and to explain traditional practices for extracting citrus flavor beyond just juicing (see the section on preserving citrus, page 207).

Citrus trees live for about a century. The fruit you're juicing now might be from a tree patronized by Donn Beach, Trader Vic, or even Constantino Ribalaigua Vert himself.

this condition at the store, it's ready to go. If the store's pineapples are not yet ripe, they can ripen in your kitchen.

Cut off the top and bottom of the pineapple so the fruit stands flat. Cut off the skin with a sharp knife. Remove the dark black circles known as "eyes," as juicing these imparts a woodier flavor and makes the juice spoil faster.

Alternatively, if you plan to make a habit of juicing pineapples or featuring them in garnishes, a pineapple corer is a handy tool.

With a juicer: Cut the fruit into long strips and run it through a masticating juicer. A large amount of foam will form on top. Use a spoon to hold back the foam while pouring the juice through a fine strainer into a bottle.

Without a juicer: Cut the fruit into chunks and place the chunks in a bowl or shallow baking sheet. Break up the pineapple with a potato masher or muddler. This will release some juice and soften the fruit. Transfer the mashed pineapple and its juice to a blender. Blend the pineapple on high until pureed. Pour the puree through a nut milk bag. Squeeze the bag to release the juice into a bottle.

### JUICING A BELL PEPPER WITHOUT A JUICER

Bell peppers work in a masticating juicer. But in the absence of such equipment, you can still get results by finely shredding the pepper on a cheese grater, then placing the shreds in a nut milk bag and squeezing. It's a bit of work, but should produce enough juice for your drink.

### JUICING AN APPLE

Apples require a masticating juicer. To preserve the color, add 0.5 gram of ascorbic acid per 250 milliliters of apple juice. Ascorbic acid is another name for vitamin C, so if you can't find it in powdered form, you can make some by crushing a vitamin C tablet.

## Tools

Cocktail construction involves a panoply of tools. Some are essential for even the most basic bartending activities, and some have specialized, advanced applications. There's no need to rush out and buy everything at the beginning of this adventure. Choose the tools you need to accomplish recipes you want to try and build from there.

### MEASURING

#### Jigger

The main devices for measuring liquids behind the bar, jiggers come in a wide variety of styles and shapes—some of which are more decorative than functional. The design should help you consistently hit the exact measurement needed, and it's great to have jiggers with multiple measurement lines for flexibility. Some find that a wide-mouthed bell design has an advantage, but choose whichever jiggers you prefer.

#### Teaspoon Set

When you need to get in between the measures on your jigger, teaspoons are the way to go. Choose a set with ¼ teaspoon, ½ teaspoon, 1 teaspoon, and 1 tablespoon.

#### Dropper

An eyedropper is used to measure ingredients needed in minute amounts (it's generally accepted that the theoretical ideal drop is 1⁄20 milliliter). Typically, a dropper comes integrated into the cap of a bottle. Having a few 2-ounce amber glass bottles with droppers will be handy.

#### Dasher

Bitters that you purchase may have a dropper cap or a dasher cap. For homemade bitters, we recommend a wider dash top with a stainless steel spout embedded in a cork. Any bottle that can handle a speed-pour spout should be able to handle them. Dasher tops tend to work best when the bottle is about half full, so resist the urge to overfill.

#### Measuring Cup

Used primarily to measure crushed ice, this cup is vital for nailing the dilution of a flash-blended drink or creating the perfect texture for a frozen drink. Consider an 8-ounce plastic cup with a handle. Of course, the measuring cup can also be used to measure larger amounts of liquid.

#### Graduated Cylinders

Graduated cylinders are more accurate than measuring cups for precise needs; 50-milliliter and 100-milliliter sizes are the most useful.

#### Scale

A digital kitchen scale capable of measuring at least 5 pounds, which displays in grams and is accurate to at least a tenth of a gram, is necessary for the recipes in this book.

#### Refractometer

Necessary for the powerful syrup calibration known as sugar adjusting (see page 185), these devices measure the amount of solids (in our use case, sucrose) in a solution. Cheap analog versions are available for about $20, but electronic ones, costing about $150, are much easier to use. As there are many types of refractometers for different applications, make sure its scale is delineated in Brix, with a range of around 0–85.

#### Micropipette

The micropipette is a highly calibrated measuring device used in labs, and we use it for the most precise measurements, typically for volumes under 5 milliliters. This is necessary when measuring ingredients for juice clarification (see pages 217–218). If, for example, you need to measure exactly 2.65 milliliters of something, this is your answer.

### BUILDING

#### Shaker Set

Once upon a time, shaken drinks were manifested inside a Boston shaker: a metal shaker tin partially encasing a pint glass. In the full swing of the cocktail revival, a tin-on-tin system has largely replaced it. Two metal tins are lighter, allowing the bartender to shake harder, and the elimination of glass makes it safer. Choose a set of stainless steel tins where the larger half is about 28 ounces.

This system also has the added benefit of working with a drink mixer: simply use the larger half of the shaker to build your flash-blended drinks.

#### Mixing Glass and Bar Spoon

The setup for stirred cocktails is simpler than their shaken, frozen, or flash-blended cousins. One simply needs a glass in which to prepare the drink and a spoon to mix it.

In the era of Boston shaker dominance, the glass was simply the pint glass without the shaker tin. Today, many specialized mixing glasses are available. Go as ornate or utilitarian as you wish; the flavor is not affected.

Bar spoons also come in a wide variety of shapes and sizes due to the last decade's proliferation of bar gear companies. All you need is a sturdy spoon with a firm spiral that fits comfortably between your fingers. A spoon of around 40 cm in length offers clearance above the mixing glass, making it easier to rotate.

### Drink Mixer

Colloquially known as a milkshake machine or flash blender, the electric drink mixer swirls and aerates the liquid inside a shaker tin. You don't need a vintage or expensive mixer to pull this off. We suggest the Hamilton Beach DrinkMaster, which retails for around $50 and features the same industrial design cues as vintage models. See the flash blending section (page 36) for more information.

### Blender

To execute frozen cocktails properly and produce syrups effectively, you need an electric blender with significant power and variable speed control. Vitamix is the gold standard for a flexible, powerful blender, but any blenders with variable speed control will get the job done.

### Muddler

This blunt-force tool has various applications. Primarily used for crushing fresh fruit, a good muddler can also effectively break up ice to create cracked ice. Choose a model made from food-grade plastic, which is dishwasher safe. Wooden muddlers tend to splinter over time.

### Atomizer / Spray Bottle

A pump-style spray bottle accommodating 3 to 4 ounces is useful for the occasional spritz.

### Milk Frother

An electric handheld milk frother is your secret multitasker behind the bar. It can dissolve raw sugar into cocktails. It can prewhip egg whites, making them easier to measure in a jigger. It can perform as an electrified swizzle stick.

There are dozens of budget versions of this tool that can be picked up for a few bucks in the housewares section of your grocery store. These cheaper models will break after a few months. Alternatively, spend a few dollars more and get a model with a stronger motor and rechargeable battery.

### Hand Blender / Immersion Blender

A big sibling to the milk frother, the hand blender will provide more power for blending certain ingredients.

### Lewis Bag and Mallet

For crushing ice, a zip-lock plastic bag wrapped in a towel can be used in place of a purpose-built bag.

### GE Profile Opal Ice Maker

If you find yourself in thrall to the flash-blended drink, it may be time to clear counter space for this efficient and consistent source of crushed ice.

## FILTERING

### Hawthorne Strainer

A proper cocktail strainer has several requirements. It should have a short handle for ease of grip. It should fit comfortably on top of a shaker or mixing glass. It should have a tight coil to prevent leaking instead of straining. Finally, it should have a sturdy finger tab for stabilization while pouring.

**Fine Mesh Strainer**
Primarily, this tool is used to filter pulp from squeezed juices or muddled fruit. Up drinks can be poured through this strainer, but that is a personal judgment call. Constantino Ribalaigua Vert finely strained his Daiquiris to ensure a silky texture and to eliminate ice crystals. Other folks find comfort in ice crystals dancing atop a Daiquiri.

Regardless of your position on this organoleptic schism, stick with a strainer on the smaller side, around 3 inches in diameter, to fit over the glasses you will be serving.

**Basket Coffee Filter**
The reusable basket filter from a coffee maker, such as from the manufacturer GoldTone, can be used for an extremely fine strain of bitters, infusions, or juices. It sits comfortably on top of a quart container for easy pouring.

**Nut Milk Bag**
This bag is another fine straining tool, which can also be squeezed for applications where some physical force is needed.

## EXTRACTING

**Citrus Press**
The needs of home and commercial bars are vastly different in regard to this tool. Home bartenders should choose a hand press that's sturdy and can handle various sizes of fruit. One designed for oranges should work for anything from limes to grapefruits. It will also double as a mold for ice shells (see page 118).

In a commercial setting, a tabletop manual press keeps up with volume. Unlike an electric juicer, the manual press slowly extracts the juice, preserving the important oils in the peel. The more aggressive electric versions can pull bitter pith instead.

**Masticating Juicer**
A masticating juicer opens up multiple avenues to fresher ingredients. This type of juicer can handle pineapples, apples, and even ginger, squeezing every possible ounce out of the produce. We detail alternative methods without the juicer (see page 27), but this equipment is highly efficient with much less effort.

**Whipped Cream Dispenser / Cream Whipper**
This device is used to whip cream with pressurized gas, but that's not what we use it for. The pressure of the gas can also infuse flavors into spirits, accomplishing more in minutes than a traditional infusion can do in weeks. (See the Banshee on page 45 for further discussion of the nitrous infusion technique.)

**Vacuum Sealer**
An inexpensive vacuum sealer will speed up creation of syrups, infusions, and oleosaccharum.

**Centrifuge**
The Spinzall is the first centrifuge designed specifically for kitchen use. Developed by Dave Arnold, it allows the clarification of juices using techniques he pioneered at his bar, Booker and Dax. There are alternative solutions that don't require this expensive bit of kit, but again, they will not be as efficient or effective. Consider the centrifuge as something to work up to.

## GARNISHING

**Peeler**
In kitchen parlance, this would be a vegetable or potato peeler, but for bartenders, it's for making citrus peels for garnish.

For bar use, the peeler should have several features. Its blade should be serrated, allowing it to grip the fruit better and prevent cuts to your fingers. The blade should be sharp, to last a long time. And the handle should be ergonomic, with a grip that works when pulling the peeler toward you.

#### Channel Knife

Channel knives create twists or ribbons that spritz a nice amount of oil onto a cocktail. When the garnish is specified as "channeled," produce it with this knife.

#### Zester Grater

If a recipe calls for freshly grated nutmeg or cinnamon, you will need this tool.

### STORING

#### Lidded Containers

These may be the hardest working pieces of equipment in the kitchen. Storage can quickly become an issue when building a library of ingredients. Having a stack of plastic containers with lids will help organize all these juices and syrups in your refrigerator. Stock up on a few in 8-ounce, 16-ounce, and 32-ounce sizes.

#### Glass Bottles

For easier pouring, you need bottles—use them for the ingredients you grab regularly. These can be recycled from previous use or you can invest in 250-milliliter bottles, which should fit in any fridge. Glass bottles are easy to wash and, unlike some plastics, won't affect the ingredient within it. Screw tops are easiest to work with.

#### Squeeze Bottles

For the easiest pouring of all, especially for thicker ingredients like coconut mix, we recommend plastic squeeze bottles.

### GLASSWARE

Each recipe indicates the style and capacity of glass used, but the ultimate presentation of the drink, including glassware choice, is up to you.

Glasses, with the exception of Old Fashioned glasses, should be chilled in the freezer before use. These are the styles and approximate sizes we specify throughout the book:

#### Coupe and Cocktail

- Saucer-shaped coupes, both 6 ounces and 10 ounces
- The iconic Nick and Nora, 5 ounces
- Goblet with a footed base, 10 ounces

#### Old Fashioned

- Old Fashioned glass, 12 ounces
- Double Old Fashioned glass, 16 ounces

#### Highball

- Tall, thin highball glass, 12 ounces
- Pearl Diver glass, a decorative variant, 12 ounces
- Collins glass, a larger highball, 15 ounces
- Zombie glass, even larger to accommodate the eponymous drink, 16 ounces

#### Miscellaneous

- Decorative punch glass, 8–10 ounces
- Red wine glass, 14 ounces
- Hurricane glass, 15 ounces
- Glass or ceramic mug, 16 ounces
- Stemmed Pilsner glass, 16 ounces
- Large snifter, 22 ounces

# PREPARATIONS

This section explains several methods of physically combining ingredients into a finished cocktail.

Flash blending, the employment of an electrically driven spindle mixer, is a foundational technique from an earlier age of tropical drinks that has become less common these days. We will make the case for its return to your repertoire.

Shaking, the hearty exertion by which so many bartenders are judged, will be broken down by the particular needs of three categories of cocktail.

Frozen blender drinks, another historically significant category relying on the electric motor, are capable of delivering the exceptional texture critical for many recipes.

Finally, we detail the devising of ice molds—glittering prizes on which to rest your liquid achievements.

# FLASH-BLENDED

Flash blending has been overlooked by the craft cocktail revival, but it plays an important historical role in the tropical canon worthy of its own revival. Flash blending was the next leap ahead in technique after the cocktail went mainstream in the nineteenth century. The advent of electric mixers provided bartenders with a robotic exoskeleton, producing superhuman forces able to shape cocktails into new textures and frosty depths of temperature. Electric mixers got their start in the soda fountains driven by the temperance movement, but found their true calling in moving the mixed drink forward. The cocktail went electric.

Flash blending can be thought of as mechanically assisted swizzling. Instead of manually turning a swizzle stick around in a glass, you have a 1,500 rpm motor doing it for you. It's a fast method of dilution, aeration, and chilling that cannot be replicated by human hands.

The mixer circulates and aerates, because it uses a spindle or paddle rather than the blender's thin, sharp blades. It chops just enough of the ice to drop the temperature quickly, creating a layered drink with whole ice on the bottom, chopped ice in the middle, and an aromatic foam on the top. With ice in these three different roles, the drink is kept cold with less ice, preventing over-dilution.

Over-dilution can be a problem with practices common to many craft cocktail bars. These bars focus on a few systems that can be applied to a large number of drinks. This reasonable approach allows bartenders to make more drinks without having to learn additional techniques. But sometimes the techniques don't fit the drinks.

If a bar primarily specializes in pre-Prohibition classics rather than tropicals, their crushed ice drinks will be based on the julep, topped with a dome of crushed ice. That works in a julep, which is essentially 3 ounces of sweetened liquor, but the extra water can destroy a tropical drink made from a selection of intricately balanced ingredients.

Crushed ice drinks don't dilute like normal cocktails: They're often too watery or too strong. Sometimes a bar will try to solve this, not by changing the drink, but by asking customers to change their behavior. They serve a frozen swizzle drink, knowing it has a window of at most 10 minutes of drinkability, and say, "Drink it fast!" It's not a great example of hospitality; guests should be allowed their own pace, and most people aren't in the habit of slamming every cocktail put before them.

Flavors in the drink are meant to evolve and open up over time, not become drowned out by extra dilution. Using flash blending gives crushed ice drinks a larger window in which to be enjoyed.

Flash blending isn't just about using a mixer

with a spindle instead of a blade. It's about balancing amounts of ice between the mixer and the glass. By measuring ice as part of the recipe, you won't need to top up with more ice at the end, which kills the head on the cocktail.

With a measured amount of pure ice already in the glass, less ice can be used in the tin, resulting in a more aerated drink, since there are fewer solids to move around. After much experimentation, we found this formula works best: a full cup (8 ounces) of crushed ice in the tin, and half a cup (4 ounces) of crushed ice in the glass. After blending, the contents of the tin, including partially melted ice, are poured into the glass. However, there are exceptions: a few of the following recipes are strained, and some adjust the amount of ice. Our standard process for flash blending follows.

### Flash Blending 101

- Combine all ingredients in a mixing tin.
- Select glass. Measure and place ice in the glass.
- Measure and place ice in the tin.
- Place the tin into position with the mixer; the mixer's spindle should be in the middle of the liquid and ice mixture.
- Run the mixer on full power for 5 seconds; the tin should frost.
- Pour the entire contents of the tin, including ice, over the ice in the glass.
- Add garnish, if applicable. Because of the small pieces of floating ice, flash-blended drinks should be served with straws.

# Tropical Itch

*Unveiling bold flavors*

Heavy flavors like mango and cinnamon glory in the additional aeration flash blending brings, making the Tropical Itch an excellent illustration of the technique. Were it shaken, the purees would remain thick but the rest of the drink would be too watery; flash blending pulls it all together.

There are multiple traditions for the Tropical Itch recipe, created during the fiercely competitive bar climate at the height of tropical drinks' popularity in the mid-twentieth century. Serving tropical drinks was a big business pursued by restaurateurs worldwide, and poaching secret recipes and knowledgeable staff from competitors was the bar world's echo of the espionage underpinning the ongoing Cold War. The massive Hilton chain made a pact with Trader Vic to install his eponymous saloons in key hotel properties, while also hiring legendary bartender Joe Scialom to develop recipes for their resorts in Europe and the Caribbean. Keeping up in this arms race, Hilton nemesis Sheraton responded with a deal to bring the Kon-Tiki bar-restaurants to its thirsty lodgers.

Thus, a drink called the Tropical Itch was invented by Scialom, based on rum, vodka, and mango. A different drink of the same name came from Harry Yee at the Hawaiian Village Hotel (later also to come under Hilton's control) based on bourbon, rum, and passionfruit. A Kon-Tiki version was inspired by Scialom's but with gin instead of vodka.

In the Kon-Tiki formulation, the Tropical Itch shows that rum and gin can go together, but we felt it needed a boost to unlock the mango, which is where the pear eau-de-vie steps in (in fact, it usurped the need for gin at all). Mango and pear are often found complementing each other in herbal tea blends, a source of inspiration for the canny bartender. Eau-de-vie wasn't a common ingredient in the 1950s when the original was developed, but in every other aspect this version of the drink is classically designed.

The flavor of mango is enhanced by complementing it with almond, an observation that tropical bartender Bob Esmino made to Jeff Berry (see Berry's book *Sippin' Safari* for further discussion) and which we have always taken to heart. The ginger in falernum further meshes with almond. This sequence of connections comes together to scratch this particular itch.

RECIPE CONTINUES

**5 drops salt solution** (see page 27)

**6 drops almond extract**

**2 dashes Angostura aromatic bitters**

**¾ ounce mango puree** (see below)

**¾ ounce strained lime juice**

**¼ ounce falernum** (see page 232)

**½ ounce cassia cinnamon bark syrup** (see page 65)

**1 ounce Barbancourt White Rhum**

**1 ounce Purkhart Pear Williams eau-de-vie**

**Grated cassia cinnamon, for garnish**

**Mango slice, for garnish**

- Combine the ingredients in a mixing tin with 8 ounces of crushed ice. Flash blend for 5 seconds and pour unstrained into a chilled Hurricane glass (15 ounces) with 4 ounces of crushed ice.
- Dust with grated cassia cinnamon. Garnish with a mango slice. Historically, this drink would also have been garnished with a miniature back scratcher. Serve with a straw.

---

## Mango Puree, 25 Brix

Commercial fruit purees work in this drink recipe (for mango, we prefer the Perfect Purée brand, though Boiron is a brand that works well for other fruits). If these brands aren't available, look for a product with minimal water content and not much added sugar or ingredients other than the fruit itself.

However, for those willing to go that last mile, here's a homemade puree that can't be beat, and is less expensive (but that's because you're doing the work). It comes in at a sweetness of 25 degrees Brix. (See pages 185–187 for the grand explanation on Brix values.)

Mango puree can also bring tropical delight to a Bellini.

**300 grams Ataúlfo or Champagne mango, peeled, seeded, and cut into 2-inch chunks**

**150 grams water**

**90 grams white sugar**

**1.5 grams citric acid**

- Combine the mango and water in a blender. Blend on low speed, slowly adding the sugar. Once the sugar is fully dissolved, add the citric acid. Citric acid preserves the acidity of the fruit while extending the puree's usable life.
- If not to be used immediately, seal and refrigerate for use within 1 week, or freeze for later use. Makes 1 pint.

# Sub-Mariner

*Blended carbonation*

Carbonated drinks can't be shaken, as a closed container plus agitation equals an explosive mess. But for richer flash-blended cocktails, soda water is an important lengthener. Soda water opens up a drink, lowering sweetness as it provides bubbles, allowing the ingredients' full flavor to come across in a lighter mix. It's a common technique across the menu at the Tiki-Ti, as we'll also see in drinks like the Bird of Paradise (page 199) and Ray's Mystique (page 239).

The Sub-Mariner is an unconventional gin and juice with the feeling of a New England–style IPA. It's designed for the exploration of the new world of nontraditional gins with unusual botanicals. Gins outside of the typical London dry style, with fruitier or spicier notes, are the right match for this recipe.

Suntory's peppery Roku Gin is one interesting possibility that opens up a beautiful contrast with the fruit notes. Bimini Gin incorporates grapefruit, hops, and coriander—all perfect for tropical combinations. Another compelling choice, Monkey 47 Schwarzwald Dry Gin, is floral with inspiration from Germany's Black Forest.

The level of carbonation with this process is subtle, analogous to a lightly sparkling *frizzante* wine. With the Sub-Mariner's heavy hit of pineapple, carbonation also conjures a thicker head of foam, amplifying the cocktail's aroma while mounting a brilliant presentation to boot.

**5 drops salt solution** (see page 27)

**¾ ounce strained lemon juice**

**1 ounce strained pineapple juice**

**1½ ounces grapefruit punch syrup** (see page 216)

**2 ounces gin of your choice** (see discussion above)

**1½ ounces soda water**

**Grapefruit slice, for garnish**

**Pineapple leaves, for garnish**

- Combine the ingredients in a mixing tin with 8 ounces of crushed ice. Flash blend for 5 seconds and pour unstrained into a chilled Collins glass (15 ounces) with 8 ounces of crushed ice.
- Garnish with a grapefruit slice and pineapple leaves. Serve with a straw.

# Special Daiquiri No. 1

*Tropical aperitifs*

The best menus do not simply list cocktails but instead categorize them by culinary objective. Cocktails arrive at the time in an evening appropriate for each: before the meal, as an amuse-bouche, or complementing (or in place of) dessert. (See the next recipe, the Banshee, for that final division.)

The menus of midcentury tropical restaurants had this arrangement, often additionally assembling drinks by strength. Drinks from the "strong" category, like the Zombie or Rum Barrel, may have been more often examined in cocktail books, but those intended as smaller, lighter aperitifs offer their own pleasures. These smaller-sized drinks have become something of a lost art, with the Mai-Kai alone currently preserving the practice (with its Shark Bite and Special Reserve Daiquiri). Flash-blended aperitifs are small like an up drink, but morph over time like a rocks drink—except not very much time, as it's just a few sips until dinner.

Let's consider Don's Special Daiquiri from Don the Beachcomber, with its focus on passionfruit and honey. One important aspect for its execution is the use of passionfruit puree, rather than bottled juice (sometimes labeled "nectar"). This approach was pioneered by Jeff "Beachbum" Berry and also popularized by the influential Mezcal Mule at PDT.

Commercial passionfruit juice has a lot of sugar already added, along with water and citric acid—it acts more like a syrup, which limits what you can do with it. The puree is closer to cutting open a fresh piece of fruit. Passionfruit typically contains about 3 percent acid, half as tart as lemon or lime (see the section on acid adjusting, page 172, for more), and the puree retains this acidity, allowing us to treat passionfruit like an acid rather than a sweetener. Now there's space in the spec to fill with a different sweetener. Here it's honey, a complex ingredient on its own.

Honey's high viscosity makes it hard to pour and even harder to incorporate into cocktails, so cutting it with water to make a syrup is essential. However, honey already has a fair amount of water (around 18 percent of its mass), so the amount of water that needs to be introduced to make a honey-based syrup is much lower than it would be for a sugar-based syrup.

To promote honey's complexity of flavors, we favor a stronger syrup at 66 degrees Brix. If you have a refractometer (see Tools, page 29), you can calculate the amount of water required for the sweetness of your specific honey. Otherwise, the following recipe provides a reasonable approximation. (See the section on sugar adjusting, page 185, for further discussion.)

RECIPE CONTINUES

As is common in the Don the Beachcomber oeuvre, the recipe exhibits a custom blend of rums to achieve a summation of characteristics not available in any one rum. The three rums here exemplify different traditionally Jamaican profiles (with the Denizen also incorporating lighter rum from Angostura in Trinidad) that work together in harmony.

Special Daiquiri No. 1 is named with a number on the end, in the style of the various Daiquiri interpretations available at the Havana popularizer of that drink, the bar known as El Floridita (see page 58). As for the Special Daiquiri No. 2 and beyond, that's up to you. Take advantage of the space opened up by the passionfruit puree by replacing falernum and honey with other sweeteners and substituting favorite rum blends of your own.

**5 drops salt solution** (see page 27)

**1 teaspoon passionfruit puree** (such as Boiron or Goya)

**½ ounce strained lime juice**

**¼ ounce honey syrup** (see below)

**¼ ounce falernum** (see page 232)

**½ ounce Denizen Aged White Rum**

**½ ounce Two James Doctor Bird Jamaica Rum**

**½ ounce Appleton Estate 8 Year Old Rum**

- Combine the ingredients in a mixing tin with 8 ounces of crushed ice. Flash blend for 5 seconds and pour unstrained into a chilled goblet (10 ounces).
- Optionally, garnish with an ice shell (page 118). Serve with a straw.

---

## Honey Syrup, 66 Brix

**69 grams water**

**300 grams orange blossom honey**

- Boil water in a saucepan, starting with slightly more water than you need, as some will be lost during boiling. After boiling, weigh the water to be sure you have 69 grams.
- Add the honey to a separate container, then pour the boiling water into the honey. Stir until uniform. Bottle and refrigerate. It will keep for 4 weeks in the refrigerator. Makes around 12 ounces.

# Banshee

*Dairy and texture*

In the tropical restaurants of yore, just as you were on the verge of surrender, the waiter would once again present the cocktail menu, this time turned to its ultimate page: an enumeration of revitalizing postprandials incorporating dairy and chocolate. Donn Beach offered his Rum Cow, perhaps with an affectionate thought of New Orleans and its celebrated Brandy Milk Punch. Trader Vic built on this with the Banana Cow. After a night of quaffing rounds of drinks based on a plethora of citrus juice, it might be necessary to counter with something to settle the stomach.

Today's bars have largely jettisoned the tropical dessert category. One venue that has not, largely because it has survived every drink trend since 1938, is Bryant's Cocktail Lounge in Milwaukee, Wisconsin. It was there that bartender-owner Bryant Sharp conceived of cocktails like the Pink Squirrel (it's pink), the Blue Tail Fly (it's blue), and the Banshee.

Unlike Vic's Banana Cow, which dilutes its banana with a troubling 5 ounces of milk, the Banshee is a banana-centered sibling to dainty dairy delights like the Alexander and the Grasshopper. We've always liked it better with half-and-half instead of straight cream. But the real inspiration was ordering a Grasshopper from New Orleans bar legend Paul Gustings when he was behind the stick at Tujague's. Paul adds Cognac to create an Improved Grasshopper and it more than lives up to the name.

This version of the Banshee follows Paul's pattern for the Grasshopper, with banana liqueur replacing crème de menthe and Hamilton Demerara rum replacing the Cognac. The rum is not here to brazenly assert its presence but to fortify the other ingredients.

Flash blending dairy drinks confers several advantages. A bit more dilution makes the creaminess lighter and less overwhelming. The consistent chilling over the life of the drink enables you to enjoy it at a more leisurely pace; nobody wants to slam an ounce and a half of cream, and that cold, creamy drink isn't going to taste better when it warms up. Flash blending your Banshee will also create layers of texture in a manner that isn't usually found in dairy cocktails.

To layer the chocolate flavors, we're using both crème de cacao and chocolate bitters. You could use any of several quality commercial bitters, but to really kick things up a notch, Dave Arnold's recipe for bitters is simple to make—and simply amazing. It will also introduce you to a powerful technique, also originated by Dave, called nitrous infusion.

RECIPE CONTINUES

**5 drops salt solution** (see page 27)

**1 dash Dave Arnold's chocolate bitters** (see below)

**1 ounce half-and-half**

**1 ounce banana bunch liqueur** (see page 147)

**½ ounce Hamilton Demerara 86 Rum**

**1 ounce Tempus Fugit Crème de Cacao**

**Grated nutmeg, for garnish**

- Combine the ingredients in a mixing tin with 8 ounces of crushed ice. Flash blend for 5 seconds and pour unstrained into an Old Fashioned glass (12 ounces) with 4 ounces of crushed ice.
- Dust with grated nutmeg. Serve with a straw.

---

## Dave Arnold's Chocolate Bitters

### Nitrous Infusion

Dave Arnold pioneered a clever method of rapidly infusing flavor into spirits using a whipped cream dispenser (sometimes called a cream whipper). This device uses nitrogen gas in small chargers to raise the pressure of cream, instantly turning it into whipped cream, like a reusable version of the Reddi-wip can. But Dave realized that you could use the pressure of the whipper to infuse any flavor into alcohol. He called this nitrous infusion or rapid infusion.

Dave used rapid infusion in his recipe for chocolate bitters, which was deployed at Existing Conditions. There are some excellent chocolate bitters on the market, but give this recipe a try—it's on another level.

Traditionally, cacao nibs take a long time to infuse, and along the way the more unpleasant bitter notes begin to dominate over the chocolate flavors. The rapid infusion focuses on the top notes of the nibs, capturing only a beautiful chocolate aroma—so starting with a highly aromatic ingredient is crucial. Many cacao nibs we tested exhibited a flavor flatline, with only the barest rumor of an aroma. Valrhona *grue de cacao,* also known as cacao or cocoa nibs, have a consistently strong chocolate nose, making them ideal candidates for infusion.

Mace is added here for its spicy affinity with chocolate. Gentian and quassia are commonly used as bittering agents.

After booze and flavorings are added to the cream whipper, the mix is pressurized by nitrous oxide ($N_2O$) chargers. Under pressure, the vodka and nitrous oxide are forced into a solution with the cacao nibs and other ingredients. Then, when the canister is vented, the return to atmospheric pressure boils and expands the nitrous in the solution, extracting more flavor into the mix.

There are also applications where a traditional infusion would be preferred over the rapid technique. For an example, see the Cardamom Tincture on page 162.

**3 grams mace**

**1.5 grams dried gentian**

**1.5 grams quassia bark**

**100 grams Valrhona cacao nibs**

**350 milliliters 80 proof neutral vodka**

- Break up the mace. Combine all the ingredients in a cream whipper. Charge with two 7.5 gram $N_2O$ chargers. Allow the mixture to infuse for 1 hour.
- Vent all at once, with the spigot pointed up into a container to catch any spray. Let the mixture settle in the whipper until bubbling stops (around 5 minutes).
- Strain out the liquid, pressing the solids to extract the most liquid. Fine strain and bottle. Will keep indefinitely; does not need to be refrigerated. Makes 10 ounces.

# Winter in L.A.

*Blended egg whites*

Los Angeles is a region known for its indistinguishable seasons. But that only applies to the weather, not to the farmers' market. This drink is an homage to winter holiday traditions amidst the Southern California climate, starting with the bright profile of a summer drink and rebuilding it for cold weather with rich notes of spice.

Citrus is beautifully expressed in a simple sour, especially with added texture from an egg white. Flash blending simplifies the incorporation of egg whites. The texture of a flash-blended sour is light and velvety, as if it had been run through a nitro tap, with a head that sips like Guinness. Your rotator cuffs will thank you for avoiding the debate on all the different methods of hard shaking—let the electric mixer do the work.

One important improvement to egg white drinks is the application of gum syrup instead of regular simple syrup. Acacia gum, a derivative of tree sap, gives more heft and texture to the syrup. And as acacia gum is an emulsifier, it holds the egg white better in solution. Many nineteenth-century recipes used them together, and we recommend doing so, too. (See page 197 for more on gum syrups.)

If you prefer your L.A. without smoke, swap out the mezcal for a pisco such as Macchu Pisco.

**5 drops salt solution** (see page 27)

**½ teaspoon Bittermens New England Spiced Cranberry Bitters**

**½ ounce egg white**

**½ ounce strained tangerine juice**

**¾ ounce strained lime juice**

**¾ ounce gum syrup** (see page 197)

**2 ounces Alipús San Luis Del Rio Mezcal**

**Grated cassia cinnamon, for garnish**

- Combine the ingredients in a mixing tin. Flash blend without ice for 5 seconds. Add 12 ounces of crushed ice to the tin and flash blend for 5 seconds. Double strain into a chilled goblet (10 ounces).
- Dust with grated cassia cinnamon.

# Penang Punch

*Herbs without tears*

Fresh herbs, especially mint, are an exciting addition to a drink. But putting herbs in the drink mixer results in a ripped-up salad floating in chewy chunks throughout the glass. It's not pretty and it's not delicious. You can avoid this pitfall the way the Tiki-Ti and the Mai-Kai do: muddle the mint in the bottom of the glass first, then blend everything else and pour it on top. The drink receives the desired mint oils, but the leaves aren't agitated into expressing negative flavors, let alone their shredded remains.

The original Penang Punch didn't include mint, which was a later innovation in the Mai-Kai's version, known as the Zula. The mint oil acts to dry out the drink, working in concert with the herbaceous qualities of the absinthe. Over the years, we've tried it with different combinations of rums, but we're especially pleased with this lineup. For something aged but still dry and aromatic, we looked to the English Harbour from Antigua. Barbancourt White, sometimes overlooked in favor of the company's better-known Barbancourt 5 Star, has an unusual profile with similarities both to molasses-based rum and Martinican rhum agricole. It plays well with pineapple and passionfruit.

The Penang Punch, also known as the Penang Afrididi, was on the first menu at Don the Beachcomber but has been less often revived than other contemporaneous classics. The coupled crafts of muddling and flash blending makes that easy to correct.

**8 to 10 mint leaves**

**5 drops salt solution** (see page 27)

**¼ ounce strained lime juice**

**½ ounce passionfruit puree**

**½ ounce strained pineapple juice**

**½ ounce strained orange juice**

**½ ounce cane syrup** (see page 52)

**1 teaspoon Vieux Pontarlier Absinthe**

**1½ ounces Barbancourt White Rhum**

**1½ ounces English Harbour 5 Year Old Rum**

**Mint sprig, for garnish**

**Pineapple slice, for garnish**

**Pineapple leaf, for garnish**

**Vieux Pontarlier Absinthe spray**

- At the bottom of a chilled Hurricane glass (15 ounces), muddle the mint. Add 8 ounces of crushed ice to the glass.
- Combine all other ingredients in a mixing tin with 8 ounces of crushed ice. Flash blend for 5 seconds and pour unstrained into the glass.
- Garnish with a mint sprig speared to a pineapple slice and a pineapple leaf. Spray the mint sprig with absinthe from an atomizer 2 times. Serve with a straw.

RECIPE CONTINUES

## Cane Syrup, 66 Brix

Cane syrup can refer to two distinctly different ingredients that largely operate in a similar way when balancing sweet and sour.

*Sirop de canne* from Martinique is derived from boiled sugarcane juice that has been reduced to a rich syrup, usually 60 Brix. Rhum agricole producers often make the syrup with extra sugarcane juice pressed for fermentation. This process adds a subtle, grassy quality to the sweetness.

Some cocktail bars make their own cane syrup, which is simply a rich syrup (66 Brix) made with sugar derived from evaporated cane juice (often labeled in grocery stores as organic cane sugar). This method will bring texture and a slightly caramelized flavor but will lack the vegetal notes of the Martinique version.

As the two styles feature a similar level of sweetness, they can be used interchangeably, depending on what works best for you. Recommended brands of Martinique *sirop* are Petit and Rhum J.M—or make your own cane syrup with the following recipe.

**200 grams organic cane sugar**

**100 grams water**

- Combine the sugar and water in a saucepan. Bring the mixture to a simmer, stirring until the sugar is fully dissolved. Store in a bottle. It will keep for 4 weeks in the refrigerator. Makes about 10 ounces.

# SHAKEN

All drinks need proper dilution, chill, and aeration. Different methods of preparation achieve this in different ways, but with their own emphasis. Shaking a drink promotes aeration, which in turn develops texture and aroma.

Shaken drinks are meant to be enjoyed right away. Flash-blended drinks can develop over time as the ice melts, but shaken drinks are at their peak when served.

After performing many tests, Dave Arnold determined that no real difference is made by the style of shaking, in terms of temperature and dilution, assuming the drink is shaken for about 12 seconds with reasonable force and a judicious quantity of hard ice. So shake like you mean it! As Richard Boccato reminds new bartenders, "You are trying to wake it up, not rock it to sleep."

Shaking is a blunt instrument, but it can be tuned, especially for aeration and texture. The following shaking techniques emphasize appropriate aeration for the style of drink in addition to its needs in terms of temperature and dilution.

First, we'll look at up drinks, a foundational form. Then we'll analyze shaking styles indigenous to Trader Vic's and Tommy's Mexican Restaurant in San Francisco, and the hybrid shake derived from their union. Finally, we'll discuss how to optimize shaking for the particular demands of Collins-style drinks.

Note that ice needs to acclimatize a bit after coming out of the freezer; at freezer temperature, it's too brittle to withstand shaking. If the ice breaks apart too fast, it blunts the effects of our differently-sized cube setup (explained below). The simple solution is to take the ice tray out of the freezer when you begin making the drink.

## UP

An up drink is shaken with ice, then strained into a glass without ice. The aeration it gets in the shaker is especially important for an up drink, since the texture derived from aeration is all you have in the glass besides the liquid itself. Aeration also enhances aroma, which is a huge part of how a cocktail is perceived.

Two types of ice are used together in the shaker with this method. Large ice cubes whip air into the drink as it is shaken, providing proper aeration. However, larger ice takes longer to melt, which can provide a challenge with dilution and temperature. Shaking with two small cubes (providing dilution) alongside one large cube (providing texture) hits the sweet spot, delivering a tipple that has perfect composition, temperature, and alcohol content. Dave Arnold considers this approach "your best chance of providing consistent dilution and texture."

# Daiquiri

*Sugar versus syrup*

The Daiquiri has been a font of inspiration for generations of tropical drinks, reaching its maturity in the hands of legendary Havana bartender Constantino Ribalaigua Vert in the 1930s. As Audrey Saunders has written, "it's one of the most fragile, challenging drinks around. It's a stark, naked drink that doesn't lie, and if you don't get it right, it's blatant at the first sip."

The Daiquiri features a delicate balance of ingredients that showcases the properties of each, and for that it has become a favorite of today's craft bartenders, for whom it acts as a yardstick for mixing ability. However, while the classic Cuban style is based on granulated sugar, when you order a Daiquiri in a craft bar, it's most likely to contain simple syrup instead, probably due to craft bars' focus on pre-Prohibition drinks that call for syrups, and the application of the same template onto the Daiquiri. Whether Daiquiris are better with granulated sugar or simple syrup is hotly debated, and the passions on both sides have yet to be quenched—even by all the Daiquiris at stake. However, as is often the case, we have an exhaustively researched opinion.

Using syrup instead of granulated sugar adds extra water, which can drown out delicate flavors in the rum. Also, as the proof of most white rums available today is significantly lower than their vintage counterparts, the water content of the rum will already be higher, so lowering the amount of water in other ingredients is essential for balance. Therefore, try your Daiquiri with granulated sugar.

Consider that if a sour is being made with a base spirit such as whiskey or gin, there are high-proof bottlings that can be used, like 100 proof Rittenhouse or 94.6 proof Tanqueray. Today we don't have a similarly high-proof, clean, Cuban-style rum to put into a Daiquiri, so instead of removing water from the rum, we can remove it from the syrup. One tablespoon of sugar is equivalent in sweetness to ¾ ounce of 50 Brix syrup, so our syrupless recipe still conforms to Audrey Saunders's widely adopted spec of 2 ounces of rum and ¾ ounce each of lime juice and simple syrup.

An important reason bartenders prefer syrups to granulated sugar is that the standard shaking process chills the drink more quickly than the sugar can be dissolved, and the result is sugar congregating at the bottom of the glass instead of sweetening the drink as it should. Dry shaking (shaking without ice) can dissolve sugar into the drink, but that adds a cumbersome extra step to the process. Tech-savvy bartender Daniele Dalla Pola offers a neat solution: the milk frother. This coffee accessory, nothing more than a small motorized whisk, is a versatile tool, and a surprisingly brief buzz with a frother can dissolve all the sugar a drink needs.

RECIPE CONTINUES

Sugar is not the only variable in a Daiquiri. There are different types of lime. There are an astonishing number of rums. And don't forget the ice.

We'll remove two variables right away: lime choices are a bit constrained, as in the United States the most prominent lime is the Persian, although Key limes and, to a lesser extent, makrut limes are also on the market. (Generally, wherever you are in the world, locally available limes will work.) As for the ice, the Daiquiri is a perfect model for our strategy of one large cube and two small cubes in the shaker.

Which leaves us with rum. The classic Daiquiri is made with light Cuban rum. But this presents us with two problems. First of all, as Americans, we have no access to Cuban rum. (If you believe a Daiquiri can only be made with Cuban rum, this means no bar in America has made one since the embargo began in 1962.) Secondly, today's Cuban rum is not the same as the rums that existed during the Daiquiri's heyday.

Our suggestion is simple: Use whichever rum you prefer. If seeking to approximate a light Cuban, try Don Q Cristal, Angostura White Oak, or Santa Teresa Claro. There are also contemporary rums created with the Daiquiri in mind, such as Probitas, Equiano Light, Hamilton White 'Stache, and Denizen Aged White. Wray & Nephew or Rum-Bar Overproof make for deceptively quaffable variations. And there's no good reason not to use longer-aged rums or rhum agricole, although taking the Daiquiri in those directions may also be an opportunity for experimenting with other sweeteners; some suggested pairings are included in the variations that follow.

The simple, beautiful Daiquiri is a world unto itself. You might explore it for the rest of your life.

**5 drops salt solution** (see page 27)

**1 tablespoon sugar**

**¾ ounce strained lime juice**

**2 ounces white rum of your choice**

- Combine all the ingredients except the rum in a shaker, and whisk with a milk frother until the sugar is fully dissolved. Add the rum and 1 medium and 2 small ice cubes. Shake and strain into a chilled coupe (6 ounces).

## VARIATIONS

After our defense of granulated sugar in Daiquiris, here are three more with sugar—and three with syrups. The rum dictates the type of sweetener to match it with. Lighter rums favor granulated sugar, but heavier-bodied ones can stand up to syrups. Start exploring!

**2 ounces Don Q Reserva 7, ¾ ounce lime juice, 1 tablespoon organic cane sugar, 5 drops salt solution**

**2 ounces Appleton Estate 12 Year Old, ¾ ounce lime juice, ¾ ounce gum syrup, 5 drops salt solution**

**2 ounces Flor de Caña 4 Year Old, ½ teaspoon Wray & Nephew Overproof, ¾ ounce lime juice, 1 tablespoon white sugar, 5 drops salt solution**

**1 ounce Brugal Especial Extra Dry, 1 ounce Rum-Bar Gold, ¾ ounce lime juice, 1 tablespoon organic cane sugar, 5 drops salt solution**

**2 ounces Rhum J.M Blanc, ⅞ ounce lime juice, ½ ounce cane syrup, 5 drops salt solution**

**2 ounces Doorly's XO, ¾ ounce lime juice, ⅜ ounce Demerara syrup, 5 drops salt solution**

# Hemingway Daiquiri

*The snow ice of Kilimanjaro*

Among the many regular customers holding up the bar at Ribalaigua's El Floridita was noted writer and drinker Ernest Hemingway. He became more than familiar with the many subtle variations on the Daiquiri that El Floridita offered. As described in the 1934 edition of El Floridita's cocktail guide, they were: No. 1 (the classic, described on page 55, from which the others were derived), No. 2 (curaçao and orange juice), No. 3 (maraschino and grapefruit juice), and No. 4 (maraschino alone).

Ingredient enhancements were not the only distinction among the drinks. They were also prepared in specialized ways, with Nos. 1 and 2 shaken and strained, No. 3 shaken and strained over shaved ice, and No. 4 ending up over shaved ice but first going through an electric blender.

However, the precise approach to the No. 3 has fluctuated over the years. El Floridita's published 1934 recipe specified shaking and serving frappé (referring to the shaved ice presentation, from the French for an iced drink). But for expediency, even at El Floridita itself, the drink became frozen. Finally, in recent years, the drink has been served up, like a Daiquiri No. 1. The dilution of the drink, of course, differs with each approach to its ice.

But more about that in a moment. Back to Hemingway, who took to ordering the No. 3, but without sugar, and with double the rum, in the belief that this would not exacerbate his diabetes. In the 1939 printing of El Floridita's bar manual, this variant was published as an "E. Henmiway [*sic*] Special." From its big hit of booze and Hemingway's self-selected nickname, the bartenders also dubbed the drink a Papa Doble.

Let's be clear: A formula with no sugar, several acids, and a bunch of rum is nowhere close to a balanced drink. We wonder if this off-menu order would be as widely known if it had been attributed to a noncelebrity. As it is, a needy customer's questionable request has made its way into the canon. But not actually in the form Hemingway quaffed it.

Constantino's snowy shaved ice makes a significant impact on how the drink is perceived: The slushier consistency opens the aromatics and tames the ingredients much more than the high-acid version produced by simply straining into a coupe. Yet the latter is how it's made in craft cocktail bars today. The influential turning point may be Charles Schumann's *Tropical Bar Book* (1986 in German, 1989 in English), where he lists the "Ernest Hemingway Special"—exactly the Cuban ingredients, though in different proportions, but without mention of the special ice preparation. It became a shaken and strained drink like many others.

From there, Dale DeGroff featured the drink at the Rainbow Room, bestowing upon it its most evocative name—the Hemingway Daiquiri. However, Dale made the crucial addition of simple syrup, analogous to the teaspoon of sugar in Constantino's original Daiquiri No. 3. This process is a bit like adapting *My Fair Lady* into *Pygmalion*, but it brought the elements back into harmony, letting the syrup do in the shaken form much of what the shaved ice achieved in the original. It's Dale's version that has propagated to the infinity of bars seeking the same high standards he employed at the Rainbow Room. As currently practiced, the drink is essentially a shaken version of the Daiquiri No. 3, with Hemingway's changes rolled back even as his memory lingers on.

Our homage to Dale and Constantino follows their framework, but with the addition of citrus syrup. In the Daiquiri No. 3, sugar is dissolved into grapefruit juice; a grapefruit punch syrup simply does that in advance. (Punch syrups are discussed on pages 207–208.) Importantly, this syrup will always be measured to the right amount of sweetness, rather than varying with every fruit. Equally important, it gets flavor from the peel, where most of citrus's character lies. In this way, we're letting lime be the sole acid, freeing grapefruit to take on the role of sweetener. While the Brugal Extra Dry isn't what would have been used historically, its crispness fits with the current perception of what this drink should be, thanks to Dale DeGroff's reconditioning of Ernest Hemingway's special call.

*"That's all we do, isn't it—look at things and try new drinks?"*

—ERNEST HEMINGWAY, "HILLS LIKE WHITE ELEPHANTS," 1927

**5 drops salt solution** (see page 27)

**½ teaspoon Luxardo Maraschino**

**½ ounce strained lime juice**

**½ ounce grapefruit punch syrup** (see page 216)

**2 ounces Brugal Especial Extra Dry Rum**

**Grapefruit twist, for garnish**

- Combine all the ingredients in a shaker with 1 medium ice cube and 2 small ice cubes. Shake and strain into a chilled coupe (6 ounces). Express a grapefruit twist over the drink and discard.

# Yellow Bird

*Finely tuned flavor*

Today's liquor brands engage with bartenders and consumers alike with mountains of logoed swag, a jammed calendar of sponsored cocktail competitions, and armies of celebrity consultants. In the 1960s, traditional booze marketing hadn't embraced these techniques—except for that ambitiously ahead-of-its-time liqueur, Galliano.

European herbal liqueurs were in vogue in America in the 1960s, briefly squeezing their way into trendy cocktails. Drambuie found success with the Rusty Nail, a favorite of the Rat Pack, while Chartreuse tried and failed (the Swamp Water just didn't connect; for more on that see the Swamp Fire, page 155). Galliano hired recipe consultants to crank out Galliano-tinged variants on standard drinks like the Screwdriver (add Galliano and it's a Harvey Wallbanger, the most famed of these inventions) and the Alexander (the less-celebrated Golden Cadillac). Another such corporate creation was an expansion of the Sidecar called the Yellow Bird. Despite its fame, and its publication in cocktail manuals far and wide, its attribution is unknown; it may be the first internationally successful drink created by a cocktail consultant.

The Yellow Bird, as found in Galliano brochures of the period, was classically designed, featuring 1½ ounces white rum, ½ ounce Galliano, ½ ounce triple sec, and the juice of 1 lime. In the years since, the recipe has picked up extra juices such as pineapple and orange in its transformation into a "resort drink," but it's the original Sidecar variant that deserves rediscovery.

Don't be afraid of the ⅜- and ⅝-ounce measurements. On your jigger, ⅜ is halfway between ¼ and ½ ounce, and ⅝ is halfway between ½ and ¾ ounce, so the amounts are easy to eyeball. These finer gradations appear throughout the book in recipes where precise amounts of flavor make a vast difference in the result. (As an illustration of their power, according to legend, Sasha Petraske ordered custom jiggers with a ⅜-ounce marking due to his recipes' reliance on exactitude.)

**5 drops salt solution** (see page 27)

**1 dash orange bitters** (see page 62)

**⅝ ounce strained lime juice**

**1 teaspoon lime cordial** (see page 221)

**⅜ ounce Cointreau**

**⅜ ounce Galliano L'Autentico**

**1½ ounces Denizen Aged White Rum**

**Sugar for rim, optional**

RECIPE CONTINUES

- Combine all the ingredients in a shaker with 1 medium ice cube and 2 small ice cubes. Shake and strain into a chilled coupe (6 ounces).
- A sugar rim is optional, in honor of the drink's heritage from the Crusta and Sidecar.

## ORANGE BITTERS

After too long an absence, there are once again a plethora of orange bitters on the market. For these recipes, you might want to try a 50-50 mix of Regan's Orange Bitters No. 6 and Fee Brothers West Indian Orange Bitters—a combination of spicy and sweet with wide acceptance in the craft cocktail world. Alternatively, Angostura Orange Bitters offers an all-around orange peel profile that also excels.

# Outrigger

Jeff "Beachbum" Berry created this cocktail as a means to slip aged rum into a Sidecar. It's an excellent showcase for aged rhum agricole, adding a Martinique flair to the traditional French cocktail.

**5 drops salt solution** (see page 27)

**1 dash orange bitters** (see above)

**⅝ ounce strained lemon juice**

**1 teaspoon lime cordial** (see page 221)

**¾ ounce Clément Creole Shrubb**

**1½ ounces La Favorite Rhum Agricole Vieux or Clément VSOP Rhum Agricole Vieux**

**Sugar for rim, optional**

- Combine all the ingredients in a shaker and shake with 1 medium ice cube and 2 small ice cubes. Strain into a chilled coupe (6 ounces).
- A sugar rim is optional.

# Sunset Suite

*Metropolitan aquavit*

The New York Sour, a bourbon sour with a float of red wine, experienced a resurgence in New York City in the 2010s, no doubt partially thanks to the name, but more so from the focus it received in the bars of Julie Reiner. In addition to her pioneering Flatiron Lounge and Clover Club, she managed the glamorous Monkey Bar at the Hotel Elysée.

"The New York Sour is mulled wine meets Whiskey Sour," Julie told us. "People love the look of the wine slowly merging on top. Aesthetically, it's a really beautiful drink, and just as tasty. I serve it for Thanksgiving just about every year."

Our drink is a tropical remodeling of the New York Sour with a slight Scandinavian holiday flair. With the wine float a must, Krogstad Aquavit emerges as a capable pairing, as its notes of caraway and star anise imbue it with a mulled wine quality. Doubling down on this concept, the sweetener is cinnamon syrup. Trader Vic's Fog Cutter, with three base spirits and a sherry float, is the closest tropical analogue, further defining the formula.

With the spices as the bass note and the aquavit singing treble, mid-tones come from a duo of aged rums. Santa Teresa provides dryness for the spices to emerge from, while Clément provides a vegetal contrast. Returning to the Fog Cutter, a drop of sherry harmonizes. Pinot Noir as the float brings a tannic element, keeping the drink dry and refreshing, while adding a deep red horizon.

The Sunset Suite of the Hotel Elysée was the home of playwright Tennessee Williams for the last fifteen years of his life.

**5 drops salt solution** (see page 27)

**¾ ounce strained lime juice**

**½ ounce cassia cinnamon bark syrup** (see below)

**¼ ounce Emilio Hidalgo "Morenita" Cream Sherry**

**⅜ ounce Krogstad Aquavit**

**½ ounce Santa Teresa 1796 Rum**

**½ ounce Clément VSOP Rhum Agricole Vieux**

**⅜ ounce Pinot Noir**

**Grated nutmeg, for garnish**

- Combine all the ingredients, except the wine, in a shaker with 1 medium ice cube and 2 small ice cubes. Shake and strain into a chilled coupe (6 ounces). Float the wine by pouring it slowly and carefully over the back of a spoon. The specific gravity of the wine will allow it to float on top of the drink.
- Dust with grated nutmeg.

RECIPE CONTINUES

## Cassia Cinnamon Bark Syrup, 50 Brix

Don the Beachcomber's opening menu in 1934 featured drinks with an extensive array of syrups, but cinnamon syrup may be the most revelatory. Cinnamon adds not just spice to a cocktail, but also layers of umami and fruit. But for it to work correctly in complex tropical drinks, the right cinnamon must be used.

Common supermarket cinnamon sticks are usually Sri Lankan or Ceylon cinnamon. Unfortunately, this variety is too subtle when boiled in a syrup. Instead, try cassia, a type of cinnamon much more common in mainland Asia, where it is used in everything from chai to pickling liquid to five-spice powder.

Toasting the bark coaxes out more flavor, opening the aroma and releasing oils within the bark.

This recipe results in a flavored simple syrup at 50 degrees Brix. To apply the same template to other spices, be sure to weigh the ingredients. The spice component is 6 percent of the weight of the water. (See the section on sugar adjusting, starting on page 185, for more on degrees Brix and proper measuring for sweetness.)

**15 grams cassia cinnamon bark, broken into ½-inch pieces**

**250 grams water**

**250 grams organic cane sugar**

- Toast the cinnamon bark in a saucepan over medium-low heat until aromatic, about 1 to 3 minutes. Add water and sugar. Bring the mixture to a simmer, stirring occasionally, then cover and reduce heat to low. After 15 minutes, remove from heat and let it sit for 12 hours.
- Strain and bottle. It will keep for 4 weeks in the refrigerator. Makes 16 ounces.

# Heroes and Villains

*Savory rum and fresh produce*

Over the past few years, American liquor store shelves have expanded to include rums with unusually savory profiles: bottlings like Paranubes, KoHana Koho Mahai'ula, and St. George Spirits Agua Libre. They showcase flavors such as sea salt, olive, and black garlic. Long fermentation periods replace rum's more common banana and ripe fruit notes and metamorphose it into this much brinier species of spirit.

At the same time, the craft cocktail movement has embraced its savory side, experimenting with vegetal flavors where once there was only fruit. A drink that excels at this idea is the Bowery Fix, by Naren Young from Saxon and Parole in New York. A sour with layers of yellow bell pepper, Thai chile, and herbaceous Chartreuse, its savory qualities enliven the drink's mezcal and Tequila base. Similarly, at ZZ's Clam Bar, a standout on the cocktail menu was the Jalapeño, Thomas Waugh's transmutation of Jerri Banks's trailblazing Juniperotivo into a spicy Margarita. It showed how peppers and pomegranates could be formidable allies.

Heroes and Villains applies these approaches to the tropical palette, like Donn Beach stalking the Hollywood Farmers Market. There's no reason that a tropical drink must only concern itself with tropical fruit stalwarts like banana, passionfruit, and coconut, when the flavors of bell pepper, cucumber, and basil can be just as compelling. There's room in the tropical family to explore it all.

In this recipe, the black olive notes found within Dakabend Oaxacan Rum are matched with the bold juniper of Tanqueray, the spice notes of which are amplified by ginger and Bénédictine. Orange bell pepper brings a touch more sweetness than the yellow variety found in the Bowery Fix.

Pomegranate-inspired grenadine syrup is an ingredient that has been kicking around in mixed drinks since the 1890s, but it's spent most of that time as an artificially colored sweetener with little or no fruit flavor. The craft cocktail revival's insistence on fresh juices and syrups unlocked the vibrancy of pomegranate flavor in cocktails for the first time in generations.

**5 drops salt solution**
(see page 27)

**6 drops Bittermens Winter Melon Bitters**

**½ ounce orange bell pepper juice**

**¾ ounce strained lime juice**

**1 teaspoon ginger syrup**
(see page 83)

**¼ ounce grenadine**
(see page 68)

**½ ounce Bénédictine**

**¾ ounce Dakabend Oaxacan Pot Still Rum**

**¾ ounce Tanqueray London Dry Gin**

RECIPE CONTINUES

- **Combine all the ingredients in a shaker with 1 medium ice cube and 2 small ice cubes. Shake and strain into a chilled goblet (10 ounces).**

## Grenadine, 50 Brix

As syrups go, this one is surprisingly controversial. Originally a pomegranate syrup from France, it has spent more of its life as a red-dyed sugar syrup of no particular flavor. Many learned scholars debate how this affects classic cocktails that call for the ingredient. However, we can sidestep those concerns. The recipes in this book that include grenadine are all expected to be based on freshly juiced pomegranates, and the drinks made with it take full advantage of that flavor.

Bottled pomegranate juice is wildly inconsistent from brand to brand. Popular labels taste one-dimensional, while obscure imports are closer to marinades than juices. The color of bottled juice is off, leaving many classic red cocktails a burnt sienna at best.

For a produce-driven drink, you want the real thing. But it seems like every bar mentor proclaims how difficult it is to extract fresh pomegranate juice. Is there a secret to doing it anyway? Of course!

Pomegranates are not unlike citrus fruits and can be juiced with a simple citrus hand press. The seeds stay in the shell and are pressed like the vesicles of a grapefruit. The same method is used in the Republic of Georgia, where roadside pomegranate stands dot the countryside. With just a knife and a citrus press, fresh pomegranate juice can be yours.

Slice off the top and bottom, and then cut the fruit in half along its equator. This will leave you with two halves that can each fit into the press. Place the pomegranate seed-side down into the press. If using a handheld press, use the larger version for oranges.

Pomegranate season in the United States generally lasts from October through January, with the majority of the produce coming from California. Pomegranates have a long shelf life and can be found up to a month past their season. If you want to squirrel away juice for the summer months, simply freeze the freshly extracted juice in a sealable container.

**250 grams freshly pressed pomegranate juice**

**162 grams white sugar** (estimated; see Note)

**1 gram citric acid**

**2 long orange twists**

- **Add the pomegranate juice to a blender. Blend on medium speed, gradually adding the sugar to the juice, until the sugar is fully dissolved. Add the citric acid. Express oils from orange twists in the syrup, then discard.**
- **Bottle and refrigerate. It will keep for 1 week in the refrigerator. Makes around 10 ounces.**

**NOTE:** *The recipe's sugar content (50 Brix) is an estimate based on the average degrees Brix of pomegranate fruit (18 Brix). For instructions on determining a more precise level of sweetness based on the actual fruit you have, please refer to the sugar adjusting formula found on page 186.*

## HYBRID

The following drinks feature a new method we call the hybrid shake. It incorporates two kinds of ice and is inspired by two legendary Bay Area bars.

Drinks at Trader Vic's are made in every way imaginable. But for certain drinks that needed something different, Vic created a method of agitation unique to his bars. Crushed ice is used in the shaker, which is gently and rhythmically rocked, ending with a direct dump into the glass. This provides a slow and steady dilution that allows sour-style cocktails to thrive longer on the bar.

Vic's special shaking method is integral to many classics of the canon, like the Scorpion, Fog Cutter, and that apotheosis of cocktails, the Mai Tai. But it needs to be used precisely to achieve its results. With crushed ice it's easy to over-shake and therefore over-dilute.

A related technique that's more forgiving of user error can be found at the San Francisco shrine to agave, Tommy's Mexican Restaurant. When Julio Bermejo, son of Tommy, developed his house Margarita, the eponymous Tommy's Margarita, he created a spec now imitated around the world. His showcase for great Tequila substituted agave nectar for the previously obligatory triple sec. But it also had its own shaking style: every Margarita is briefly shaken in a large pitcher with cracked ice, then emptied into an Old Fashioned glass. The slightly agitated ice contributes just the right amount of water to the Margarita, balancing the rich agave nectar.

Like Vic's shake, the Tommy's method controls dilution and opens up flavor. It can also stand up to a more aggressive shake familiar to cocktail bartenders, and still provides delicious results.

But there may be an even better way, combining the best elements of Tommy and Vic in what we'll call the hybrid shake. "Crushed dilutes so quickly that it's hard to stop shaking at the exact right moment, whereas shaking with Kold-Draft cubes is very consistent," Dave Arnold told us. To bring that crucial consistency, we'll shake the drink with hard ice rather than the faster-melting crushed, then pour unstrained and add crushed ice to the glass.

First, build the drink in the cocktail shaker. Then shake the mixture with four small cubes, which aerate and moderately dilute the drink. Pour the entire contents of the tin, unstrained, into a wide-mouthed glass, such as a double Old Fashioned, wine glass, or snifter. Top with a measured amount of crushed ice.

# Mai Tai

*The cocktail's Platonic ideal*

If the Daiquiri is the prototype for the tropical canon, the Mai Tai is the epitome of its midcentury popularity. Unlike some of the classics we are reconsidering, it does not suffer from any defect in its conception. But it is difficult to make for another reason: entropy.

When Trader Vic concocted the first Mai Tai, he used ingredients available to him. But, as ingredients are wont to do, they didn't stay available. Vic had to change the base rum several times in his restaurants' specs as old stock was depleted. The original rum in the Mai Tai was Wray & Nephew 17 Year Old, now elevated to mythic status, and which may have been manufactured on only one occasion. Its heavily flavorful Jamaican profile, so prominent in the early twentieth century, no longer held wide appeal in a world increasingly dominated by vodka.

In order to give the Mai Tai more of what it lost with the disappearance of the old Wray & Nephew, Vic eventually began using two rums of complementary characters, an approach that continues to be a preferred key to the Mai Tai puzzle. (Typically, these will be a heavier-bodied Jamaican and a Martinican rhum agricole.)

This illustrates a sometimes-underappreciated aspect of the craft cocktail revival, which is that you can't always make a historical recipe as it's presented in an old book. Brands of spirits don't exist or their product formulas have changed. Agricultural ingredients are different today. A contemporary bartender has to reinterpret, not just repeat. There are many possible solutions, each with its own justification.

In this particular Mai Tai reinterpretation, the hybrid shake is the keystone. Like many tropical drinks made in a craft bar context, the Mai Tai is often burdened with the "snow cone" dome of ice that ultimately kills it with over-dilution. The amount of ice is both precisely measured and much reduced in our version. The lower dilution also gives greater prominence to the citrus, necessary for a proper Mai Tai profile.

Changing the method of dilution is only one of the many translations needed to refurbish this standard. As we've described, proper rum substitution was a problem that even Vic had to solve more than once. In recent years, the Denizen Merchant's Reserve Rum was created specifically to fill an aromatic role in the Mai Tai, which it does admirably well. But in chasing the legendary Wray & Nephew, we wanted heavier molasses at the fore, as exemplified by Coruba. The inclusion of rhum agricole acknowledges its popularity in recipes for the Mai Tai during its first era of revival in the 1990s.

RECIPE CONTINUES

Once you're using multiple rums, why not allow two orange liqueurs to harmonize as well? Grand Marnier offers a spicy bass note to the Clément's juicier treble.

The 2 teaspoons of liqueurs plus ⅝ ounce of orgeat equals about 1 ounce of total sweetener, balancing the same amount of lime juice.

Many people float a spent lime shell in the glass. As an improvement on the unwieldy, bobbing semi-spheres, we suggest only a wedge with its juice removed—and at the bottom, not floating on top. Its oils will then coat the ice and suffuse through the drink.

New versions of this pivotal cocktail are constantly advanced and debated by bartenders worldwide. It is nigh on impossible to improve on a drink as iconic as the Mai Tai, but with its collection of small adjustments, rediscovered techniques, and precise flavor pairings, the Mai Tai you are about to make will banish all others from your heart.

**1 lime wedge**

**5 drops salt solution** (see page 27)

**1 ounce strained lime juice**

**⅝ ounce orgeat** (see below)

**1 teaspoon Grand Marnier**

**1 teaspoon Clément Creole Shrubb**

**¼ ounce La Favorite Rhum Agricole Vieux**

**½ ounce Coruba Rum**

**1½ ounces Denizen Merchant's Reserve Rum**

**Mint sprig, for garnish**

**Orchid, for garnish**

**Lime twist, for garnish**

- Squeeze a lime wedge to remove the juice, discard the juice, and place the spent wedge in a double Old Fashioned glass (16 ounces). Combine the remaining ingredients in a shaker with 4 small ice cubes. Shake and pour unstrained into the glass. Top with 8 to 10 ounces of crushed ice.
- Garnish with the mint sprig, orchid, and lime twist.

## ORGEAT

Orgeat is an almond syrup with a long history in mixed drinks. For an authentic midcentury profile, we recommend the Latitude 29 brand from Orgeat Works Ltd.

Alternatively, substitute any commercial or homemade orgeat you admire, as long as it's around 66 Brix.

# London Sour

*Tropical Scotland*

Rum is not the only tipple in the Caribbean. Especially in its English-speaking nations, Scotch holds enough sway to have fostered many local twists, such as in a highball with coconut water. (See the Romero on page 129 for a stirred take on the tradition.) Trader Vic approached from the other direction, placing bourbon whiskey at the center of a Mai Tai derivative, known as the Eastern Sour. For the opening of his restaurant in London's bustling Mayfair in 1963, he subbed Scotch and dubbed it the London Sour.

Some formulations of the London Sour call for 1½ or even 2 ounces of orange juice, but this drink is not a Screwdriver and doesn't shine under such conditions. Instead of dominating with orange, let it subtly combine with almond and Peychaud's cherry and anise notes to contrast the smoky and briny qualities of Scotch.

For the Scotch, try the Compass Box Artist Blend, with its strong apple and vanilla culminating in a spicy finish. It's common today to finish Scotch sours with a hint of smoky Islay malt whisky, as in the influential Penicillin. Here, try the salty, savory Talisker from the Isle of Skye, which propels the almond.

**1 lemon wedge**

**1 orange wedge**

**5 drops salt solution** (see page 27)

**2 dashes Peychaud's Bitters**

**½ ounce strained orange juice**

**¾ ounce strained lemon juice**

**½ ounce orgeat** (see page 72)

**¼ ounce Talisker 10 Year Old Single Malt Scotch Whisky**

**2 ounces Compass Box Artist Blend Scotch Whisky**

**Orchid, for garnish**

- Squeeze a lemon wedge and an orange wedge to remove the juice, discard the juice, and place the spent wedges in a double Old Fashioned glass (16 ounces). Combine the remaining ingredients in a shaker with 4 small ice cubes. Shake and pour unstrained into the glass. Top with 8 ounces of crushed ice.
- Garnish with an orchid.

# Silver Lake Smash

*In a muddle*

The Tiki-Ti, the legendary bar on Sunset Boulevard in the Silver Lake neighborhood of Los Angeles, opened by Ray Buhen in 1961, has an infamously extensive menu. (Further discussion of this important bar begins on page 238.) Among its many nuanced classics are a few hoists that are simply easy to appreciate.

The Tiki-Ti offers a duo of sweet and sour combos seemingly derived from the Lemon Drop, which invaded the bar world back when ferns dominated the landscape: the Lemon Head (with a vodka base by default but also available with the vastly more flavorful Lemon Hart Demerara Rum) and the Sweet Tart (the same formula but with vanilla-inflected Whaler's Rum). We will not dwell on the fact that the Lemon Drop, Lemon Head, and Sweet Tart all are drinks whose names and raison d'être come from old-time candy. Instead, we will focus on how the drinks are constructed, and how they got that way.

Jerry Thomas's *How to Mix Drinks* of 1862 recorded many bar practices for the first time. In the description of the Whiskey Cobbler, slices of orange are shaken in the tin along with the drink. While not muddling per se, it amounts to the same: abrading citrus peel for oil and flesh for juice. Six score years later, Dale DeGroff read these instructions and experienced an epiphany. A few pages earlier in the same tome is the Whiskey Smash, what Thomas calls "a julep on a small plan." DeGroff had the inspiration to combine muddled lemons, in the style of the Cobbler, with the mint and sugar of the Smash, resulting in a drink he designated as a Whiskey Smash, though his formula shared only a partial lineage with that drink.

Today, it's a popular offering on craft cocktail menus, often erroneously attributed fully to Thomas. In fact, the crucial part is the muddling, which was where DeGroff placed the emphasis. "I should have called it the Whiskey Smash No. 2," Dale told us with his characteristic grin. "I never really thought Mint Juleps were so great. I mean, you're drinking water, sugar, and bourbon. Can I add a little bit of flavor? That's what this is all about."

DeGroff's transformation of the Smash is reflected in our approach to the Tiki-Ti's lemony beverage. Fresh quarters of lemon must be muddled with gum syrup to make a kind of à la minute oleosaccharum.

This drink showcases citrus, both fresh lemons and preserved lime peel in lime punch syrup (see page 213), but it's also a great platform for exploring the subtleties of the aged Don Q Reserva 7. The rum's character shines through the citrus in this combination, with its longer time in the barrel contrasting congenially with the drink's brighter tones.

**5 to 6 lemon quarters**

**5 drops salt solution**
(see page 27)

**½ ounce lime punch syrup**
(see page 213)

**½ ounce gum syrup**
(see page 197)

**2½ ounces Don Q Reserva 7 Rum**

- Muddle the lemon quarters in a shaker. Add the remaining ingredients and 4 small ice cubes. Shake and taste for balance, adjusting with lemon or gum syrup as needed. Pour unstrained into an Old Fashioned glass (12 ounces). Top with 8 ounces of crushed ice.

# Piña Brava

*Caipirinha style*

Brazil's beloved Caipirinha brings together muddled limes, sugar, and cachaça, the local rendition of rum. The style is simple and elegant and invites innovations like switching base spirits or including other fruits.

At the Rainbow Room, Dale DeGroff embraced the Caipirinha with gusto and helped popularize it in New York and the universe beyond. He made alluring additions like sour cherry that showed the flexibility of the form. Here is our homage to such practices.

The conception is somewhere between the proto-Caipirinha referred to in Charles H. Baker Jr.'s *The Gentleman's Companion* as the Añejo Candido, and an off-menu request from an Existing Conditions regular for a large hit of Angostura in her Pineapple Daiquiri.

This drink calls for a slightly different approach to ginger than the syrup found in our Heroes and Villains (page 67) and El Diablo (page 81): namely, ginger oleosaccharum, which brings a softer, more floral ginger flavor, allowing the ginger to retreat into the wings and let the pulpiness of the lime play the starring role. (See pages 207–208 for a full discussion, including the oleo recipe.)

Since limes are central to this drink, and limes can be especially acidic or very dry, always taste test before serving. If necessary, balance the drink with more lime or sweetener.

**6 to 8 lime quarters**

**5 drops salt solution** (see page 27)

**4 dashes Angostura aromatic bitters**

**¼ ounce pineapple gum syrup** (see page 197)

**½ ounce ginger oleosaccharum** (see page 208)

**2 ounces Santa Teresa 1796 Rum**

- Muddle the lime quarters in a shaker. Add the remaining ingredients and 4 small ice cubes. Shake and taste for balance, adjusting with lime or ginger oleosaccharum as needed. Pour unstrained into an Old Fashioned glass (12 ounces). Top with 8 ounces of crushed ice.

Opposite: Silver Lake Smash (left); Piña Brava (right)

## Caipirinha

Our adaptation of the classic comes with a choice: either the Novo Fogo Silver Cachaça, at 80 proof, or the more recently introduced Bar Strength version, at 86 proof. That extra little kick makes a big difference. Reckon you'll have to try both or be left forever wondering.

In the drink's native Brazil, as well as bars worldwide, debate rages as to whether sugar or syrup should be employed—the same controversy facing the Daiquiri. At Milk & Honey, they compromised with a bit of both: a small amount of sugar in the tin acts as an assisting abrasive in muddling the limes, while syrup provides body.

**6 to 8 lime quarters**

**2 teaspoons white sugar**

**5 drops salt solution** (see page 27)

**⅜ ounce gum syrup** (see page 197)

**2 ounces Novo Fogo Silver Cachaça or Novo Fogo Bar Strength Silver Cachaça**

- Muddle the lime quarters and sugar in a shaker. Add the remaining ingredients and 4 small ice cubes. Shake and straw taste for balance, adjusting with lime or syrup as needed. Pour unstrained into an Old Fashioned glass (12 ounces). Top with 8 ounces of crushed ice.

## COLLINS

The classic Collins amounts to a fizzy lemonade. It derives some of its dilution and chill from being served with ice and soda, so it needs a special shaking style to compensate for the different style of service. In addition to the higher dilution of a Collins, its bubbles force the bartender to think about long drinks differently than their up counterparts. These drinks have their own requirements for perfect balance, which we'll explore in this section.

Whipping the citrus, syrup, and spirit components in a shaker with one large ice cube introduces air bubbles and some water. Since more ice and water is waiting in the glass, the shaking is more for aeration than total temperature or dilution. Only a brief shake is required, until the shaker tin is cold but not frosted. But do make sure it's cold! If the mixture is too warm when poured into the glass, the ice will melt and the soda will go flat, as carbon dioxide stays dissolved better at lower temperatures.

Never shake with fizzy liquid in the shaker, but once the shaking is done, add the soda water or sparkling wine to the shaker and then strain everything into the glass. Don't strain without the soda and then add it on top, as the soda will not be well mixed. This would force you to stir the drink as well, which would only serve to eliminate precious bubbles.

# El Diablo

*Tequila archaeology*

Once relegated to obscurity, El Diablo now stands as one of the few classic cocktails that Tequila can call its own. Or can it?

The recipe's origins seem straightforward. Trader Vic included a Mexican El Diablo in his *Book of Food and Drink* of 1946, where he noted it as one of his own formulas. It was served at both the Trader Vic's chain and his later Mexican eatery, Señor Pico. The drink's spotlighting of Tequila was innovative; the spirit was largely unknown outside of Mexico and Southern California. When the craft cocktail revival began, El Diablo was quickly embraced as first in line behind the Margarita in the small agave pantheon. The cassis brought exuberance contrasting ginger's spice and accentuating Tequila's vegetal notes. It was a nuanced easy drinker.

But there are earlier sources for the drink. A now-obscure 1940 cocktail book, *The How and When,* published by Chicago liquor store Marco's, featured a Diablo cocktail under a section marked "Tropical Specialties." The recipe in this book was copied verbatim from Ronrico's own marketing brochures, which date from either 1939 or 1940. Thus, the Diablo seems to have first emerged from that marketing source as a showcase of Ronrico's rum offering.

The components to Vic's cocktail of 1946 are identical to the Diablo of 1940, but with a base of Tequila instead of Ronrico white rum. So why did Vic alter the Diablo's spirit base? He was, after all, a man who sold a lot of rum. But the answer may lie with another cassis and lime cocktail on the scene. The Tequila Sunrise had been the signature drink of the Agua Caliente resort in Tijuana, Mexico, since the 1920s. It looked identical to the Diablo, with soda water instead of ginger ale, though its color came from dashes of both cassis and grenadine. The resort recommended this drink to ease its norteamericano guests into the local spirit. As an incantation from their 1933 brochure has it, Tequila is "[t]he Worshiped Drink of the Aztecs . . . Wholesome . . . Pleasing . . . Forceful . . . Refreshing . . . Invigorating . . . Appetizing." Note that this early version of the drink bears only passing resemblance to the orange juice monster the Eagles later glorified for reasons best known to themselves.

Perhaps Vic contemplated these two beverages and, in his archetypical way, combined their strengths. He dropped the grenadine from the Sunrise and added the ginger ale from the Diablo, left Tequila at its heart, and El Diablo was born.

RECIPE CONTINUES

In adapting this drink, our major change was to furnish an addictive spicy burn by replacing ginger ale with ginger syrup, a move common to the Sasha Petraske constellation of bars. But we've also returned to the Agua Caliente version with a touch of raspberry syrup in addition to crème de cassis.

The use of more syrups in our version must be balanced by a larger amount of citrus. Lemon juice instead of lime promotes the crème de cassis and raspberry, which in turn stand up to the bolder ginger syrup. With these small innovations, the diabolical progeny of Vic, Ronrico, and the Agua Caliente can be worshipped once again.

**5 drops salt solution** (see page 27)

**1 dash cardamom tincture** (see page 162)

**¾ ounce strained lemon juice**

**⅜ ounce ginger syrup** (see page 83)

**⅜ ounce raspberry syrup** (see page 201)

**¼ ounce Clear Creek Crème de Cassis**

**2 ounces Siete Leguas Blanco Tequila**

**3 ounces soda water**

**Lemon wheel, for garnish**

- Combine all the ingredients, except the soda water, in a shaker. Shake briefly with 1 medium ice cube. Add the soda water to the shaker. Strain into a chilled red wine glass (14 ounces) filled with small ice cubes.
- Garnish with a lemon wheel.

## Ginger Syrup, 50 Brix

Barman Toby Maloney created this syrup for Milk & Honey as a replacement for ginger ale and ginger beer in classic cocktails. It later found fame as a vital ingredient to the modern classic devised at that bar, the Penicillin. Its flavor is bolder and spicier than the ginger syrups that would have been known during the midcentury tropical drink boom.

Ginger is tough stuff, so an electric juicer is required for this recipe. The recipe also requires brief freezing, as this helps to separate the juice from the thick ginger paste.

The syrup comes in at our usual 50 Brix for greatest flexibility. (See the section on sugar adjusting, starting on page 185, for more on degrees Brix and proper measuring for sweetness.)

**125 grams ginger juice**

**114 grams white sugar** (estimated; see Note)

- Peel the ginger and cut it into vertical strips. Run each strip through an electric juicer, collecting into a container, until you have the required weight of juice. Place the container of juice in the freezer for 20 minutes. Strain the resulting separated juice with a fine mesh strainer into a blender. Blend the juice on low, gradually adding the sugar to it until well mixed. Bottle the juice, which will keep for 1 week in the refrigerator. Makes 8 ounces.

**NOTE:** *The sugar amount is based on an average degrees Brix of ginger juice (4.5 Brix). For best results, adjust the strained ginger juice using the sugar adjusting formula found on page 186.*

# Santa Cruz Royal Cobbler

*Cobbler style*

While Champagne drinks are not often seen in the tropical canon, they were a fixture of mixed drinks during their zenith in the nineteenth century. This was especially true of punches and cobblers, which were often served—just like later tropicals—on crushed ice. And since adding sparkling wine to a cocktail is almost always an elevation (accordingly, doing so adds "royal" to the name of a drink), here's a tropical Champagne Cobbler for your delectation.

The cobbler was among the lost styles of drink rehabilitated during the craft cocktail revival, especially in the work of Dale DeGroff. (See the Silver Lake Smash, page 74, for a discussion.) This style of drink is spirit or wine served over "cobbled" ice, referring to its small, rounded shape (think cobblestones)—another name for crushed ice. In its classical form, the Cobbler involved prodigious citrus or berry garnishes. With DeGroff's retooling, in addition to its display as the garnish, fresh fruit is muddled as part of the drink.

Our recipe takes the cobbler format and coalesces it into a famous rum drink of similar vintage, the Knickerbocker. The original plan Knickerbocker boasts raspberry syrup and aged rum, usually along with lemon or lime juice and orange curaçao, a familiar-seeming spec that presages Donn and Vic by almost a century.

In our version, loganberry liqueur amplifies the qualities of the raspberry. It's a trick pulled from another Champagne drink, the great Dick Bradsell's Russian Spring Punch, which explores crèmes de cassis et framboise in tandem with freshly muddled raspberries.

The loganberry, a hybrid of the North American blackberry and European raspberry, is named after amateur botanist James Harvey Logan (1841–1928), a California Superior Court judge based in Santa Cruz County.

**4 raspberries**

**5 drops salt solution** (see page 27)

**¾ ounce strained lemon juice**

**½ ounce cane syrup** (see page 52)

**½ ounce Clear Creek Loganberry Liqueur**

**1 ounce Chairman's Reserve Rum**

**1½ ounces dry sparkling wine** (preferably Champagne)

**Lemon wheel, for garnish**

**Raspberry, for garnish**

**Mint sprig, for garnish**

- Muddle the raspberries at the bottom of a shaker. Add the remaining ingredients except for the sparkling wine. Shake briefly with 1 medium ice cube. Add sparkling wine to the shaker, then double strain into a chilled Collins glass (15 ounces) filled with crushed ice.
- Garnish with a lemon wheel, raspberry, and mint.

# Mojito

*The magic of the milk frother*

The Mojito is another elegantly simple creation from Cuba, a long drink with mint, lime, sugar, and rum. To maintain its elegance, use the traditional method of building the drink instead of shaking it. The challenge (as ever) is arriving at the right amount of dilution from the ice versus the soda water added to finish the cocktail. A key to nailing that balance is the enlistment of granulated sugar rather than syrup, and utilizing a milk frother to help integrate it. (See our discussion on the Daiquiri, page 55.)

The milk frother becomes your battery-powered swizzle stick and muddler in one. It's a lighter, more delicate flash blender as much as it is a more powerful human hand. It will chill the drink without ripping the mint apart.

Craft versions of the Mojito also struggle with the choice of ice. Some bars use cubed ice and serve it like a traditional Collins, while others use crushed ice and serve it like a swizzle. But for a Mojito to shine, it needs cracked ice. In this recipe, several cracked cubes are combined with a topping of crushed ice. The float of crushed ice provides a stable crown to hold the mint, while the cracked cubes keep the drink from overwatering.

Try using white or organic cane sugar. The white sugar provides a cleaner finish whereas the organic cane sugar offers a touch of molasses.

Don Q Cristal is a widely available rum that approximates a dry Cuban, but you may also want to try Denizen White, Barbancourt White, or Equiano Light.

**5 drops salt solution** (see page 27)

**1 tablespoon organic cane sugar**

**¾ ounce strained lime juice**

**10 to 12 mint leaves**

**2 ounces Don Q Cristal Rum**

**2 ounces soda water**

**Mint sprig, for garnish**

**Lime wheel, for garnish**

- Combine sugar, lime juice, and salt solution in a chilled Collins glass (15 ounces). Whisk with a milk frother until the sugar is fully dissolved. Add the rum and mint leaves. With the frother now powered off, use its end to muddle the leaves, lightly pressing them while moving the leaves up and down the sides of the glass.
- Crack 5 small ice cubes with the back of a spoon and add them to the glass. Pulse blend with the milk frother until the liquid is chilled. Add soda water and top with 6 to 8 ounces of crushed ice.
- Garnish with a mint sprig and a lime wheel.

# Kingston Zing

*Caribbean highballs*

At Booker and Dax, Dave Arnold confronted a problem: highballs going flat. His solution was incredibly effective and just as complicated.

In a mixed drink, alcohol and bubbles are in competition. Dave's solution was to bring them together at the last possible moment before serving. He created a Rube Goldberg apparatus to facilitate this. The cocktails were batched in advance and stored in single-serving bottles kept cool in a chilled bath. When the order came in, the bottle would be carbonated à la minute via a hose connected to a $CO_2$ canister. The freshly carbonated cocktail was then poured into an iced Collins glass along with a touch of freshly squeezed lemon or lime juice halfway through the pour. When everything came together, the result was the most effervescent and refreshing highball yet devised. But the equipment list is not for everyone. This recipe represents our downsized take on the technique.

Wray & Nephew Overproof Rum and Ting grapefruit soda are two pillars of Jamaican drinking culture, separately and together. But as acquiring Ting in many parts of the world is as difficult as constructing a pressurized $CO_2$ supply, here's an approach for home use that avoids both.

When room temperature alcohol touches ice, the cubes start to weep water, leaving less room for carbonation. To avoid this, both your spirit and your glassware should come from the freezer and be as cold as possible. Frosty liquor preserves the bubbles, allowing the remaining mixers to be added halfway through building the drink. The recipe emulates the sweetness of sodas, typically 10 to 12 Brix.

The special steps for this process involve only briefly stirring, and not shaking, the ingredients other than spirit and soda, then combining everything together in a glass with ice. All the dilution comes from the soda water.

If possible, make your grapefruit punch syrup with white rather than pink fruit so as to more closely correspond to the Ting profile. And, if you do have Ting, leave out the juice and syrup, but build the drink as described in the rest of the spec, to make your Wray and Ting more brisk and bubbly than ever. Or replace the rum with 2 ounces of blanco Tequila from the freezer to make a delightfully chilly Paloma.

**5 drops salt solution** (see page 27)

**6 drops Bittermens Hopped Grapefruit Bitters**

**⅜ ounce strained lime juice**

**½ ounce grapefruit punch syrup** (see page 216)

**1½ ounces Wray & Nephew Overproof Rum** (freezer temperature)

**Soda water**

**Channeled lime twist, for garnish**

**Grapefruit slice, for garnish**

RECIPE CONTINUES

Kingston Zing

- Combine all the ingredients, except the rum and soda water, in a shaker. Whisk with a milk frother (or, if not available, stir until uniform) and set aside.
- Fill a chilled highball glass (12 ounces) with small ice cubes. Add the rum, then add the soda until the glass is ¾ full.
- Pour the contents of the shaker into the glass while holding the glass at a 45-degree angle. Top with soda until the glass is full. Agitate the mixture with a single brisk dip of a bar spoon.
- Garnish with a channeled lime twist and a grapefruit slice.

# Rum and Tonic

What the Wray and Ting is to Jamaica perhaps finds an analogue with the Rum and Tonic in Barbados. It's important in sailing culture and serves as the official drink of Barbados Sailing Week.

Nowadays there are an endless multitude of fancy Gin and Tonic interpretations, but not enough love is given to the rum version. Here's a delicious variation using the highball technique we've outlined, involving Tomr's Tonic syrup. (You can read more about that ingredient in the Bay of Pigs recipe, page 133.)

The idea of a splash of maraschino in a Gin and Tonic was cribbed from Janet and Avery Glasser's house spec when they opened the Spanish-inspired bitters bar Amor y Amargo in New York.

**5 drops salt solution** (see page 27)

**12 drops Bittermens Boston Bittahs**

**⅜ ounce strained lime juice**

**½ ounce Tomr's Tonic syrup**

**½ teaspoon Luxardo Maraschino**

**2 ounces Mount Gay Black Barrel Rum** (freezer temperature)

**Soda water**

**Orange slice, for garnish**

**Channeled lime twist, for garnish**

- Combine all the ingredients, except the rum and soda water, in a shaker. Whisk with a milk frother (or, if not available, stir until uniform) and set aside.
- Fill a chilled highball glass (12 ounces) with small ice cubes. Add the rum, then add the soda until the glass is ¾ full.
- Pour the contents of the shaker into the glass while holding the glass at a 45-degree angle. Top with soda until the glass is full. Agitate the mixture with a single brisk dip of a bar spoon.
- Garnish with an orange slice and a channeled lime twist.

# FROZEN

Frozen blender drinks have been chronically misunderstood by the craft cocktail revival. Even in the resurgent wave of bars specializing in tropical drinks, blenders are rarely seen. Perhaps it's their association with poorly balanced drinks found in resorts, boardwalks, and Bourbon Street, or perhaps it's because today's historically minded bartenders want to do everything by hand. But when the blender was new, it was a cutting-edge appliance offering innovations on how food and drink were prepared, like a sous vide immersion circulator or centrifuge today.

The breakthrough that made it possible was the 1905 invention of a lightweight, high-speed motor small enough for domestic use. Its creator, Chester Beach, teamed up with marketing man Louis Hamilton and inventor-investor Fred Osius to form the Hamilton Beach Manufacturing Company in Racine, Wisconsin, in 1910. They embedded their motor in a wide range of electric appliances new to the home, including hair dryers, sewing machines, fans, floor polishers, and meat grinders. In 1911, they released their first paddle-based drink mixer, which fueled the fashion in soda fountains, but also found its way into bar use. (See the section on flash blending starting on page 36.)

The first liquefying blender, with spinning blades at the bottom, was designed in 1922 by Stephen Poplawski, also of Racine, Wisconsin. The concept caught the attention of Osius, who worked to develop an improved version. Seeking a cash infusion, he contacted big band frontman Fred Waring, a successful entertainer who had earlier studied engineering, apparently willing to overlook the fact that he was not from Racine. Waring appreciated the notion of the blender, but not Osius's glitch-laden redesign. Waring handed it off to a colleague, Ed Lee, who was able to resolve the mechanical obstacles, and industrial designer Peter Müller-Munk, who outfitted the device with an art deco envelope of glass and chrome. In 1937, the Waring Miracle Mixer hit the stage, offering home (and bar) blending backed by Waring's marketing dollars. In 1938, the name was abbreviated to the Waring Blendor—yes, with an "o," which the company clung to well into the 1960s.

Throughout these early years, from small-town soda fountains to El Floridita to New York nightclubs, electric mixers and blenders enticed imbibers with concoctions the texture and temperature of which were not like that of drinks they had enjoyed before. Frothy. Thick. Silky. And above all, as Balzac presciently noted, "cold as the stones on which sorrowing hearts had caused to be carved their regrets." American drinking turned up the current on its long-established love affair with ice.

To reclaim the blender, first we have to deal with syrup, which may be the main reason for the downfall of frozen drinks. When you use syrup in a blender recipe, you're taking on water from two sources. To rise above the dilution, much more syrup needs to be added to get your point across. But syrup is a poor sweetener to balance water, since it also contains water, so you can never really get where you need to be. Abandon syrup and return to granulated sugar, which dissolves into the water already in the drink mix, and the resulting beverage will balance more like a traditional shaken drink. With the problem solved, opportunities abound.

We recommend starting with a "dry blend," meaning without the ice. A dry blend uses the blender's power to dissolve the sugar into the other ingredients, creating a uniform product ready for the addition of ice. This step is especially important in blender recipes that include heavier ingredients, like whole fruit or coconut cream.

Even though we're using a blender, it's vital to work with crushed ice and that the amount of ice be measured, allowing a proper interpretation of the recipe and consistent fill levels across multiple rounds of drinks.

If your crushed ice is uniform in shape, as from a home Opal machine or a commercial Scotsman machine, measuring it by volume is fast and accurate. This works for both flash-blended and frozen drinks. But with crushed ice from a refrigerator's ice maker or a Lewis bag, the shards will be dissimilar. For the accuracy demanded by the delicacy of frozen drinks, the ice must be measured by weight instead. In the following recipes, weights are specified (in grams, to avoid any confusion with ounces as a measurement of volume, as ice is usually specified by volume in non-frozen recipes). However, if you will be using an Opal machine, the equivalent volumes are 10 ounces for 142 grams and 12 ounces for 170 grams.

Crushed ice also places less stress on the blender mechanism than solid ice does. No matter how powerful your blender's motor, the easier it can liquefy the ice, the more pleasingly frozen the cocktail will be. With chunkier ice the blender's motor has to run longer, which actually heats up the cocktail.

If a multispeed blender is available, we suggest a special technique called the four-ten-two-seven rule. Run the blender in four stages, for five seconds each. Start the blender out at speed level four, then crank it up to the maximum at ten. Then go down to two, in order to get the tiny pieces of ice that were just jumping around. Then back to seven for one more jolt of speed. It adds up to make sure all the ice is thoroughly blended.

# Frozen Daiquiri

*Replicating high-end texture*

Part of Havana bar El Floridita's enduring reputation as "the Cradle of the Daiquiri" is undoubtedly the result of head barman Constantino Ribalaigua Vert's range of Daiquiri variations and the range of techniques exhibited to make them, with some versions shaken and some created using the then-new technology of the electric blender.

Today, frozen drinks are often seen as low-brow, but they started out as an advanced culinary application. For example, in the 1962 manual *International Cocktail Specialties,* Madison Avenue drinks maven James Mayabb describes the frozen, shaved ice Daiquiri at the Plaza Hotel: "In the highly regarded bastion of elegance, New York's Plaza, this Society favorite is served in 'the season.' . . . Serve in saucer champagne glass. Cut very thin wedges of fresh lime, using about 6 slices to form a 'crown' around edge of glass. One giant strawberry in center. Serve with straws." This lavish presentation indicates the esteem the drink was held in by "Society." (More on strawberries gliding their way into Daiquiris in the next recipe.)

The blender may not be returning to the Plaza anytime soon, but the frozen cocktail's reputation is on the mend, as evidenced by the large frozen drink machines that have been steadily creeping into the cocktail landscape. These devices freeze a cocktail uniformly, creating a sorbet-like mix suggesting a luxury version of the convenience store slushy. As they produce large batches rather than individual drinks, these machines are appropriate only for the busiest bars, so we return our attention to the original device: Can a regular blender produce cocktails as dependable and delicious as drinks from the slushy machine?

Starbucks, of all entities, proves that the answer is yes, as they crank out consistently creamy frozen drinks using traditional blenders. But their advantage isn't the equipment, it's an extra ingredient: xanthan gum, a thickening agent that sometimes replaces gluten in gluten-free products. A small amount of xanthan gum makes a big difference in stabilizing frozen drinks, resisting the ice's tendency to separate to the top. We can create a top-notch slushy texture with any blender as long as we exercise care with ingredient proportions, as even small differences in the ratio of water affect how the drink freezes.

In your Frozen Daiquiri, experiment with different rums. We suggest a slightly aged rum, but it also works with unaged rums, overproof, agricole, or your own blend—whichever you prefer. The Cuban Havana Club is not available in the United States, but try it if you can get it.

RECIPE CONTINUES

**5 drops salt solution** (see page 27)

**1½ tablespoons sugar mix** (see below)

**¾ ounce strained lime juice**

**2 ounces rum of your choice**

**¼ teaspoon xanthan gum**

**Lime wheel, for garnish**

- Combine all the ingredients, except the xanthan gum, in a blender. Dry blend (without ice). Once the sugar is fully dissolved, slowly add the gum while continuing to blend. Add 170 grams of crushed ice while continuing to blend. Pour into a large, chilled coupe (10 ounces).
- Garnish with a lime wheel.

---

### Sugar Mix

While for many rum, lime, and sugar combinations we prefer the clean sweetness of white sugar, in certain applications a sugar mix with more molasses character can make a delicious difference. The team at Lost Lake often used this combination.

**Equal parts by weight of organic cane sugar and turbinado sugar**

## Floridita Daiquiri

Arguably, the world's first famous frozen drink was Constantino Ribalaigua Vert's Daiquiri No. 4. It is here adapted to our particular frozen techniques.

**5 drops salt solution** (see page 27)

**2 teaspoons white sugar**

**¾ ounce strained lime juice**

**¼ ounce Luxardo Maraschino**

**1½ ounces white rum of your choice**

**¼ teaspoon xanthan gum**

**Lime wheel, for garnish**

**Cherry, for garnish**

- Combine all the ingredients, except the xanthan gum, in a blender. Dry blend (without ice). Once the sugar is fully dissolved, slowly add the gum while continuing to blend. Add 142 grams of crushed ice while continuing to blend. Pour into a chilled goblet (10 ounces).
- Garnish with a lime wheel speared to a cherry.

# Frozen Strawberry Daiquiri

*Frozen fruit fruition*

If the Frozen Daiquiri has been seen as ignoble, that goes a hundred times for the Frozen Strawberry Daiquiri, which has served as the poster child for the despised era of syrupy, frigid booze bombs after the cocktail's collapse. This is tragic, as the Frozen Strawberry Daiquiri used to *be* somebody.

The celebrated *Stork Club Bar Book* by Lucius Beebe, published in 1946, opines that "the Stork will compound as many drinks with Cuban rums as there are days in the year" but emphasizes three "which are as dominant in their field as Martinis or Scotch and soda in theirs"—the Frozen Daiquiri, the Cuba Libre, and the MacArthur Cocktail. (We didn't know what that one was, either, but reading the provided recipe clarified that it wasn't a lost classic.)

Isolated from the book's celebrity-filled pages is an appendix of drink suggestions from the Stork's staff. It is here that Edward G. Johnson, a waiter captain, endorses the Frozen Strawberry Daiquiri, made with "3 or 4 ripe strawberries." Beebe seems to be distancing himself from the drink by relegating it to the back of the book, but in fact, its availability at the bar was a draw, as evidenced by Walter Winchell's syndicated column of July 25, 1940, where the last of his verbless recommendations (two of which are about hot dogs) is: "The peach or strawberry daiquiri at the Stork."

The Ronrico distillery produced a series of bar guides in the 1940s and '50s with a wide range of cocktails, desserts, and entire meals that their rums would augment. The 1944 edition of *The Rum Connoisseur* immediately makes its case for the primacy of what they call the Ronrico West Indies, known outside their marketing department as a Frozen Daiquiri, in the Floridita No. 4 style. On the very next page, horizons broaden with the introduction of the "Famous Ronrico Frosted Fresh Fruit West Indies," four Frozen Daiquiri variations embellished with the flavors of pineapple, mint, apple, and strawberry.

(Ronrico also notes that, properly made, the drink in question "is a Cocktail, NOT a Sherbet.")

These 1940s references show that the Frozen Strawberry Daiquiri was correctly seen as a delicacy, just as the Frozen Daiquiri itself. Its genesis was probably a bit later than the Havana heyday of Frozen Daiquiris. As Florida is a major source of strawberries, perhaps the combination originated in a Miami hotspot, where its notoriety trickled down to Miami-based Ronrico, and further into recipe brochures, newspaper columns, and history.

RECIPE CONTINUES

Blending whole fruit gives the benefit of its texture, but the sugar needs to be knocked down accordingly. Contrasting the fruit flavors in our version is the boldly savory Uruapan Charanda Blanco Rum. It all balances out to something magnificent.

The drink can be made year-round with strawberries from your grocer's freezer aisle. But its true luxury is conveyed only by the exhilaration of fresh strawberries at the height of their season. Be sure to mark your calendars to make the Frozen Strawberry Daiquiri then, but take along one final tip: To cement the drink's frosty texture, even fresh strawberries should be frozen for at least 8 hours.

**5 drops salt solution** (see page 27)

**60 grams frozen strawberries (about 2 large or 3 small, stems removed)**

**1 tablespoon sugar mix** (see page 94)

**¾ ounce strained lime juice**

**2 ounces Uruapan Charanda Blanco Rum**

**¼ teaspoon xanthan gum**

**Strawberry, for garnish**

- Combine all the ingredients, except the xanthan gum, in a blender. Dry blend (without ice). Once the sugar is fully dissolved, slowly add the gum while continuing to blend. Add 170 grams of crushed ice while continuing to blend. Pour into a large, chilled coupe (10 ounces).
- Garnish with a sliced or whole strawberry.

# Dark Star

*Chocolate and citrus*

Chocolate and citrus are an exquisite juxtaposition beloved in confectionery but somehow underutilized in the cocktail canon. Among the few examples of such drinks are the Floridita, the 20th Century, and the Tortuga (see the Yacht Rock, page 259).

Our approach layers several chocolate flavors: crème de cacao delivers the sweet vanilla tones often associated with chocolate, while Dave Arnold's essential bitters provide a backbone of the spicier side of chocolate, and the infused rum showcases the rich aroma of high-quality cacao. The choice of Mount Gay Black Barrel emphasizes caramelized fruit notes, which bolster the fruitiness of the nibs. Together, the ingredients heighten the contrast of chocolate and citrus, making the drink exceptionally compelling.

**5 drops salt solution** (see page 27)

**3 dashes Dave Arnold's chocolate bitters** (see page 46)

**1 tablespoon sugar mix** (see page 94)

**¾ ounce strained lime juice**

**½ ounce Tempus Fugit Crème de Cacao**

**1½ ounces cacao nib-infused rum** (see below)

**¼ teaspoon xanthan gum**

**Grated dark chocolate, for garnish**

- Combine all the ingredients, except the xanthan gum, in a blender. Dry blend (without ice). Once the sugar is fully dissolved, slowly add the gum while continuing to blend. Add 170 grams of crushed ice while continuing to blend. Pour into a large, chilled coupe (10 ounces).
- Garnish with grated dark chocolate.

## Cacao Nib-Infused Rum

This infusion is made with the same nitrous technique as Dave Arnold's Chocolate Bitters (see page 46). The infusion gains a strong aroma of the cacao, injecting masses of chocolate flavor into the spirit without any accompanying sugar.

Try this infused rum in an Old Fashioned or slip it into an Espresso Martini. Of course, it's a great sipper on its own.

**75 grams Valrhona cacao nibs**

**500 milliliters Mount Gay Black Barrel Rum**

- Combine all the ingredients in a cream whipper. Charge with two 7.5 gram $N_2O$ chargers. Shake the whipper for 30 seconds and then let it rest for 2 minutes.
- Vent all at once, with the spigot pointed up into a container to catch any spray. Let the mixture settle in the whipper until bubbling stops (around 5 minutes).
- Fine strain and bottle. Will keep indefinitely; does not need to be refrigerated. Makes 16 ounces.

# Hibiscus Pacific

*Margarita fresca*

In areas of the Mexican diaspora, aguas frescas are a ubiquitous refreshment that offer a palette of fruit flavors. One of the most intriguing is *agua de jamaica,* derived from the roselle variety of hibiscus. Even a dried hibiscus flower has an abundance of acidity, with a tartness akin to cranberry or citrus once it is infused. It's used extensively in Caribbean cuisine, where its English name is sorrel.

In a classic Margarita, orange liqueur offers an additional hit of citrus. But this drink brings the acidity of hibiscus directly into an infused Tequila. With that power at the helm, an extra citrus bump is not necessary, so we're free to explore new flavors in the liqueur slot. We opted for Del Maguey Crema de Mezcal, a blend of mezcal from San Luis del Rio and *miel de maguey,* an unfermented syrup of roasted agave, which adds fruity notes as well as a lovely layer of smoke, enhancing the drink's agave profile.

**5 drops salt solution** (see page 27)

**1½ tablespoons sugar mix** (see page 94)

**¾ ounce strained lime juice**

**½ ounce Del Maguey Crema de Mezcal**

**1½ ounces hibiscus-infused Pueblo Viejo Reposado Tequila** (see page 102)

**¼ teaspoon xanthan gum**

**Lime wedge, for garnish**

- Combine all the ingredients, except the xanthan gum, in a blender. Dry blend (without ice). Once the sugar is fully dissolved, slowly add the gum while continuing to blend. Add 170 grams of crushed ice while continuing to blend. Pour into a large, chilled coupe (10 ounces).
- Garnish with a lime wedge.

RECIPE CONTINUES

### Hibiscus-Infused Tequila

This infusion has the benefit of a quick turnaround, with the full-strength spirit essentially "boiling" out the flavor of the dried flowers at room temperature. This recipe was modified from one used at PDT.

**15 grams dried hibiscus flowers**

**375 milliliters Pueblo Viejo Reposado Tequila**

- Steep the hibiscus in the Tequila for 90 minutes. Fine strain and bottle.

## Frozen Margarita

Mariano Martinez is a pioneer after our own detail-obsessed hearts. His East Dallas Tex-Mex restaurant, Mariano's Hacienda, served piquant and popular Margaritas, but in the high-volume heat of the moment, the quality sometimes slipped. Seeking consistent results for his customers, in 1971 Martinez devised the world's first frozen Margarita machine, adapting a soft-serve ice cream dispenser for a new, boozy career. Today that machine resides in the Smithsonian's National Museum of American History and its progeny have conquered the globe.

To salute both the ingenuity of Mariano Martinez and the drive toward consistently delicious drinks everywhere, here's our frozen template applied to the traditional Margarita. Please rise for the national anthem (which is, of course, "Qué de raro tiene" as performed by Vicente Fernández).

**5 drops salt solution** (see page 27)

**1 tablespoon sugar mix** (see page 94)

**¾ ounce strained lime juice**

**½ ounce Cointreau**

**1½ ounces Pueblo Viejo Blanco Tequila**

**¼ teaspoon xanthan gum**

**Lime wheel, for garnish**

**Salt for rim, optional**

- Combine all the ingredients, except the xanthan gum, in a blender. Dry blend (without ice). Once the sugar is fully dissolved, slowly add the gum while continuing to blend. Add 170 grams of crushed ice while continuing to blend. Pour into a large, chilled coupe (10 ounces).
- Garnish with a lime wheel and, optionally, a salt rim.

# Slushy Dog

*Translating a classic to the blender*

Many classic cocktails have been adapted for the frozen drink machine, but attuning shaken drinks to the blender is a greater challenge due to the rush of dilution that accompanies the pulverization of ice. Drinks most amenable to blender conversion are those with ingredients that can be concentrated, which explains the use of sugar in place of syrup.

Grapefruit seemed to be a flavor that would stand up to the blender process, so we looked to the quintessential grapefruit cocktail, the Salty Dog. It's served long with vodka or gin and a large measure of grapefruit juice, and is differentiated from the similar Greyhound by the presence of a salt rim, which tames the bitter edges of the grapefruit. In the classic Salty Dog, grapefruit juice brings both acidity and sweetness, but not really enough of either for balance. In order to succeed as a frozen sour, the grapefruit needed to drift toward a more fully acidic role, with sugar making up the difference.

Using the technique of acid adjusting, we can focus the grapefruit juice into an acidic component akin to lime. A more acidic juice means less is needed. (Acid adjusting is explained in detail starting on page 172.)

Note that white sugar is specified; the added molasses of Demerara and organic cane sugars would obscure the grapefruit.

This drink was directly inspired by the Gin and Juice served at Booker and Dax, which adapted the Greyhound/Salty Dog to its carbonated drink style. The Slushy Dog is the same idea conceived along the lines of our frozen style.

The drink is a natural for brunch.

RECIPE CONTINUES

**5 drops salt solution**
(see page 27)

**1 tablespoon white sugar**

**1 ounce grapefruit juice, acid adjusted to lime**
(see below)

**1½ ounces Fords Gin**

**¼ teaspoon xanthan gum**

**Grapefruit slice, for garnish**

**Salt for rim, optional**

- Combine all the ingredients, except the xanthan gum, in a blender. Dry blend (without ice). Once the sugar is fully dissolved, slowly add the gum while continuing to blend. Add 170 grams of crushed ice while continuing to blend. Pour unstrained into a chilled goblet (10 ounces).
- Garnish with a grapefruit slice and, optionally, a salt rim.

---

## Grapefruit Juice, Acid Adjusted to Lime

A full explanation of acid adjusting beings on page 172.

- Strain the grapefruit juice. Mix the acid (in proportions below) until the powders dissolve, then bottle. It will keep for 3 days in the refrigerator.
- To adjust grapefruit juice to the acidity of lime, to each 100 milliliters of juice add:
  2.0 grams citric acid
  2.0 grams malic acid

Your
Piña Colada.
Enjoy
it!

# Piña Colada

*Rehabilitating the resort staple*

Rupert Holmes and Warren Zevon came to regret ever mentioning them, but Piña Coladas remain frozen favorites. With a few revisions, we can lift them high above the mass-produced poolside product.

The drink is about pineapple first and foremost—the clue is in the name—yet the drink is often presented with a lurch toward overwhelming creaminess. The true Piña Colada should be pineapple accented by coconut. Once you accept that, the drink makes sense. Additionally, it must be prepared as an unapologetic frozen drink; shaken versions with crushed ice are a weak reverberation. The team at Painkiller (later PKNY) understood all this, and took the fore on reestablishing this beverage.

Sometimes a bartender will add lime juice to a Piña Colada in an attempt to tart up the pineapple. But, of course, it also adds the taste of lime, which is a third wheel in a drink that should showcase the flavors and textures of pineapple and coconut. Acid adjusting, which allows pineapple juice to achieve the same acidity as lime juice, is the real solution. (See page 172 for our explanation of acid adjusting.) Adding frozen pineapple chunks provides both sweetness and texture, while the simultaneous use of pineapple juice showcases the acidic aspect of the fruit.

As for the coconut component, the canned coconut cream Coco López is an excellent product. However, the addition of a small amount of coconut milk improves the texture and lowers the sweetness to the strength of standard simple syrup, while also curtailing the viscosity that can make coconut cream difficult to work with.

Adding Angostura is a permutation from the mind of Dale DeGroff. It's a subtle hit of spice that works in the background. Think of how delicious a spoonful of Angostura bitters would be on a slice of fresh pineapple.

We like the complexity of Scarlet Ibis punching through the richness, but a more traditional rum approach would be Don Q Gold. Or substitute a 100 proof vodka and you have yourself a Chi-Chi.

RECIPE CONTINUES

**5 drops salt solution**
(see page 27)

**2 dashes Angostura aromatic bitters**

**60 grams frozen pineapple**
(about 3 chunks)

**½ ounce pineapple juice, acid adjusted to lime**
(see page 180)

**1½ ounces coconut mix**
(see below)

**1½ ounces Scarlet Ibis Trinidad Rum or Don Q Gold Rum**

**¼ teaspoon xanthan gum**

**Pineapple wedge, for garnish**

**Pineapple leaves, for garnish**

- Combine all the ingredients, except the xanthan gum, in a blender. Dry blend (without ice). Once the sugar is fully dissolved, slowly add the gum while continuing to blend. Add 170 grams of crushed ice while continuing to blend. Pour into a chilled highball glass (12 ounces).
- Garnish with a pineapple wedge and pineapple leaves.

---

## Coconut Mix, 50 Brix

The suggested combination is a 3:1 ratio of López to milk, which should end up around 50 Brix depending on the brand of coconut milk used. Weighing will ensure an even more accurate measurement of sweetness. (See the section on sugar adjusting, starting on page 185, for more on degrees Brix and proper measuring for sweetness.)

**142 grams coconut milk**

**425 grams Coco López**

- Mix the ingredients together until uniform. (Due to the thickness of Coco López, a hand blender will help.) Pour into a squeeze bottle. It will keep in the refrigerator for 2 weeks. Makes 20 ounces.

# Cloud Forest

*Freezing fresh herbs*

While many classic drinks call for muddled mint, Donn Beach employed the blender to pulverize and disperse the herb in his Missionary's Downfall. Because the leaves freeze before they can brown, they lend the drink a brilliant green glow.

The Cloud Forest is the Missionary by way of Booker and Dax, where a popular drink was the Thai Basil Daiquiri (or T.B.D.), which showcased an innovative nitro-muddling technique. Nitro-muddling involves rapidly freezing an herb with liquid nitrogen, then grinding it with a muddler. The result is an herb powder with fresh, strong flavors that is easily incorporated into a cocktail.

Granted, the easy part comes only after the bit with giant tanks of liquid nitrogen and all the related safety gear. For those of us without such labs at home, a blender can be used to pulverize the herbs in a spirit, as the alcohol inhibits the enzyme that causes the color change. For a shaken drink like the T.B.D., the herb-liquor mix can then be transferred to a mixing tin and combined with the juice, syrup, and ice for shaking—but for the Cloud Forest we'll do the whole drink in the blender to create its distinctive frozen texture.

With spicier, anise-like notes not present in sweet basil, Thai basil is a complex ingredient worth exploring in cocktails. Coconut pairs well with it (as countless curries demonstrate), so we find ourselves contemplating a Colada format. The ascorbic acid (otherwise known as vitamin C) in lime further preserves the basil color against oxidation and provides the requisite tartness. Even though it contains coconut cream, the herbaceous qualities of the drink dominate. You can think of it as an amuse-bouche or palate cleanser.

The Cloud Forest also highlights judicial use of vodka in a cocktail, lengthening and fortifying a flavorful mixture without getting in its way. Any 100 proof vodka will do, but in a world of countless disappointing "craft" vodkas without much to recommend them, one product stands out to us—not for a difference in flavor, but for one in texture. Black Cow Vodka, fermented and distilled from whey left over from cheesemaking, has a subtle mouthfeel reminiscent of a milk-washed spirit straight out of the bottle. While its flavor is still neutral, allowing the Thai basil and coconut to stay central, the added texture calls to mind the chopped pineapple from the original Missionary's Downfall.

The drink's name is prompted by the cloud forests of Thailand's Doi Inthanon National Park, verdant and exhilarating.

RECIPE CONTINUES

**5 drops salt solution** (see page 27)

**14 to 16 Thai basil leaves**

**½ ounce strained lime juice**

**1½ ounces coconut mix** (see page 108)

**1½ ounces 100 proof vodka or Black Cow Vodka, if available**

**¼ teaspoon xanthan gum**

**Thai basil sprig, for garnish**

- Combine all the ingredients, except the xanthan gum, in a blender. Dry blend (without ice). Once the sugar is fully dissolved, slowly add gum while continuing to blend. Add 170 grams of crushed ice while continuing to blend. Pour into a chilled goblet (10 ounces).
- Garnish with a sprig of Thai basil.

# Frosty Buck

*The slushy machine you already own*

This chapter has detailed how blender drinks benefit from the use of granulated sugar instead of syrups. But what about drinks where syrup is irreplaceable because it is conveying a core flavor in addition to sweetness?

The buck, a drink format of spirit, citrus, and ginger beer or ale, is a style where the sweetness comes wrapped in flavor. Making your own ginger syrup affords much more control than commercially produced ginger beers, but there is still the challenge of integrating it into a frozen drink without over-dilution.

The way a frozen drink machine works suggests how it could be done, even without such a machine. The slushy machine slowly and uniformly freezes a mixture, then keeps it circulating to stay that way. We can replicate those steps with two appliances you already have: the freezer and the blender.

The same results produced by a slushy machine can be achieved by batching the cocktail with water and sealing it in an airtight container in the freezer. The slow, uniform freezing process yields a different ice crystal structure than what's found in a regular blender drink. Moreover, ice doesn't need to be added later—the drink becomes its own ice.

When the mixture is suitably frozen, the blender can then perform the circulation needed to create the drink's uniformity. Only a short blend is required, as the drink is already frozen (and remember, longer blending will melt it). It should take about 3 to 5 seconds of blending for the mixture to resemble a slushy drink.

Lime juice is added fresh to ensure a crucial citrus bite. Since it doesn't contain fruit juice, the batch can slumber in the freezer until you're ready to serve.

The rum blend for this drink is Coruba for body and Black Barrel for aromatics, with the two forming a strong base for the spice component. You can also try the same formula with gin, whiskey, or vodka.

The following specification can be scaled up to four servings for easier blending. In a pinch, you can also shake the frozen mixture in a tin, which will break it up into drinkable consistency.

**3 drops salt solution**
(see page 27)

**1 dash cardamom tincture**
(see page 162)

**⅜ ounce lime cordial**
(see page 221)

**⅜ ounce ginger syrup**
(see page 83)

**1 ounce Mount Gay Black Barrel Rum**

**1 ounce Coruba Rum**

**3½ ounces water**

**⅜ ounce strained lime juice**

- Place all the ingredients except the lime juice in an airtight container and stir until uniform. Freeze for 12 hours. The mixture should be firm when taken out of the freezer.
- Break up the frozen mixture with a fork and stir again to ensure uniform freezing. (This step replicates the churning of the frozen drink machine.) Freeze for an additional 12 hours.
- When ready to serve, combine the frozen contents of the container and lime juice in a blender. Blend for 3 to 5 seconds on low-medium speed until uniformly slushy.
- Pour into a chilled goblet (10 ounces).

# Ice Molds and Shaved Ice

The aesthetics of the original "rhum rhapsodies" at Don the Beachcomber were built on a dual foundation: gorgeous glassware and elaborate ice.

Donn sourced glassware from purveyors of the day, such as the Dunbar Glass Corporation in Dunbar, West Virginia, which in the 1930s produced an art deco juice glass known by many arcane catalog numbers until glassware historian Hazel Marie Weatherman dubbed it "the Aramis." This geometric, ribbed tumbler became familiar to tropical drink fans when Donn employed it in the Pearl Diver, by which name the glass itself is now commonly known.

The crown for such masterpieces in glass was equally glimmering molded ice. Together, the drinks' presentation was as regal as it was fantastical.

The key to molded ice is the texture of the ice used. Successful ice molds must be made from shaved ice, sometimes called snow ice, which is the finest type of ice. Even crushed ice consists of pieces too large to be properly formed into solid shapes.

While it may be more familiar to Americans as the snow cone, shaved ice is a culinary tradition throughout Asia. As early as the seventh century, Chinese nobles ate a form of shaved ice sweetened with palm sap. This dessert made its way across Asia, morphing into each culture's own icy delight, including Japanese kakigōri and the halo-halo of the Philippines.

Manufacturing the ice's pillowy texture required specific equipment. In Japan, rugged iron kakigōri machines contain a sharp, angled blade that shaves down a block of ice spun by a hand crank. Donn Beach acquired several of these Japanese ice shavers to generate ice for his molds, but importation of the machines was interrupted by World War II. Later tropical drink palaces, like the Mai-Kai, would rely on snow cone machines or ice makers from oyster bars.

Jeff Berry championed the return of the ice shaver to tropical bars, while Dave Arnold added a drink category to the menus at both Booker and Dax and Existing Conditions that highlighted the ice's unique texture. Bartenders at these venues would pour half a drink into a coupe. Then, with the same type of heavy iron machines Donn Beach had used, they would shave ice right into the glass (and in front of the customer). The first finely shaved layers would melt instantly in the glass, but additional shavings would build into a looming, frigid mountain. The rest of the drink was then poured on top, disappearing the mountain completely into the drink and filling the glass right to the rim. After this impressive presentation, the drink's final form was slushy, exhibiting the dilution of a frozen cocktail with the finer texture of the powdery ice.

If your bar top or budget won't support another cast-iron contraption, there are alternatives. As Jeff Berry explained, "Today all it takes to render snow ice from crushed is to run the crushed ice through a food processor, a much cheaper and speedier alternative to old-school ice shavers." In addition to your food processor, numerous single-purpose electric ice shavers are also available, sometimes referred to as snow cone machines. Handheld electric ice shavers that look like pepper grinders, such as the Otona Kakigori Automatic Shaved Ice Maker, are particularly effective in producing the ice needed for sturdy molds.

# Manta Ray

*Ice shell*

One of the most alluring of a host of alluring beverages available at the Mai-Kai is the Moonkist Coconut, offering more dimensions of spicy and savory notes than the typical coconut drink. While the Mai-Kai is famously secretive about its methods, the Moonkist Coconut was described in a 1959 *Esquire* profile of the bar, making it one of the few Mai-Kai recipes to be officially declassified. A full, historical spec to work from was a rare opportunity. After close study, we present the Manta Ray, which follows its progenitor's lofty ambitions.

As the Mai-Kai's offerings are based on the Don the Beachcomber canon, the Manta Ray is a careful pastiche of some of Donn's greatest hits: honey and ginger, as in the Queen's Road, plus peach and mint from the Missionary's Downfall.

Rum and gin are paired in some of the canon's favorites, such as the Fog Cutter and Ray's Mistake (we discuss these in our recipes for the Scarlet Fog, page 233, and Ray's Mystique, page 239). Finding the right combination requires some calculation, as every rum has its own flavor notes just as gins have their botanical profiles. We found a happy match between Fords and Barbancourt. Fords's jasmine elements work well with the peach and coconut while its citrus notes suit the lime and mint. Barbancourt's full flavor rounds out the drink.

The muddling technique here is the same as in the Penang Punch (page 50).

**6 mint leaves**

**5 drops salt solution** (see page 27)

**2 dashes Angostura aromatic bitters**

**½ ounce strained lime juice**

**½ teaspoon honey syrup** (see page 44)

**1 teaspoon ginger syrup** (see page 83)

**¾ ounce coconut mix** (see page 108)

**¼ ounce Giffard Crème de Pêche de Vigne Liqueur**

**¾ ounce Barbancourt 5 Star Rhum**

**¾ ounce Fords Gin**

**Grated cassia cinnamon, for garnish**

**Lime twist, for garnish**

- Muddle the mint leaves on the bottom of a large, chilled coupe (10 ounces). Fill the glass with 4 ounces of crushed ice.
- Combine the remaining ingredients in a mixing tin with 8 ounces of crushed ice. Flash blend for 5 seconds and pour unstrained into the glass.
- Dust with grated cassia cinnamon. Garnish with a lime twist and an ice shell (see page 118). Serve with a straw.

## ICE SHELL

The production of ice molds can seem intimidating. Here's a quick and efficient method for making an ice shell for drinks that works à la minute.

Presentation-oriented bars like Artesian in London have used tabletop citrus presses to form ice shells. Crushed ice is placed where the citrus ought to be and the handle is lowered, forcing the ice into the shape of a hollow half sphere. That nest would be floated on top of a cocktail, providing a platform for further garnishes to be added. The citrus presses, designed for limes, produced ice shells that were small and delicate.

For our ice shell, we'll use the same idea, but with a hand squeezer designed for oranges. The larger size gets us closer to the original Beachcomber molds.

The key is using the correct type of ice. Crushed ice doesn't compact enough from the pressure of a hand squeezer, so molds made with crushed ice tend to fall apart. Here's where we need to pull out an electric ice shaver to make finer snow ice. Fill your squeezer with snow ice, press down, and presto, you've constructed a beautifully delicate but appropriately sized ice shell. Push the side of the shell gently, and it will start to slide out of the press. When it's peeking over the edge, scoop it out.

# Field of Mars

*Ice cone*

Whiskey doesn't figure into many tropical drinks, so it's easy to get trapped in the framework of those drinks where it does appear, such as the Starboard Light and the Port Light. Like a number of Trader Vic drinks, they're tropical Whiskey Sours, easy to appreciate and easy to tinker with.

Here's another crack at the template where each ingredient suggests the next. Cherry and apple go well together; apple and whiskey go well together. And one of the most rapidly growing markets for Scotch is Southeast Asia, where makrut lime leaves receive many culinary applications. These overlapping observations suggested the elements of a new recipe.

Cherry-inflected red fassionola syrup is the start. Tartness comes from Granny Smith apple juice. The herbal flavors of lime leaf exhibit the freshness of the apples, joining their malic acid forces. It all sits on that bed of Scotch, which can stand up to these aggressive flavors.

As makrut lime leaves are both hard to come by and not long lasting, a nitrous-infused tincture technique preserves their attributes for as long as possible. The same technique works with other herbs, too. (See the Banshee on page 45 for a discussion of nitrous infusion.) Try the lime leaf tincture in a Gin and Tonic, a Daiquiri, or drinks with coconut.

Maria Ann Sherwood "Granny" Smith was a nineteenth-century Anglo-Australian midwife and orchardist, whose property in New South Wales abutted public land known as the Field of Mars. This term refers to a parade ground used by the military, but it nicely evokes our crimson-hued beverage and its space-age ice cone.

**5 drops salt solution**
(see page 27)

**¼ teaspoon makrut lime leaf tincture**
(see herb tincture, below)

**¾ ounce Granny Smith apple juice**

**¾ ounce strained lemon juice**

**½ teaspoon cane syrup**
(see page 52)

**¾ ounce red fassionola**
(see page 244)

**2 ounces Compass Box Artist Blend Scotch Whisky**

- Combine all the ingredients in a mixing tin with 8 ounces of crushed ice. Flash blend for 5 seconds and strain over an ice cone in a double Old Fashioned glass (16 ounces). Insert a straw into the ice cone.

RECIPE CONTINUES

### Herb Tincture

For this drink, we'll be making a makrut lime leaf tincture, but the same template applies to any herb you want to transform.

**500 milliliters 192 proof neutral spirit** (such as Lvov Spirytus or 190 proof Everclear)

**75 grams herb leaves (for example, makrut lime leaves, cilantro leaves, or others)**

- Place the neutral spirit and leaves in a blender. Blend until the herb is finely chopped and the liquid is green.
- Place the blended mixture in a cream whipper. Charge with two 7.5 gram $N_2O$ chargers. Shake the whipper for 30 seconds and then let it rest for 10 minutes. Vent rapidly, then let the mixture settle in the whipper until bubbling stops (about 10 minutes). Fine strain and bottle. It will keep indefinitely, and does not need to be refrigerated. Makes 16 ounces.

## ICE CONE

The ice cone is a presentational beacon that outfits your drink with elan as well as chill. But first you have to make one. Barware purveyor Cocktail Kingdom offers Beachbum Berry's Navy Grog Cone Kit, which provides specialized tools to turn out effective cones. But for those desiring a greater challenge, here's how our forebears did it with a glass and metal straw.

A Pilsner glass yields the appropriate conical shape, but the ice cone's delicate tip doesn't survive long after serving. With a highball glass, the ice mold is burlier but cylindrical; you might call it an ice buoy.

Hold an 8-inch metal straw in the center of a chilled 12-ounce highball glass, then pour shaved ice into the glass. When the glass is halfway full with ice, pack the ice down and around the straw. Repeat this process, pouring a bit more shaved ice into the glass and packing it firmly around the straw, until the glass is full. Remove the straw, revealing a shaft through the ice. Turn the glass upside down to remove the mold. Place the mold in the freezer for an hour before using it in a drink with a standard serving straw.

# Colonial Grog

*Ice-lined glass*

This Don the Beachcomber recipe from 1944 was unearthed by Jeff "Beachbum" Berry in the private papers of Mariano Licudine, the Beachcomber bartender who would later achieve fame as the drinks developer at the Mai-Kai. (On the Mai-Kai's menu, the Colonial Grog appears in disguise as the Samoan Grog.)

Maple syrup makes a rare appearance in a tropical drink, but fits in admirably here. The average maple syrup clocks in at about 66 Brix, in the range of a cane syrup, but with a darker, woodier pungency.

"It's just such a good example of how Donn Beach was constantly pushing himself to find and fold new ingredients into old templates," Jeff told us. "Using maple syrup as the sweetener instantly sets the Colonial Grog apart from all of Donn's many other Planter's Punch variations, and shows how a little imagination can go a long way in drink assemblage."

With this recipe Donn turned from his usual South Pacific themes to romanticize the colonial period of New England; the drink was sometimes described on his menus as involving "Very Old New England Rum." Such rum was still produced into the 1970s and has undergone a resurgence today, but for this version we're going even deeper into American drinking history.

Maple syrup and molasses were staples of colonial taverns—alongside rum, the spirit of choice in America's early days. Port, Madeira, sherry, and other imported fortified wines were also important in the period, so our version incorporates that colonial compulsion as well, by way of two cask-finished rums of unusual provenance.

Dos Maderas PX 5+5 is a blended rum sourced from Barbados and Guyana, aged for five years in the Caribbean in American oak and finished for an additional five years in Pedro Ximénez sherry casks in Spain. The Navazos Palazzi Oloroso Cask rum takes a molasses-based rum of an unspecified Caribbean origin and ages it for ten years in used Oloroso sherry casks. The Dos Maderas offers a wetter sherry flavor while the Navazos Palazzi is dry and woody. If the Navazos is not readily available, try English Harbour 5 Year Old Rum from Antigua.

Finishing the wine profile, Noilly Prat Extra Dry Vermouth brings acidity and crispness. The layering of these wine flavors is in line with both Donn's intentions and the cravings of the colonials.

RECIPE CONTINUES

**5 drops salt solution** (see page 27)

**3 dashes Angostura aromatic bitters**

**½ ounce strained lime juice**

**½ ounce strained orange juice**

**½ ounce maple syrup** (Grade A Dark Color and Robust Flavor), see Note

**½ teaspoon St. Elizabeth Allspice Dram**

**½ ounce Noilly Prat Extra Dry Vermouth**

**½ ounce Ron Navazos Palazzi Oloroso Cask Strength Rum or English Harbour 5 Year Old Rum**

**1½ ounces Dos Maderas PX 5+5 Rum**

**Grated nutmeg, for garnish**

- Combine all the ingredients in a mixing tin with 6 ounces of crushed ice. Flash blend for 5 seconds and pour unstrained into an Old Fashioned glass (12 ounces) lined with crushed ice.
- Dust with grated nutmeg. Serve with a straw.

**NOTE:** *The current designation of "Grade A Dark Color and Robust Flavor" is analogous to the former "Grade B" moniker and should not be confused with other iterations of "Grade A." This version of the syrup offers more maple flavor cutting through the sweetness.*

## ICE-LINED GLASS

The Colonial Grog featured one of Donn's more ingenious ice molds, the ice-lined Old Fashioned glass. This technique used the angles of the glass to create a lining of ice that crests over the rim of the glass. The resulting thin sheet of ice cradles the cocktail in a chilled, eye-pleasing package.

To make one, start with a chilled Old Fashioned glass. Fill it slightly more than halfway with shaved ice. Using a muddler or large spoon, press down on the center of the ice, creating a hole. Widen the hole by pressing the ice against the walls of the glass, keeping it uniform by pressing in each direction in turn. Add more shaved ice and repeat until the ice rises above the rim.

The ice above the glass will be very delicate. In order to secure these beautiful waves of ice, center a small shaker tin in the middle of the glass. Mold the lifted ice against the shaker. Slip the shaker out carefully. Place the glass in the freezer to harden the ice lining.

When served, a straw will be necessary to reach into the drink beyond the raised ice lining.

# EXPANSION

The shaken sour is the most common application for tropical drinks. But the tropical category ought to be a big tent. The world has a lot of tropics; the category has the flexibility to encompass all genres.

Can tropical perspective be added to drinks with no juice, to stirred drinks, to drinks with a savory character? Read on.

# Stirred

In the American mid-twentieth century, when tropical drinks freely roamed the land, stirred drinks like the Martini and the Old Fashioned also experienced a peak in popularity. But the styles, while equally in vogue, were rarely seen in the same company.

Now, as tropical drinks have once again risen in popularity, they have proliferated into craft cocktail bars—even those bars without a tropical focus—where they are served alongside pre-Prohibition favorites. Cross-pollination has developed among the different styles, with imaginative bartenders appropriating falernum as the sweetener in an Old Fashioned, or stirring a Martini-style drink with rhum agricole.

We've seen tropical ingredients end up in stirred drinks, but as stirred drinks themselves gain more fans, tropical bars should take the opportunity to adapt those styles to their own strengths. Stirred tropicals, overlooked in the times of tropical drinks' greatest popularity, represent a frontier of new possibilities. Among its advantages, a stirred tropical can show off the nuances of a complex sweetener, which would be lost in a tall drink.

We've divided the drinks in this section by the classic category of the stirred drink they most resemble: the Old Fashioned, the Martini/Manhattan, and the Negroni. They may be stirred and poured over ice, stirred and served up, or stirred in the glass with a large rock.

## OLD FASHIONED

The Old Fashioned is the Ur-cocktail, so named because it had already been around for ages by the time cocktails reached wide popularity in the late nineteenth century. It is the Eozoic bedrock of stirred drinks.

Its form is spirit, sugar, water, and bitters. It's a dignified showcase for spirits, softening their edge. However, it's the inclusion of bitters that most distinguishes the Old Fashioned, adding another dimension of complex spice. Isn't a Rum Old Fashioned, spiced with Angostura bitters made from Caribbean botanicals, already a tropical drink?

In recent years, Old Fashioneds with variations in base spirit, sweetener, and bitters have proliferated, many following in the wake of Phil Ward's Oaxaca Old Fashioned. A specifically tropical connection was made by Julie Reiner at Lani Kai, where she offered the Tree House, merging rye, rum, macadamia, and chocolate, bridging the traditional and tropical. Combinations like these show the tropical possibilities in an Old Fashioned setting.

# Romero

*Stirring on a rock*

The Romero is built like a late nineteenth-century Improved Whiskey Cocktail, which took the Old Fashioned pattern and added more layers of flavor through liqueurs. Here the liqueurs will be tropical.

Trader Vic's menus indicated "a whisper of almond" in his canonical Mai Tai and Scorpion Bowl, as he assigned the nut to an ongoing central role in tropical drinks. In the realm of stirred cocktails, almonds play a part in simple drinks like the Godfather, a basic combo of blended Scotch and Amaretto. It did for Disaronno what the Rusty Nail did for Drambuie: move a lot of product in 1970s fern bars.

The two-ingredient Godfather is close to an Old Fashioned, and serves as the starting point for this tropical Scotch exercise. While pairing Scotch with Amaretto was natural enough in the States, teaming Scotch with coconut water is a common Caribbean refresher. The Romero makes a unified Old Fashioned out of both Scotch combinations.

Instead of almond, we'll engage walnut. It pairs well with earthy flavors, so our Scotch is Bruichladdich The Classic Laddie, an unpeated Islay malt with an especially grain-forward profile. It will be the fire on which we roast the walnuts. However, if you prefer your walnuts more heavily roasted, split the Classic Laddie with a smokier Scotch such as Talisker or Bruichladdich's Port Charlotte.

Horror film director George A. Romero is, of course, the "Godfather of the Dead." Perhaps the aroma of this drink will conjure candy bars at a drive-in double feature. (For some reason, we're thinking we might mix a Zombie next.)

**3 drops salt solution** (see page 27)

**4 dashes Dave Arnold's chocolate bitters** (see page 46)

**¼ teaspoon Kalani Coconut Liqueur**

**½ teaspoon Demerara syrup**

**¾ teaspoon Nux Alpina Walnut Liqueur**

**2 ounces Bruichladdich The Classic Laddie whisky**

- Combine the ingredients in an Old Fashioned glass (12 ounces). Stir with a large ice cube until chilled.

# Violet Chachki

*Tropical fernet*

The bitters that you dash into your Old Fashioned are referred to as nonpotable bitters, since their highly concentrated bitterness makes them suitable only as an accent rather than the main beverage. But replacing them with a bitter spirit designed to be enjoyed on its own, like an Italian amaro, opens up a vast new stretch of Old Fashioned possibility.

A particularly popular category of amaro is fernet, a bitter liqueur strongly flavored with a blend of herbs, which vary from brand to brand. When we say popular, we mean especially with bartenders—witness the hearty revival of fernet-forward drinks like the Toronto or Hanky Panky.

Prime Meats in Brooklyn was known for a range of bitter cocktails, developed by head bartender Damon Boelte, that incorporated the leading fernet brand Fernet-Branca. While sampling one, a guest from Amsterdam revealed that back home he liked to drink fernet with violet syrup. It seemed like a discordant match, as both ingredients could dominate a drink on their own. How could dual dictators learn to peacefully rule the same land?

The trick was finding the right fernet. Luxardo's version is a bit drier than Branca, and contains savory notes, like cardamom, that harmonize with crème de violette. To arrange the drink in an Old Fashioned mold, it needed a base spirit strong enough to stand up to these two powerhouses. The vegetal, high-proof Rhum J.M is equal to the task.

Black pepper as the garnish was suggested by Jim Kearns when this drink was served at Slowly Shirley. It intensifies the arugula-like spiciness of the Luxardo Fernet and J.M Blanc combination.

This drink is served up, bringing its template closer to the Whiskey Cocktail than the Old Fashioned, though the serve is their major distinction. In its up form, the aromatics of the rum and amaro are better perceived. The black pepper becomes more intense as the drink warms.

Violet Chachki is a renowned drag queen, burlesque artist, and aerialist who shares fashion and mystery with this cocktail.

**3 drops salt solution** (see page 27)

**½ ounce Giffard Crème de Violette Liqueur**

**½ ounce Luxardo Fernet Amaro**

**1½ ounces Rhum J.M Blanc 100 Proof**

**Freshly ground black pepper, for garnish**

- Combine all the ingredients in a mixing glass filled with small ice cubes. Stir and strain into a Nick and Nora glass (5 ounces).
- Garnish with several turns of freshly ground black pepper.

# Bay of Pigs

*Cuba Libre, stirred*

The Bay of Pigs is a drink that transforms the Cuba Libre into an Old Fashioned, much as the 1961 Bay of Pigs invasion was meant to do with the real Cuba.

The Cuba Libre, known to capitalists as a rum and Coca-Cola with lime, is a classic highball, but as Coke is only a couple of steps from being a kind of nonalcoholic amaro, we thought it could be telescoped into the Old Fashioned format. The Filmograph cocktail, outlined in Ted Haigh's *Vintage Spirits and Forgotten Cocktails,* and consisting of brandy, lemon syrup, and kola tonic, was the initial impetus for this drink.

West Africa's kola nut is the basis for kola tonic, but, of course, it's also the second half of the famous name of Coca-Cola. Like cocaine, kola nut is no longer a component of Coca-Cola, which now uses artificial flavors to get somewhere in the vicinity.

Instead of kola tonic, we'll turn sugarcane-based Mexican Coke into a syrup, which we call a "grog concentrate" from similar flavors in Trader Vic's version of the Navy Grog. (See page 205 for the tale.) The tonic component comes courtesy of inventive bartender Tom Richter's Tomr's Tonic syrup. Tom developed the ingredient to bring natural cinchona bark back to the Gin and Tonic, which had long languished among high-fructose corn syrup and artificial flavors. His syrup is meant to be added to club soda to create tonic water, but here we're using it in concentrated form. (You can find it sold online, including from Tom's own site. See page 89 for its application in the Rum and Tonic.)

The cordial and concentrates bring acidity, which isn't traditionally part of an Old Fashioned, but helps to replicate the bite of the bubbles in a Cuba Libre, here absent. The acidity differentiates the Bay of Pigs from other Old Fashioneds, just as lime transforms a rum and Coke into a Cuba Libre. The clarified cordial makes this possible, as we'll see in other stirred drinks such as the Beachcomber Negroni, Classic Gimlet, and Improved Rum Cocktail.

To get a bit closer to the characteristics of the aged Cuban rums of yore, we're calling for a blend of Don Q Cristal, which replicates the lightness of a traditional Cuban, and Chairman's Reserve, which despite not being in the Cuban tradition brings more of the molasses-forward qualities that would have been found in an early twentieth-century Cuban rum.

A traditional Old Fashioned is stirred in the glass with a big rock of ice. For the Bay of Pigs, we indicate stirring in a mixing glass with cubed ice before serving over the usual big rock because, unlike the traditional Old Fashioned, the Bay of Pigs contains a much higher level of acid, which must be balanced by more dilution to prevent its dominance.

RECIPE CONTINUES

**3 drops salt solution** (see page 27)

**2 dashes Angostura aromatic bitters**

**½ teaspoon Tomr's Tonic syrup**

**¼ ounce lime cordial** (see page 221)

**¼ ounce grog concentrate syrup** (see page 206)

**1 ounce Don Q Cristal Rum**

**1½ ounces Chairman's Reserve Rum**

**Channeled lime twist, for garnish**

- Combine all the ingredients in a mixing glass filled with small ice cubes. Stir and strain into an Old Fashioned glass (12 ounces) with a large ice cube.
- Garnish with a channeled lime twist.

## MARTINI/MANHATTAN

The gin and dry vermouth Martini and the whiskey and sweet vermouth Manhattan are nonidentical twins born in America in the 1870s or '80s. Entire books have been written on these titans of tippling, but we'll keep it brief. For a scintillating look at the cultural significance of the Martini, we recommend *Martini, Straight Up* by Lowell Edmunds. All his other books are on ancient Greek and Roman literature, but the Martini is just as classic a subject.

The form is spirit, vermouth, and bitters, through which the Manhattan and Martini show the importance of aromatized wine as an ingredient. Building on the Old Fashioned, the Martini and Manhattan add vermouth, which lengthens modifiers and highlights base spirits in new ways. Vermouth also brings with it some acidity and a range of botanicals, possibilities that are explored in the following drinks.

# El Presidente

*More than Cuba's Martini*

As ever, Cuba is the font of libationary imagination. This truly tropical stirred drink arose on its shores sometime around 1915, when it first appeared in print in John B. Escalante's *Manual de Cantinero*. While often mistaken for a rum Martini in the years since, the original drink holds more mystery.

"Upside down" or "inverted" variants of cocktails, where a low-proof ingredient (for example, vermouth) is used in greater measure than a high-proof one (for instance, rum), are popular with both bartenders and bar-goers today, offering an experience that's lower in alcohol but still rich with flavor—and especially aroma.

"Aroma molecules are . . . more chemically similar to alcohol molecules than they are to water, so they tend to cling to alcohol, and are quicker to evaporate out of a drink when there's less alcohol to cling to," Harold McGee wrote in a 2010 *New York Times* piece. "This means that the more alcoholic a drink is, the more it cloisters its aroma molecules, and the less aroma it releases into the air. Add water and there's less alcohol to irritate and burn, and more aroma release."

The original El Presidente from 1915 was there first, specifying two parts of vermouth to one of rum. The Cuban original called for vermouth de Chambéry, a specific style from the Alpine outpost of Chambéry with a distinct flavor profile that was long missing from the American market. We're fortunate that there are now two such vermouths available, Dolin Blanc and Comoz Blanc Vermouth de Chambéry. The restitution of this ingredient makes a huge difference in the drink's success.

Dolin suggests elderflower, vanilla, plenty of citrus, and a thin thread of bitterness from wormwood. Comoz proceeds in a similar vein, but with a stronger wormwood note, and a finish of stone fruit and cherries. In El Presidente, the attributes of the Comoz mesh with the other ingredients in a manner tailor-made. For the rums, Hamilton is dry but aromatic, working to support the vermouth, while Scarlet Ibis brings a bit of gravitas.

As with other inverted drinks—and like the Martini—El Presidente has evolved over the years to accommodate changing tastes. While the original was "upside down" and modern takes are usually rum-forward, in truth the vermouth to spirit ratio exists on a sliding scale. Audrey Saunders's Pegu Club was a haven for inverted drinks as well as her revitalization of the equal parts Martini (known with New York swagger as a Fiddy-Fiddy). Our Presidente takes this equitable approach, but can be easily adjusted to any ratio you prefer.

RECIPE CONTINUES

**5 drops salt solution** (see page 27)

**2 dashes orange bitters** (see page 62)

**½ teaspoon grenadine** (see page 68)

**1 teaspoon Pierre Ferrand Dry Curaçao**

**½ ounce Scarlet Ibis Trinidad Rum**

**1 ounce Hamilton White 'Stache Rum**

**1½ ounces Comoz Blanc Vermouth de Chambéry**

**Lemon peel, for garnish**

- Combine all the ingredients in a mixing glass filled with small ice cubes. Stir and strain into a chilled coupe (6 ounces).
- Garnish with a lemon peel.

# Our Man in Havana

This riff puts quinine-flavored fortified wine in place of the vermouth, and makes it the main ingredient, as in the original 1915 El Presidente. The Byrrh, with a base of red mistelle, presents a fascinating fruit contrast to the rum in a totally different way from the vermouth version.

Barbancourt's dryness is akin to an aged Cuban rum, but its fresh cane backbone correlates with the vegetal sting of quinine in the Byrrh. Orgeat replaces grenadine to add a floral finish.

Our friend Charles H. Baker Jr. was a loyal fan of the theatrical channeled lime twist garnish, even when not entirely justified. Here its purposeful existence imbues the drink with brightness, like the ghost of fruit the cocktail does not contain.

**3 drops salt solution** (see page 27)

**1 dash orange bitters** (see page 62)

**1 dash Angostura aromatic bitters**

**½ teaspoon orgeat** (see page 72)

**1 teaspoon Pierre Ferrand Dry Curaçao**

**1 ounce Barbancourt 5 Star Rhum**

**2 ounces Byrrh Grand Quinquina**

**Channeled lime twist, for garnish**

- Combine all the ingredients in a mixing glass filled with small ice cubes. Stir and strain into a chilled Nick and Nora glass (5 ounces).
- Garnish with a channeled lime twist.

# Golden Horseshoe

*Layering botanicals*

Among the onslaught of Galliano cocktails during the 1960s and 1970s (see the Yellow Bird, page 61, for more), the Raffaello stands out. This drink by Angelo Zola, the long-tenured president of the International Bartenders Association, combines pisco and blanc vermouth, an unusual choice for the period. It seems more like a cocktail you'd find at a craft bar today.

Although containing vermouth and no juice, the Raffaello was specified as being shaken and served over ice. The Golden Horseshoe is a reimagination of that spec as the stirred, up drink it yearns to be.

Vanilla and a complex composite of botanicals are at the foundation of both blanc vermouth and Galliano. The Golden Horseshoe is engineered like a classically layered tropical drink, and every layer reinforces that Galliano and blanc vermouth duet.

Contratto Bianco vermouth is both bitter and juicy, with a strong note of chamomile, another traditional pairing with vanilla, which also finds resonance in the Bittermens Boston Bittahs. Replacing pisco is a Highland Tequila with savory characteristics and salinity, plus the black pepper power of Spanish Mahón gin—a salt and pepper sonority among the many botanicals.

To balance these conspicuous savory qualities, a liqueur complementary to Galliano was needed. Thyme liqueur, an underrated bartender's tool, works alongside Galliano's lavender aspect just as the two herbs drive many contemporary interpretations of *herbes de Provence*.

**3 drops salt solution** (see page 27)

**½ teaspoon Bittermens Boston Bittahs**

**¼ ounce thyme liqueur** (such as Bigallet or Farigoule de Forcalquier)

**¼ ounce Galliano L'Autentico**

**¾ ounce Contratto Bianco**

**½ ounce Mahón Xoriguer Gin**

**1½ ounces Fortaleza Blanco Tequila or Siete Leguas Blanco Tequila**

**Orange peel, for garnish**

- Combine all the ingredients in a mixing glass filled with small ice cubes. Stir and strain into a chilled coupe (6 ounces).
- Garnish with a flamed orange peel.

# Mr. Hoy's Manhattan

*Infusing whole fruit*

The Algonquin is a drink with an enigmatic past and an unusual recipe that weaves rye, vermouth, Angostura, and pineapple. Its favor during the cocktail revival may have more to do with its narrative than its composition. It's time to admit that it isn't a great drink.

To the ears of many cocktailians, the name Algonquin conjures up the wit, bonhomie, and alcohol enthusiasm of the literary members of the Algonquin Round Table, who lunched for years at the eponymous New York hotel. While it is not entirely evident that the drink is named after the hotel, that's what we all want to believe.

From the end of Prohibition in 1933 until his untimely death in 1941, G. Selmer Fougner wrote an incomparable newspaper column, "Along the Wine Trail," a daily feature of the *New York Sun.* In addition to bringing his readership up to speed on a few thousand years of wine and food history (of which Americans were only beginning to become aware), he regularly fielded questions from imbibers seeking the recipe to a cocktail they'd encountered in the wild. Therefore, his column is often the earliest printed source for recipes, and so it is with the rye and pineapple Algonquin.

Fougner's April 14, 1934, column responds to the reader query, "Are the Manhattan and the Old Fashioned the only good cocktails which may be made with rye whisky?" with a curation of six recommendations, including the "New Algonquin." From there the drink was collected in numerous other cocktail guides including the influential *Fine Art of Mixing Drinks* by David Embury, from whence it has been rediscovered by today's bartenders. Yet, it remains a disconcerting combination not befitting the august Algonquin name. Pineapple juice brings sweetness, but it also brings a lot of dilution, as does the dry vermouth, and the rye is not strong enough to counter them. Instead, it ends up losing its spicy edge in the deluge.

Let's apply our principles to resuscitate the concept. Instead of remaining locked up in juice, pineapple flavor can be concentrated directly into the rye through infusion. With the volume of the juice removed, the whiskey and vermouth are free to relate to one another as they would in a typical Manhattan. But the recipe needs one final nudge. In another rye and dry vermouth stirred drink, the Brooklyn, amaro and maraschino play a part. Here they replace the bitters.

Hoy Wong worked as a bartender for fifty-eight years, the final thirty of which were spent at the Algonquin Hotel, before his retirement in 2009 at eighty-eight years of age. He was the oldest working barman in New York, known to all as Mr. Hoy.

We will close this discussion with a story from the career of Hoy Wong that has often been told,

RECIPE CONTINUES

but not always fully annotated. In 1961, Mr. Hoy was working the bar at celebrity hangout Freeman Chum's when the Duke of Windsor (formerly known as King Edward VIII) stepped up and called for "a House of Lords Martini in and out on toast." Mr. Hoy calmly and immediately made the drink exactly as the Duke expected, and the royal personage went away satisfied. But what the heck was that order, with its ducal spin on soda jerk slang?

"House of Lords" is the brand of gin, "in and out" is the practice of swirling vermouth in the glass and then discarding it, and "on toast" is a flamed lemon twist. Here, the skill on display does not involve the drink's execution as much as it does Mr. Hoy's ability to manifest even the most abstruse desires of his guests. We leave this as an exercise for the reader.

**3 sprays Vieux Pontarlier Absinthe**

**3 drops salt solution** (see page 27)

**½ teaspoon Luxardo Maraschino**

**½ ounce Amaro Lucano**

**¾ ounce Dolin Dry Vermouth**

**2¼ ounces pineapple-infused Rittenhouse Rye** (see below)

**Cherry, for garnish**

- Rinse a chilled coupe (6 ounces) with 3 sprays of Vieux Pontarlier Absinthe from an atomizer. Combine all the ingredients in a mixing glass filled with small ice cubes. Stir and strain into the rinsed coupe.
- Garnish with a cherry.

---

## Pineapple-Infused Rittenhouse Rye

Long infusions with fresh produce tend to result in jammy and oxidized flavors. Employing a vacuum sealer speeds up the process, keeping the fruit flavor clean and present—palpably juicy but still suitable for stirred drinks.

This is a template for infusing whole fruit in spirits; try swapping in other fruits and spirit bases with the same proportions.

**600 grams chopped pineapple**

**500 milliliters Rittenhouse Rye**

- Combine the ingredients in a vacuum seal bag, and seal with a vacuum sealer. Let mixture steep for 48 hours in the refrigerator. Fine strain and bottle. It will keep for 6 months in the refrigerator. Makes about 12 ounces.

  Please note that vacuum sealers are generally designed to work with solids, so sealing a bag of liquid comes with some challenges. The vacuum can pull out liquid as well as air. Hold the bag's opening high enough so the contents won't spill. Go slow if you can; it's preferable to use a chamber vacuum sealer or vacuum sealer with a pulse option, where smaller amounts of air can be pushed out without a full cycle. There are also machines that seal without vacuuming, an approach that also works for our purposes. It's not necessary to remove all the air to make this infusion.

## NEGRONI

The Negroni is now more than a decade into its third wave of popularity. As with just about every other mixed drink, its ultimate origins are murky, but it has repeatedly achieved fame, although not always under the same name.

The form is spirit, vermouth, and amaro. It's an interesting example of a European translation of American cocktail techniques, which themselves were made possible by European ingredients. The Negroni developed from the Americano, an Italian reinterpretation of how Americans used Italian vermouth in cocktails, with the replacement of aromatic bitters with native amaro.

An early recording of the recipe is found in 1929's *L'heure du cocktail,* by Parisian barmen J. Alimbau and E. Milhorat, under the name Campari Mixte. The recipe specifies Campari, gin, and sweet vermouth in equal parts—the version beloved today under the Negroni moniker. In the same year, *Cocktails de Paris,* by Georges-Gabriel Thenon, presented the Camparinete (attributed to another Parisian bartender, Albert of the Hotel Chatham), which doubles the quantity of gin.

The Negroni is known for its many variations today, but 'twas ever thus. *Cocktails de Paris* is bursting with drinks involving Campari, gin, and one or two more vermouths in different proportions, including the Charlie Pie, the Gloria, the Lucien Gaudin, and the Tunnel. They were all reprinted in the 1934 edition of *ABC of Mixing Cocktails* by Harry MacElhone and the same year's *World Drinks and How to Mix Them,* attributed to "Cocktail Bill" Boothby posthumously, from whence they found their way into Trader Vic's own *Bartender's Guide* of 1947. Therefore these drinks were even on Vic's radar, although his forays into the format seem to end there.

This category exemplifies the aperitif, designed to open up the palate and stimulate the appetite. Its bitter-forward profile has usually been antithetical to the fruitier focus of tropical drinks, but bartenders today are rethinking those boundaries after the worldwide success of the Jungle Bird, perhaps the first truly tropical bitter drink (and another recipe rescued by Jeff "Beachbum" Berry).

A greater variety of amari and vermouths is available today than has been for generations, which means there are even more ways of expressing the Negroni's serene social graces. Along the way, the drink has developed into a category, with new and old favorites such as the White Negroni and Boulevardier expanding its boundaries. Herein is the tropical exploration of the genre.

# De Ville

*Absinthe with the top down*

The Quill cocktail—a Negroni with its botanicals supercharged with a dash of absinthe—struck us as a drink ripe for co-option into the tropical canon. Donn's "rhum rhapsodies" made regular use of absinthe, although usually in greater quantities than classic cocktails did. Perhaps the subtle Quill could form a bridge into a new tropical aperitif format.

Two relatively recent expressions from Martini & Rossi, an intense amber vermouth and a spicy bitter, slotted into the sweet vermouth and Campari roles. The Martini bitter, with a higher presence of angostura bark than most red bitters, interacts with the absinthe similarly to the one-two punch of Angostura bitters and absinthe found in Donn's drinks.

For the absinthe, Vieux Pontarlier, brighter and higher in proof than our other commonly used brand, St. George, seemed the right fit, offering lively citrus and fennel notes. Rounding it out, we chose a split base of rums with enough age and aromatics to hold their own against the absinthe.

Over many years of manufacture, Cadillac rendered the name of its famous car with various combinations of capitalization and spacing ("de Ville," "De Ville," "deVille," and "DeVille"). In 1967, the spelling of the moment was "De Ville," and paint options included two arresting ruby shades, Flamenco Red and Ember Firemist. Our cocktail lands somewhere in between.

**5 drops salt solution** (see page 27)

**2 dashes orange bitters** (see page 62)

**1 teaspoon Vieux Pontarlier Absinthe**

**½ ounce Barbancourt White Rhum**

**¾ ounce Martini Riserva Speciale Bitter**

**1 ounce Martini Riserva Speciale Ambrato Vermouth di Torino**

**1¼ ounces Mount Gay Black Barrel Rum**

**Lemon twist, for garnish**

**Vieux Pontarlier Absinthe spray**

- Combine all the ingredients in a mixing glass filled with small ice cubes. Stir and strain into a chilled Old Fashioned glass (12 ounces).
- Garnish with a lemon twist and a spray of absinthe from an atomizer.

# Tijuana Taxi

*Building a better banana*

The last few years have brought an explosion of new liqueur brands and flavors to the market, which has been a boon to creating new recipes and innovating on classics. However, one commercially available ingredient that has yet to match our needs is banana liqueur. The new offerings come off as a bit green and bitter. They do not conjure the canonical experience of bananas for breakfast, proudly topping French toast. While the longtime stalwart, 99 Bananas, tastes strongly of artificially flavored candy, its high proof does deliver that flavor well.

Artificial banana flavor was designed to mimic the now-defunct Gros Michel cultivar, which was the dominant type of banana until disease hit the global industry in the 1950s. The current top banana, the Cavendish (which now has its own difficulties with disease), is generally considered to be less delectable than the Gros Michel. This is due to far lower levels of an ester known as isoamyl acetate, which happens to be the main ingredient in artificial banana flavor. This is a roundabout way of saying that artificial banana flavor actually tastes more like bananas than bananas do anymore.

Why not capture the best of both worlds by infusing 99 Bananas with real bananas? Freeze-dried banana slices, which are widely available, yield a better result than dehydrated or even fresh, as this process best preserves the fruit's delicate aromas. The bananas rehydrate in whatever liquid they are steeped in, resulting, in this case, in an amazing, layered banana flavor that spans the ages of Gros Michel and Cavendish. With the stacking of one banana atop another, we create our banana bunch liqueur, for which the recipe is included here.

Mezcal can walk the line between fruity, saline, and acidic in a way that shows off the banana's special qualities. Del Maguey Chichicapa or Vida mesh well here.

The dry vermouth accent was suggested by Don the Beachcomber's Tahitian Punch, an interesting application of banana and white wine.

RECIPE CONTINUES

**5 drops salt solution** (see page 27)

**6 drops Bittermens Orange Cream Citrate Bitters**

**¼ ounce banana bunch liqueur** (see below)

**¼ ounce Suze Apéritif**

**½ ounce Noilly Prat Extra Dry Vermouth**

**1 ounce Mattei Cap Corse Blanc Quinquina**

**1 ounce Del Maguey Chichicapa Mezcal or Del Maguey Vida Mezcal**

**Lime twist, for garnish**

- Combine the ingredients in an Old Fashioned glass (12 ounces). Stir with one large ice cube until chilled.
- Garnish with a lime twist.

---

## Banana Bunch Liqueur

**75 grams freeze-dried bananas, such as Trader Joe's brand**

**500 milliliters 99 Bananas liqueur**

- Combine the ingredients in a container and infuse for 24 hours. Fine strain and bottle. It will keep for 6 months in the refrigerator. Makes about 14 ounces.

# Beachcomber Negroni

*A fix for the Mix*

Donn Beach organized the bottles in his bar with two goals in mind: to assist his bartenders in making his drinks and to confound attempts by his competitors' bartenders to make them. Many recipes were executed by his team without ever knowing what was truly in bottles labeled only with code names. Most such entities were blandly numbered, but one was proudly labeled Don's Mix.

If the name wasn't intriguing enough, the mix featured in one of Donn's most beloved creations, the original 1934 version of the Zombie. When Donn seemingly took the Mix's recipe to his grave, tropical cocktailians were mourning more than just the great man's passing.

As with just about every other question arising from long-lost tropical recipes, it was Jeff "Beachbum" Berry who cracked the case. (Read his page-turning account of gumshoeing all the way to Donn's secrets in *Sippin' Safari.*) The sought-after key was revealed to be one part cinnamon syrup to two parts grapefruit juice. It unlocked the classic Zombie for the first time in decades.

But it was also a bit of prosaic bar bureaucracy. Other than to purposely confuse rivals, was there a reason to keep grapefruit juice and cinnamon syrup together? Ubiquitous deployment wasn't the case—the Donga Punch was the only other drink to use it—and plenty of drinks used cinnamon or grapefruit separately, so Donn was increasing rather than decreasing the bottles in his well. The shelf life of those bottles also shortened because juice degrades faster than syrup.

Nevertheless, the "rhum rhapsody" tradition was built on unusual flavor combinations as exemplified by ingredients like Don's Mix. Was there a way to evolve the mix to where it could be used more widely in drinks, where it conveyed its flavors more directly? Could we make a cordial that infuses the cinnamon directly into the grapefruit juice, thus cutting down on the increased water content?

Using clarified juice solves the shelf life discrepancy. Incorporating grapefruit peel raises the mixture to a pungency not found in mere juice. We have a bolder Don's Mix, with more flavor and less water, to unleash on stirred drinks in precise amounts. It's built as a spiced cordial, in line with the cordial techniques covered on pages 217–218. Reflecting its changed status, it's now Don's Remix.

That takes care of the Mix, now how about the drink itself? Campari works as well with grapefruit as it does with its more common partner, orange, so a Negroni format seemed the right place to start.

The Beachcomber Negroni follows a dry vermouth Negroni template, as in variants like the Cardinale or Lucien Gaudin, but with reduced Campari augmented with a small amount of fruit from Don's Remix and clarified lime juice. This hint of acidity gives the feel of squeezing a lime into a Wray and Ting or dropping one into a Ti' Punch. Here, the lime is invisible but its presence is clear.

RECIPE CONTINUES

The combination of rums follows Donn's trendsetting approach of blending rums of different characteristics, but with unaged and lightly aged spirits, which he rarely used. Flor de Caña contributes creaminess, Banks offers aromatics, and Wray & Nephew bestows raw power.

Unlike a standard Negroni that is built in the glass, this drink is stirred with ice and strained, as the higher acid needs a bit more water to balance.

**5 drops salt solution** (see page 27)

**¼ ounce clarified lime juice** (see template on page 218)

**½ ounce Don's Remix** (see below)

**½ ounce Campari**

**½ ounce Wray & Nephew Overproof Rum**

**½ ounce Flor de Caña 4 Year Old Rum**

**½ ounce Banks 5 Island Rum**

**1 ounce Dolin Dry Vermouth**

**Grapefruit peel, for garnish**

- Combine all the ingredients in a mixing glass filled with small ice cubes. Stir and strain into a double Old Fashioned glass (16 ounces) with a large ice cube.
- Garnish with a grapefruit peel.

---

## Don's Remix

Our re-imagining of the famed Don's Mix—cinnamon syrup and grapefruit juice—that animates the original Zombie but is too dilute to be truly versatile.

Extracting spice from the cinnamon bark requires serious boiling, but the heat will make pectins in the juice bitter. The remedy is to first rid the juice of those pesky pectins through clarification, and then amp up the acid to better resemble the tarter grapefruits of Donn's era.

**15 grams cassia cinnamon bark, broken into ½-inch pieces**

**30 grams grapefruit peel**

**250 grams clarified grapefruit juice** (see template on page 218)

**250 grams white sugar**

**5.25 grams citric acid**

- Toast the cinnamon bark in a saucepan over medium-low heat until aromatic. Add the peels, juice, and sugar. Bring the mixture to a simmer, stirring occasionally, then cover and reduce heat to low. After 15 minutes, remove from heat and let it sit for 12 hours.
- Strain the syrup into a blender, add the citric acid, and blend until the acid is fully dissolved (about 5 to 10 seconds).
- Bottle and refrigerate. It will keep for 4 weeks in the refrigerator. Makes 16 ounces.

## Donga Punch

As a bonus, here's a simple spec (shaken, not stirred!) that also uses Don's Remix. Jeff Berry discovered this long-lost Don the Beachcomber drink from circa 1939 in the personal notebooks of headwaiter Dick Santiago. It was originally served over crushed ice, but our adaptation is in an up, Daiquiri style.

**5 drops salt solution** (see page 27)

**¾ ounce strained lime juice**

**¾ ounce Don's Remix** (see above)

**2 ounces Trois Rivières Cuvée de L'Océan Rhum Blanc Agricole**

**Grapefruit twist**

**Pansy, for garnish**

- Combine all the ingredients in a shaker with 1 medium ice cube and 2 small ice cubes. Shake and strain into a chilled coupe (6 ounces). Express a grapefruit twist over the drink and discard.
- Garnish with a pansy.

# Savory

Savory flavors are associated with cooking, not bartending. But there's no strong reason for that distinction: Anything we find delicious can play a role in both food and drink, and imbibers are increasingly drawn to spicy drinks. This chapter enlists savory and spicy ingredients to expand the conception of the tropical cocktail.

For many people, the category of savory drinks begins and ends with the Bloody Mary, though on occasion, the beef broth–based Bull Shot has risen to prominence. Spicy and savory drinks only received serious attention once American palates began to embrace spicier cuisines. We can track the progress of such drinks alongside newfound interest in Southeast Asian and Latin American food in the 1980s and '90s.

A fascinating time capsule from that stage of development is *New Classic Cocktails* by Gary Regan and Mardee Haidin Regan, published in 1997. With the craft cocktail revival in its infancy, it's one of the first documents of bartenders of the era (as well as many chefs) proposing new recipes with classical foundations. Accordingly, plenty of the drinks in the book are tweaks on classics: a Margarita with mezcal and brandy, a Martini with Chartreuse, a Sazerac with Tequila. Some of the recipes seem limited by the ingredients available at the time, a keen reminder of how fortunate we are today.

A sizable chunk of the drinks described involve savory combinations of vegetation. Esti Benson's Rialto Bianco, from the Rialto Restaurant she managed in Cambridge, Massachusetts, is based on basil-infused vermouth. From the Tapika Restaurant in New York comes executive chef David Walzog and general manager Jason Lapin's creation, the Chile Rita, a straightforward Margarita enhanced with jalapeño-infused Tequila. And perhaps the grandpappy of them all, the Cajun Martini, first served at K-Paul's in New Orleans in 1980 by chef Paul Prudhomme and his wife Kay, brings jalapeño into service in a Gin Martini. It's no surprise that savory drinks were kick-started in kitchens, as chefs were already used to ordering and preparing herbs every day.

Half a century previously, Charles H. Baker Jr. was there to weigh in with the Holland Razor Blade, a Gin Sour dusted with cayenne. Even earlier, Leo Engel's 1875 manual *American & Other Drinks* contains three flips with a pinch of cayenne each. Spice has always been with us, but only recently has it been given pride of place.

As the cocktail revival got into gear circa 2005, Milk & Honey rolled out more gin savories: Gordon's Cup, a Caipirinha styling of the Red Snapper, which evolved into Gordon's Breakfast, featuring Cholula hot sauce. Shortly thereafter, Phil Ward's recipe for jalapeño-infused Tequila popped up in a range of drinks at the newly opened Death & Co. Los Angeles bar maestro Julian Cox, helming Rivera in 2010, wove chipotles, red peppers, and *sal de chapulín* (yes, that's grasshopper salt) into impeccably executed cocktails. Far from a forgotten niche, spicy and savory drinks were ringing up big sales.

"When I'm working on a new menu, I ask for feedback from the bartenders and servers about what people are asking for that we don't have an answer to," Meaghan Dorman, bar director of the Raines Law Room and Dear Irving, told us. Every time, guests are clamoring for more spice. "It challenges us, because people say, 'I've tried all your spicy drinks. What's next?' "

How about spicy and tropical? After all, in the heyday of Don the Beachcomber and Trader Vic's, a Zombie or Rum Barrel would be served alongside boldly flavored dishes. Could the seasonings found in those courses be integrated into the drinks themselves?

These especially culinary drinks offer a strong connection to the cuisines most often linked with tropical cocktails, but they also allow us to explore some unexpected cuisine pairings and the special techniques that make them work.

# Swamp Fire

*Chartreuse at the disco*

Chartreuse has been an outsized player in the craft cocktail revival, but in the mid-1970s it was a little-known French liqueur struggling to find a home in the juice-filled highballs dominating the nightclub scene. Chartreuse's importer, Schieffelin & Co., took note when rival importer McKesson used signature cocktails to drum up massive demand for their own brightly colored European import, Galliano. The Yellow Bird (page 61) and the Raffaello, reimagined here as the Golden Horseshoe (page 139), poured the canary-colored liqueur into the public consciousness, and Schieffelin set out to find an equally captivating platform for their monastically produced herbal liqueur among the Harvey Wallbangers and Tequila Sunrises.

The resulting drink was the Swamp Water, a shot of Green Chartreuse topped with pineapple juice and a squeeze of lime—a savvy combination that played into the liqueur's natural affinity with pineapple to make for easy sipping without losing herbal nuance. Schieffelin pulled out the stops on advertising, plastering a cartoon alligator across custom glassware and print ads that promised "more bang than a Wallbanger, more fire than a Sunrise." Alas, even cocktail-sippin' gators couldn't convince nightclubbers that this was true party fuel, and the Swamp Water sank out of sight.

Our version, the Swamp Fire, brings plenty of bang and fire, at long last fulfilling the advertised promise. Augmenting the Chartreuse and pineapple combo are jalapeño-infused Tequila and green chile vodka, for the feeling of both hot and sweet peppers. As the St. George Green Chile Vodka also involves lime peel and cilantro, these are echoed in the other ingredients. The drink exhibits a pepper flavor that's both broad and deep.

The structure of this drink has similarities to the Blue Leilani (page 252), though you wouldn't know it from the flavor or appearance.

RECIPE CONTINUES

**5 drops salt solution** (see page 27)

**½ teaspoon cilantro tincture** (see below)

**1 teaspoon Demerara sugar**

**½ ounce strained lime juice**

**1 ounce strained pineapple juice**

**½ ounce lime punch syrup** (see page 213)

**¼ ounce Green Chartreuse**

**¼ ounce jalapeño-infused Tequila** (see below)

**½ ounce Pueblo Viejo Blanco Tequila**

**¾ ounce St. George Green Chile Vodka**

**Pineapple slice, for garnish**

**Cilantro sprig, for garnish**

- Crack 2 small ice cubes and place in an Old Fashioned glass (12 ounces). Fill the glass with small ice cubes.
- Combine all the ingredients in a shaker with 1 medium ice cube. Shake and strain into the glass.
- Garnish with a pineapple slice and cilantro sprig.

---

## Cilantro Tincture

Follow the procedure for the makrut lime leaf tincture (see herb tincture, page 121), substituting an equal amount of fresh cilantro for the lime leaves.

## Jalapeño-Infused Tequila

This infusion is quick and easy, but capsaicin varies from pepper to pepper, so monitoring this infusion by the minute is necessary. The peppers in this infusion are mostly seeds and membranes, as that is where most of the spice is. The final infusion should have a bite to it, but the level is up to you. Our recipe draws inspiration from Phil Ward's influential pepper and agave combinations.

**3 jalapeño peppers, seeds and membranes only**

**1 deseeded jalapeño pepper, just the shell**

**1 liter blanco Tequila of your choice**

- Slice the 3 jalapeño peppers to remove the seeds and membranes. You will need the seeds and membranes from 3 peppers, and the shell from only 1 pepper. Place all of these in a container with the Tequila.
- Steep for 10 minutes. Taste to determine level of spice. If the mixture needs more spice, let it sit for an additional 5 minutes and taste again. It shouldn't need more than 15 minutes. Once the spiciness is perfect, fine strain and bottle. Makes 32 ounces.
- You may try the infused Tequila as a variation to other drinks, such as the Toro, Toro, Óle! (page 242).

# Minoan

*Olive oil in cocktails*

You like olives in your Martini; how about some olive oil in your Daiquiri?

A new, salty flavor profile for rum has erupted on the scene, with several Mexican rums with long fermentation periods offering intensely briny qualities. They offer notes of olives, grilled corn, and even herbs. We wanted to construct a sour that would match the intricacies of these rums.

The now-shuttered Marvel Bar in Minneapolis was known for its juggling of classical and innovative techniques, as exemplified by its Oliveto cocktail. The bar wizards at Marvel determined that Italian olive oil cake would be a good starting point for a cocktail, and wisely realized that egg white in the drink would emulsify the olive oil, preventing it from separating while conveying a complex texture. While the Oliveto proves its point as a sweet drink, our Minoan takes a salty route.

Among the briny Mexican rums, Paranubes is aggressively olive-forward. The beast is tamed with Manzanilla sherry, embodying the contemplation of an ocean breeze. Citrus comes from lime juice and lime punch syrup, with the oily texture of the syrup dovetailing into the lush merger of olive oil and egg white.

Choose a flavorful extra virgin olive oil, as its taste, not just its texture, will come out in the drink. Instead of salt solution, this drink is finished with olive brine, which is just flavored salt water.

The same flash-blended egg technique from Winter in L.A. (page 49) is used here. It would be quite a chore to shake, but the flash blender makes it effortless and highly aerated.

The ancient Minoan civilization was an early producer of olive oil, using it not just for food, but as a cleanser, in tanning hides, and as fuel. They missed the cocktail connection, though.

**1 teaspoon olive brine**

**½ ounce strained lime juice**

**½ teaspoon cane syrup** (see page 52)

**¼ ounce olive oil**

**½ ounce egg white**

**¾ ounce lime punch syrup** (see page 213)

**½ ounce Hidalgo "La Gitana" Manzanilla Sherry**

**1½ ounces Paranubes Oaxaca Aguardiente de Caña**

**Freshly ground black pepper, for garnish**

- Combine all the ingredients in a mixing tin. Flash blend without ice for 5 seconds. Add 12 ounces of crushed ice to the tin and flash blend for 5 seconds. Double strain into a large, chilled coupe (10 ounces).
- Garnish with freshly ground black pepper.

# Bewitched Blossom

*Li Po's Chinese Mai Tai*

The Li Po Cocktail Lounge is a veteran of the San Francisco bar scene (it's been in operation since 1937, the same year as the opening of the city's well-regarded bridge to Marin County). Named for a Tang dynasty poet known for seeking the muse through drink, Li Po's signature cocktail is the Chinese Mai Tai, a spicy spin on the Hawaiian style with a hearty dose of sriracha sauce and a shot of what is described only as Chinese liqueur. Speculated variously to be baijiu; rose-scented rice wine; or Ng Ka Py, a spirituous infusion of the root bark of *Cortex acanthopanacis,* one way or another it adds up to an umami-laden drink that underscores how tropical cocktails have been sustained and expanded through the efforts of Asian American restaurants and bars.

We wanted to apply Li Po's concept to a drink from the Don the Beachcomber canon, the Queen's Road, a Daiquiri variation already edging a bit toward the culinary through augmentation with ginger and honey. What would the power of hot sauce enable it to become?

Sriracha amplifies the ginger and honey, no doubt, but perhaps too much. We can see that other successful ginger drinks, like El Diablo and Florodora, contrast the strong hit of ginger with fruit: cassis in the case of the Diablo, and raspberry for the Florodora. For this drink, we employed strawberry, and the balance was complete. These are all bold ingredients, which the full-bodied Appleton Estate can stand up to.

The name for this drink comes from the Li Po poem "A Message to Meng Haoran."

**2 strawberries, stems removed**

**⅛ teaspoon to ¼ teaspoon sriracha sauce, to taste**

**¾ ounce strained lime juice**

**¼ ounce ginger syrup** (see page 83)

**½ ounce honey syrup** (see page 44)

**2 ounces Appleton Estate 8 Year Old Rum**

- Muddle the 2 strawberries at the bottom of a shaker. Add the remaining ingredients, 1 medium ice cube, and 2 small ice cubes. Shake and double strain into a chilled goblet (10 ounces).

# Lost Navigator

*Channeling spiced rum*

Spiced rums are as widespread and varied in the Caribbean as herbal liqueurs are in Europe. Complex infusions of barks, roots, peels, seeds, pods, and stalks express the creativity of the blender and the heritage of the region. Although such spiced rums have played a relatively small role in the tropical cocktail ecosystem, a similar artistry of spice-blending using syrups has been a critical part of the culture since the days of Donn Beach. Donn's wells were full of house-made syrups that could be mixed and matched to form endless combinations and permutations.

During Jeff Berry's long quest to recover lost cocktails of Donn's era, one of the hardest to pin down was the Nui Nui, its two syrups recorded only as "Don's Spices No. 2" and "Don's Spices No. 4." As he explains in *Sippin' Safari,* Jeff determined that No. 4 was cinnamon while chasing down a bartender's clue that No. 2 could be replaced with "spiced rum." He compared every commercially produced spiced rum and found that their most common flavors were allspice and vanilla—so No. 2 must be equal parts allspice dram and vanilla syrup.

Thanks to Jeff's tireless efforts, this Donn classic was drinkable once again, and it quickly became a favorite of the cocktail revival. But since it was his own insight into the ingredients that made it possible, the drink as we understand it owes as much to Jeff Berry as Don the Beachcomber. If someone else had made the reinterpretation of Spices No. 2, would we have a different Nui Nui today? Fortunately, we don't have to contemplate that trip into the Twilight Zone. But it does suggest that other spices might have a place in tropical recipes.

For our Lost Navigator, we retain the vanilla and cinnamon from the classic Nui Nui, but in place of allspice we turn to cardamom. At ZZ's Clam Bar in Manhattan, bartender Thomas Waugh created a drink featuring gin, Chartreuse, and cardamom tincture, and we were sufficiently delighted by the integration of this underused spice to adapt it for our own purposes. We also opted to retain Thomas's medium: displaying cardamom in a concentrated tincture instead of a syrup preserved our water allocation for other ingredients.

Our final flourish is a dusting of five-spice powder that makes the Navigator's spice-forwardness known from the start. Rather than shaking powder directly onto the surface of the drink, we dust the orchid garnishing the drink, ensuring that even as the drink is consumed the spice stays to offer its aromas. This was inspired by Trader Vic's technique of making flower garnishes do extra duty by scenting them with orange flower water. (If you're lacking orchids, dusting the surface works, too.)

RECIPE CONTINUES

**5 drops salt solution** (see page 27)

**2 dashes cardamom tincture** (see below)

**3 dashes Angostura aromatic bitters**

**½ ounce strained lime juice**

**½ ounce strained orange juice**

**1 teaspoon vanilla-sandalwood syrup** (see below)

**⅜ ounce cassia cinnamon bark syrup** (see page 65)

**1½ ounces Santa Teresa 1796 Rum**

**Channeled lime twist, for garnish**

**Orchid dusted with five-spice powder, for garnish**

- Combine all the ingredients in a mixing tin with 4 ounces of crushed ice. Flash blend for 5 seconds and pour unstrained into a goblet (10 ounces) with 4 ounces of crushed ice.
- Garnish with a channeled lime twist and an orchid dusted with five-spice powder. Serve with a straw.

---

## Cardamom Tincture

At Pegu Club, Audrey Saunders developed a range of single-flavor tinctures—a liquid spice rack—so her bar team could incorporate them in precisely tuned cocktails. "I didn't want to have just one or two notes," she told us. "I wanted an organ." Access to a dozen or so spice tinctures allowed bartenders to play the specific notes they needed in each drink, at a time when only a few bitters were commercially available, namely Angostura, Peychaud's, Fee Brothers Orange, and Regan's Orange.

In contrast to the rapid nitrous infusion method (for details, see the Banshee on page 45), which focuses on capturing the top note, this traditional type of infusion is for ingredients with deep dimensions to be displayed. "It's like cooking something low and slow versus a pressure cooker," Audrey observed.

**8 grams whole green cardamom pods**

**250 milliliters 151 proof neutral spirit** (such as Devil Spring Vodka or Diamond 151 Rum)

- Crack the cardamom pods into small pieces with a few pulses of a spice grinder. Toast the cracked pods in a saucepan over medium heat until aromatic. Let the pods cool and place them in a container. Add the neutral spirit to the container and let it steep for 48 hours. Fine strain and bottle. Makes 250 milliliters.

## Vanilla-Sandalwood Syrup

The addition of sandalwood gives this syrup a brilliant red color and an earthy edge, bringing out the best qualities of the vanilla bean.

**1 vanilla pod**

**1.25 grams food-grade red sandalwood powder**

**227 grams white sugar**

**227 grams water**

- Cut the vanilla bean in half lengthwise. Scrape the vanilla bean paste into a saucepan. Cut the vanilla stalk into small pieces. Add the cut vanilla stalk, sandalwood powder, sugar, and water to the saucepan. Bring to a boil. Cover and drop to low heat for 15 minutes. Remove from heat, keep covered, and let sit unstrained for 12 hours. Strain through a fine mesh filter, bottle, and refrigerate. It will keep for 2 weeks in the refrigerator. Makes 16 ounces.

# Kiruna Cooler

*Dill, cucumber, and coconut*

Unlike gin, which traditionally focuses on juniper, aquavit draws inspiration from a wide range of herbs and spices. Dill has a special place in Scandinavian hearts, and the dill aquavit from Gamle Ode is exceptional enough to build a drink around.

Dill and coconut come from different parts of the world, but they have found affinity in innovative contemporary vegan cooking. With the Kiruna Cooler, we apply that thinking to the format of the Coconaut, an original Jeff "Beachbum" Berry beverage. The name of our drink also derives inspiration from Jeff's original, as Kiruna is the northernmost town in Sweden and home to the Esrange Space Center. How's that for expanding the scope of tropical drinks?

First appearing in *Grog Log* in 1998, the Coconaut is an appealing mix of coconut cream, lime juice, and aged Jamaican rum. Jeff concocted it due to his dissatisfaction with the sweet-acid balance of the Piña Colada. "While playing around, I slowly realized that rum and coconut don't really need pineapple so much as they need lime," he told us. "It's a more satisfying tropical trio, which of course was not my discovery: Harry Nilsson got there first with his song lyric 'Put the lime in the coconut, then you'll feel better.' "

Along similar lines, we wanted to see how coconut cream, associated with sweeter drinks, would work when pulled in a savory direction. But swapping the rum for aquavit left out all-important body, so we split the base with aquavit and two rums of different character.

Sommeliers often cite dill and coconut as defining characteristics of American oak barrels, so a rum with a dry, woody burn to it will mesh with the other ingredients while bringing the solidity of wood back to the drink. This is the role Scarlet Ibis plays, while Banks backs up the vegetal notes.

Trader Vic himself developed the garnish used here. He noticed that cutting hashes in a cucumber makes it intensely and refreshingly aromatic, and he used that technique to add those notes to drinks that otherwise contained no cucumber. In the Kiruna Cooler, this allows the drink to start off with coconut and end with cucumber—a fascinating journey for the senses.

RECIPE CONTINUES

**5 drops salt solution**
(see page 27)

**½ ounce strained lime juice**

**1½ ounces coconut mix**
(see page 108)

**¾ ounce Scarlet Ibis Trinidad Rum**

**¾ ounce Banks 5 Island Rum**

**¾ ounce Gamle Ode Dill Aquavit**

**Dill sprig, for garnish**

**Cucumber spear, for garnish**

- Combine all the ingredients in a mixing tin with 8 ounces of crushed ice. Flash blend for 5 seconds and pour, unstrained, into a chilled Collins glass (15 ounces) with 8 ounces of crushed ice.
- Garnish with a sprig of dill and a hashed cucumber spear. (Slice an unpeeled cucumber into spears, then use your knife to cut a pattern of Xs down a spear's fleshy side.) Serve with a straw.

# Jump Up, Jamaica

*Sorrel's centrality*

In Jamaica, and throughout the Caribbean, roselle (*Hibiscus sabdariffa*) flowers and other spices are steeped in water or rum to make sorrel. It's a staple of Christmastime celebrations but is tartly refreshing at any time. Sorrel is not one recipe but an idea with hundreds of iterations. Commonalities generally include cloves, cinnamon, and ginger.

One new iteration arose by accident when Garret made a batch of sorrel but accidentally omitted the ginger. Ginger brings a needed bite to sorrel, but Garret didn't want to throw away otherwise good liquid, so he combined the gingerless batch with another experiment: serrano pepper–infused overproof rum. And what a beautiful thing these flavors are together.

The sweet and sour elements of this sorrel rum punch could reflect another Jamaican staple, the Wray and Ting, so into the recipe went lime juice, grapefruit punch syrup, and soda water. The effervescence of the soda unlocks the qualities of the sorrel, which delivers copious spice flavor even while diluted.

The name derives from a song on the soundtrack to the 1962 James Bond film *Dr. No* by Byron Lee and the Dragonaires. The band was introduced to the film crew by a young production assistant named Chris Blackwell, whose musical connections were notable enough that the label he cofounded, Island Records, would help bring reggae and ska to the world. His family also once controlled Jamaican rum giant Wray & Nephew. (The title of the song is given variously as "Jump Up" and "Jamaica Jump Up," but the lyrics do include the call to action "Jump up, Jamaica," so that's what we're going with.)

**5 drops salt solution** (see page 27)

**2 dashes Angostura aromatic bitters**

**½ ounce strained lime juice**

**1½ ounces grapefruit punch syrup** (see page 216)

**½ ounce serrano-infused Wray & Nephew Overproof Rum** (see below)

**½ ounce Coruba Rum**

**1 ounce sorrel-infused rum** (see below)

**3 ounces soda water**

**Mint sprig, for garnish**

- Combine all the ingredients, except the soda water, in a shaker with 1 medium ice cube. Shake. Add the soda water to the shaker. Strain into a chilled red wine glass (14 ounces) filled with small ice cubes and 2 to 3 cracked ice cubes on top.
- Garnish with mint.

### Sorrel-Infused Rum

**4 grams cloves**

**7 grams cassia cinnamon bark, broken into ½-inch pieces**

**128 grams dried roselle flowers (sometimes labeled as hibiscus)**

**750 milliliters Barbancourt White Rhum**

**250 milliliters gum syrup** (see page 197)

- Combine all the ingredients except gum syrup in a container and infuse for 24 hours. Strain and bottle. Add the gum syrup. It does not need to be refrigerated. Makes 32 ounces.

### Serrano-Infused Wray & Nephew Overproof Rum

Follow the procedure for making jalapeño-infused Tequila (page 157) using serrano chiles and Wray & Nephew rum.

# INNOVATION

*"Change the way drinks are made, not how people drink."*

This was the driving philosophy at Dave Arnold and Don Lee's Existing Conditions. It meant thinking differently about ingredients and how to achieve flavors, but presenting it all in forms familiar both to drinkers and bartenders.

The techniques in this section revisit crucial tropical ingredients—juices and syrups—to refine their possibilities in light of the timeless requirements of tropical drinks: that sui generis combination of sweet, sour, strong, and weak.

For example: Is orange juice a sweet component or a sour one? It's not really either, because it's neither acidic nor sugary enough to play either role alone. In a tall drink, it can act more like flavored dilution. With the practice of acid adjusting, however, you can easily make a powerful ingredient with all the orange flavor that Florida can muster.

Whether you are acid adjusting, sugar adjusting, or preserving juice in cordials, syrups, or liqueurs, these innovations are here to help you get the maximum out of your ingredients. In a cocktail bar, fresh juice is typically squeezed for service, and whatever remains is thrown out at the end of the night. The end. With the following techniques, you can either prevent that from happening by allowing juice to take a larger, central role, or you can produce marvelous new and different ingredients from the leftovers.

These techniques, based on the work of Dave and Don, were the key to liberating classic tropical recipes, which stubbornly resisted standard approaches. Welcome to the heart of the book.

# Acid Adjusting

A frequent criticism of the more intricate tropical drinks is that their multitude of flavors can get muddied. When many juices are combined, a panoply of flavors is the intent but something less than the sum of the parts may result. Along with flavor, each additional juice brings its own acidity and dilution. The bartender must then balance the extra acidity and dilution with more sugar and more alcohol. But as those elements become more prominent, more juice is needed, and the process gets stuck in an endless seesawing of upping the acid and then the sugar, each step attempting to put the drink right but only pushing it further out of whack.

What if there were a way to capture the flavor of any juice while keeping acid, sweetness, and dilution under control? Enter acid adjusting, another Dave Arnold innovation—perhaps his greatest. The method is simple: changing the acidity of one type of juice to match another by adding powdered citric and malic acid in measured amounts. The sweet and sour that works in limes and lemons can thus be transferred to the special flavors of other fruits, allowing their flavors to stand out while reducing added dilution from multiple juices.

Tropical drinks incorporate a wide range of juices, typically including pineapple, orange, and passionfruit, whereas most classic drinks stick to lemon and lime. Why do lemon and lime work so well in cocktails? Because they have higher acid than the other juices, about 6 grams of acid per 100 milliliters of juice, or 6 percent acid. In lemon juice, the whole acid amount is from citric acid, which gives citrus its identifiable flavor. Lime juice splits its acid content between the citric acid found in other citrus and malic acid, an acid also found in apples that offers that green, Granny Smith flavor.

The lemon's all-citric profile gives it a clean, lighter feel. The direct, fleeting sourness of citric acid allows lemons to pair well with longer-aged spirits, with the wood in the spirit lingering long after the acid makes its exit. Trader Vic developed many drinks with lemon juice to leverage its bright, approachable flavor that softly enrobes the palate.

Lime's split of acids sets it apart from other citrus. Malic acid has a back-of-the-throat sour component that strikes the tongue more heavily. Its tartness sticks around, and so it cooperates better with more lightly aged spirits like Tequila and gin. Lime is the assertive stalwart of tropical drinks, the weapon of choice in the Don the Beachcomber canon. Donn's heady amalgamations of flavors—often incorporating bitters, absinthe, and spices—rely on lime's bold acidity for their foundation.

The participation of lemon or lime in a drink is immediately apparent. Other fruit juices, with lower acidity, tend to struggle to be perceived distinctly. The practice of acid adjusting levels the playing field for different juices.

At Existing Conditions, Don Lee instructed

all new recruits on the mysteries of acid adjusting. The first juice tackled was orange. Orange has about the same sweetness as lemon or lime but, with about 0.8 percent citric acid and no malic acid, it is not acidic enough to carry a drink. Compare lime juice, which is about 4 percent citric acid and 2 percent malic acid. To bump orange juice up to the strength of lime juice, all that's needed is to add the difference—3.2 grams of citric acid and 2 grams of malic. Orange juice then matches the performance of lime juice but retains its special flavor.

By boosting the acidity of these fruits, we amplify their presence and concentrate their flavors. The process is simple: Measure the volume of your beginning juice, weigh out the proper amount of powdered acid (easily available online or in some grocery stores), and mix it into the juice until completely dissolved. That's it. You've mastered one of the most powerful tools for next-generation tropical drinks. Use the following table to determine which additional acids are needed.

| *Juice* | ACIDITY OF JUICE PER 100 ML | TO ADJUST TO LEMON, ADD PER 100 ML | TO ADJUST TO LIME, ADD PER 100 ML |
|---|---|---|---|
| GRAPEFRUIT | 2.0 grams citric acid | 4.0 grams citric acid | 2.0 grams citric acid, 2.0 grams malic acid |
| ORANGE | 0.8 grams citric acid | 5.2 grams citric acid | 3.2 grams citric acid, 2.0 grams malic acid |
| PINEAPPLE | 0.8 grams citric acid | 5.2 grams citric acid | 3.2 grams citric acid, 2.0 grams malic acid |

Because grapefruit already has a bit of citric acid, it's typical to adjust it to lemon, providing it that extra boost. Orange and pineapple, which tend to play second fiddle to lime in tropical recipes, can be adjusted to lime to remove the necessity of a second juice. But that doesn't mean grapefruit couldn't be adjusted to lime if that's what the drink needs.

We recommend starting with freshly squeezed juice just as you would with any cocktail. However, in a pinch, acid adjusting will work with bottled juices. Also note that it's important that the acid powders dissolve completely to achieve a uniform effect, so using a blender or hand blender, or just shaking the container, will help.

With this knowledge, you can easily adapt existing recipes to different juices. For example, try making a Tom Collins where grapefruit is the only sour component, or a Pisco Sour where pineapple is the tart element.

# PKNY

*The Soggy Dollar soother*

Jost Van Dyke is a sparsely inhabited haven among the British Virgin Islands, an archetypal fantasy of tropical seclusion. It was chosen by American expats George and Marie Myrick, pioneers in the yacht charter trade, as the site of a small beachfront hotel and bar they constructed in 1971. The unassuming Sandcastle Hotel and Soggy Dollar Bar became destinations, and their house drink, the Painkiller, became an illustrious delicacy.

As George tells it in his 2008 memoir, *Incredible Virgin Island Adventure,* prior to opening their bar, "Marie and I came up with a very tasty rum drink. Our mix consisted of orange juice, pineapple juice, and coconut cream. We added the coconut cream slowly until we said, 'Wow, this is it!' We sloshed it over some measured ounces of rum—Mount Gay or Cruzan Gold—dealer's choice. Last, but not least, ground nutmeg was sprinkled on top." He credits Marie with the inspiration to name their creation after a local bush.

The Painkiller is much in the spirit of the drinks in this book, as the Myricks were tinkering with the flaws and eccentricities of its antecedent, the Piña Colada. Their version was easier to make, as it was shaken instead of frozen, and it added an assertive rum character and spice notes. But in inserting a second juice, it supplied new complications.

It's for that reason that the drink is a perfect showcase of the acid-adjusting technique. Instead of two low-acid juices, we let the pineapple do its thing while bringing proper acidity to the show by transmuting our orange to the level of lime. Some bartenders have attempted to bolster the Painkiller's tartness by directly adding lime juice, but a third juice, with its extra dilution, only compounds the troubles.

Acid adjusting allows a lower volume of juice to do more flavor work. Dave Arnold developed the technique with orange juice in mind. "You don't really expect half an ounce of orange juice to do anything to a drink," he told us. "But once it can function as the acid foundation, you get a lot of orange flavor characteristics coming through, too."

With lower dilution, the rums also come to the fore, enhancing this drink's purported painkilling properties. To reinforce this we use a blend of rums, with Hamilton 151 bringing the beef and Smith & Cross and Coruba working in concert to approximate the strong flavors of the days when Jamaican rums ruled the waves.

To strengthen the notes of nutmeg, the complementary spice profile of Angostura bitters is added.

RECIPE CONTINUES

Finally, the drink is flash-blended to whip the enzymes and proteins in the pineapple and coconut, bringing a significantly lighter texture.

In addition to being the birthplace of the Painkiller, Jost Van Dyke had earlier been the point of origin of William Thornton (1759–1828), the architect of the US Capitol and the first superintendent of the United States Patent and Trademark Office.

Perhaps it is for this reason that, unusually among cocktails, the name Painkiller has become a registered trademark. Despite the creation of the drink and its name forty years earlier by the Myricks, Pusser's Rum Ltd. filed for trademark protection for "Painkiller" in 2011 and prevailed upon the Patent and Trademark Office to register it for alcoholic drinks and cocktail mixes. Thus armed, Pusser's dispatched cease and desist letters to bars that served drinks under the name Painkiller. Pusser's is a good rum, but this practice brought the company some infamy. A chief casualty of the legal campaign was the New York bar also known as Painkiller, whose owners were sued by Pusser's in federal court for trademark infringement. The bar settled out of court and adopted the moniker PKNY before ultimately closing in July 2013. In honor of PKNY's contributions to the advancement of tropical beverages, we've flipped the script and redubbed our recipe accordingly (although we should note it's not the same formula that was served there).

**5 drops salt solution** (see page 27)

**3 dashes Angostura aromatic bitters**

**½ ounce orange juice, acid adjusted to lime** (see below)

**1½ ounces strained pineapple juice**

**1½ ounces coconut mix** (see page 108)

**¾ ounce Smith & Cross Traditional Jamaica Rum**

**¾ ounce Coruba Rum**

**¾ ounce Hamilton Demerara 151 Rum**

**Grated nutmeg, for garnish**

**Grated cassia cinnamon, for garnish**

**Orange slice, for garnish**

**Cinnamon stick, for garnish**

- Combine all the ingredients in a mixing tin with 8 ounces of crushed ice. Flash blend for 5 seconds and pour unstrained into a chilled snifter (22 ounces) with 8 ounces of crushed ice and 3 small ice cubes.
- Dust with grated nutmeg and cassia cinnamon. Garnish with an orange slice and cinnamon stick. Serve with a straw.

---

## Orange Juice, Acid Adjusted to Lime

- Strain the orange juice. Mix the acid (in the proportions below) until the powders dissolve, then bottle. It will keep for 3 days in the refrigerator.
- To adjust orange juice to the acidity of lime, to each 100 milliliters of juice add:
  3.2 grams citric acid
  2.0 grams malic acid

# Western Sour

*Lime and bourbon problems*

California was the cradle of the midcentury tropical drink craze, with Don the Beachcomber operating from Hollywood and Trader Vic's out of Oakland. Riding in their wake was Beverly Hills socialite Steve Crane, who promoted his Kon-Tiki chain by keeping himself in the tabloids with exploits involving Hollywood celebrities, including marrying and divorcing Lana Turner two times in as many years. With marketing, rather than kitchen or bar skills, as his strength, Crane's menus drew heavily on the work done at Don the Beachcomber and Trader Vic's. Kon-Tiki's house Mai Tai closely copied Donn's Q.B. Cooler, but its menus also featured interpretations of many of Vic's non-rum cocktails. This was a category notably underemphasized at Donn's establishments. It was important at Trader Vic's and the Kon-Tiki as they were hotel bars needing to capture all guests, not only those nursing a tropical island fantasy.

Among these non-rum drinks at the Kon-Tiki was the Western Sour, derived from Trader Vic's Eastern Sour and substituting grapefruit, lime, and falernum for orange, lemon, and orgeat. The presence of lime helps the Western Sour avoid the pitfalls of another whiskey and grapefruit cocktail, the Brown Derby, whose bourbon-grapefruit-honey formulation risks runaway sweetness, runaway dilution, or both. In adding lime, though, a new problem was created in the Western Sour: the malic acid of the lime abrogates the wood notes prominent in bourbon. This effect can be pleasant in tall drinks such as the Bourbon Special (page 223), but in a sour the whole purpose of using an aged spirit is defeated.

Once again, acid adjustment allows us to have the best of both worlds. By increasing the grapefruit's acidity to that of lemon, we can achieve the balance of a traditional Whiskey Sour without need of lime, keeping the bourbon profile intact and clearing the decks for the subtle lime zest notes of the falernum.

We serve the Western Sour like a contemporary Whiskey Sour—shaken with big ice and strained over a rock—in order to let the drink open slowly.

RECIPE CONTINUES

**5 drops salt solution**
(see page 27)

**¾ ounce grapefruit juice, acid adjusted to lemon**
(see below)

**½ teaspoon cane syrup**
(see page 52)

**¾ ounce falernum**
(see page 232)

**2 ounces Elijah Craig bourbon**

**Lime twist, for garnish**

- Combine all the ingredients in a shaker with 1 medium ice cube. Shake and strain into an Old Fashioned glass (12 ounces) with a large ice cube.
- Garnish with a lime twist.

---

## Grapefruit Juice, Acid Adjusted to Lemon

- Strain the grapefruit juice. Mix the acid (in the proportions below) until the powders dissolve, then bottle. It will keep for 3 days in the refrigerator.
- To adjust grapefruit juice to the acidity of lemon, to each 100 milliliters of juice add:
  4.0 grams citric acid

# Royal Hawaiian Mai Tai

*Juice control*

When mainland tourists familiar with Californian "rhum rhapsodies" began to flood Hawai'i, they searched in vain for what they believed were native beverages, especially the Mai Tai, a drink with no genuine connection to Hawai'i or Polynesia. As a consequence, tourist-friendly versions began to appear. The original Trader Vic Mai Tai is a restrained affair, consisting of rum, lime juice, curaçao, and orgeat. Many of these new tourist versions also included a fruit that was to Hawai'i what the orange was to Florida: pineapple. (And while they were at it, they threw orange in, too.)

Today, this juice-forward variation is sometimes designated as the island-style Mai Tai, and it's still dominant in Hawai'i and resorts worldwide. Craft bartenders tend to look down on it, believing its delicate flavors disappear under a juice tsunami, but we can offer it new life through the magic of acid adjusting.

The basis comes from the drink as it was served at the Royal Hawaiian Hotel's Surf Bar around 1971, which boasted four acids, three sweeteners, and three rums. In contrast, our version is built more like an old-school Mai Tai. Pineapple becomes the only component carrying the acid. There is still lime, but oil rather than juice. It's a kind of friendship bridge between the classic Mai Tai and the Hawaiian style.

The proportions of this drink are the same as our regular Mai Tai (see page 71), which shows how acid-adjusted juice can be easily slotted into a template. In addition to a strong Jamaican rum flavor, here supplied by Coruba, the Royal Hawaiian's original spec includes Demerara and light Puerto Rican rums to add a bit of roundness. In this version, the Saint Lucian Chairman's Reserve plays that role.

Like other Vic-derived drinks, it uses the hybrid shake (see page 69).

RECIPE CONTINUES

**1 lime wedge**

**5 drops salt solution** (see page 27)

**1 ounce pineapple juice, acid adjusted to lime** (see below)

**⅝ ounce orgeat** (see page 72)

**1 teaspoon Grand Marnier**

**1 teaspoon Clément Creole Shrubb**

**¾ ounce Coruba Rum**

**1½ ounces Chairman's Reserve Rum**

**Mint sprig, for garnish**

**Orchid, for garnish**

**Pineapple wedge, for garnish**

- Squeeze a lime wedge to remove the juice, and place the spent wedge in a double Old Fashioned glass (16 ounces). Combine the remaining ingredients in a shaker with 4 small ice cubes. Shake and pour unstrained into the glass. Top with 8 to 10 ounces of crushed ice.
- Garnish with mint, orchid, and pineapple wedge.

---

## Pineapple Juice, Acid Adjusted to Lime

- Strain the pineapple juice. Mix the acid (in the proportions below) until the powders dissolve, then bottle. It will keep for 3 days in the refrigerator.
- To adjust pineapple juice to the acidity of lime, to each 100 milliliters of juice add:
  3.2 grams citric acid
  2.0 grams malic acid

# Full Fathom Five

*Calamansi*

Most fruits have been bred to increase sugar and lower acid, in line with many people's preferences. But there's one citrus where the acid adjusting is already built in. The calamansi (sometimes called calamondin in English) is a cross between a kumquat and a mandarin. It clocks in at around 4.5 to 5.8 percent citric acid, close to a lemon, but with a unique flavor of its own. While a staple of Filipino cuisine, it's largely unknown to most Americans.

At the Mai-Kai, drinks with orange juice have a particular tang that isn't easily reproduced with regular orange juice. It's unknown what they might be adding to enhance the flavor, but the calamansi's super-sour orange-ishness seemed like a possible way to re-create it. Unlike adding lime to a Painkiller, updating a Mai-Kai classic like the Deep Sea Diver (their version of Donn's Pearl Diver) with calamansi doesn't make the new fruit the star of the show; it inspires the orange to get its act together and toughen up.

In the Philippines, calamansi juice is often cut with honey, so the honey-inflected Deep Sea Diver makes sense in at least two ways. All of this, of course, would have been known to Mariano Licudine, the Filipino American bartender who helmed the program at the Mai-Kai after a tour of duty with Don the Beachcomber.

Boiron's puree makes this drink easier to concoct, although your local Asian market may have fresh calamansi to experiment with, as well.

The Pearl Diver and Deep Sea Diver are showcases for Demerara rum, so our version begins with the Hamilton 86. Barbancourt brings dry wood while the Doctor Bird adds fruity funk.

"Full fathom five" is, of course, Shakespeare's lingo for the sufficient depth for burial at sea. Remember to come up for air when sampling this delicious drink.

RECIPE CONTINUES

**5 drops salt solution** (see page 27)

**3 dashes Angostura aromatic bitters**

**¼ ounce calamansi puree** (such as Boiron)

**½ ounce strained lime juice**

**½ ounce strained orange juice**

**½ ounce falernum** (see page 232)

**¾ ounce gardenia mix** (see below)

**½ ounce Two James Doctor Bird Jamaica Rum**

**½ ounce Barbancourt 5 Star Rhum**

**¾ ounce Hamilton Demerara 86 Rum**

**Kumquats, for garnish**

- Combine all the ingredients in a mixing tin with 8 ounces of crushed ice. Flash blend for 5 seconds and pour unstrained into a chilled Pearl Diver glass (12 ounces) with 4 ounces of crushed ice.
- Garnish with kumquats on a stick.

---

## Gardenia Mix

In the catalog of Donn Beach's complicated creations, the gardenia mix stands out as particularly involved.

He devised this syrup for his Pearl Diver, which he called a "Cold Buttered Rum." The syrup represents a bit of molecular mixology before its time, as it injects melted butter into an icy variation on Planter's Punch—a revelatory feat.

But the magic starts to fade when you recognize that butter and honey do not mix naturally. The gardenia mix, like the rest of the universe, is headed for collapse. After pouring a drink involving gardenia mix, your entire toolset will be slicked with fat, and the drink will soon begin to separate, leaving a less-than-appetizing layer of milk curd floating on the surface.

Dave Arnold to the rescue. In *Liquid Intelligence,* he tackles the Cold Buttered Rum conundrum, suggesting the use of a particular compound emulsifier, common in commercial salad dressings, called Ticaloid 210 S. This proprietary mixture of acacia and xanthan gums is made by the TIC Gums company, but a do-it-yourself powder could be made with a ratio of 9 parts acacia gum to 1 part xanthan gum by weight. These emulsifiers keep the honey and butter in a uniform solution, banishing the floating curd and slippery shakers. (While we're on the subject, see the Minoan on page 160 for two ingredients, olive oil and egg white, which create a natural emulsion.)

With the fat problem burned away, we're now free to realize that it takes a lot of gardenia mix indeed to sweeten a cocktail properly. That's the second challenge: the syrup is not at standard sweetness for cocktail syrups (see the next section, on sugar adjusting, for the full story). In order to get enough honey for appropriate sweetening, a ton of butter also has to be ingested. Normally, cocktails are not croissants and a little butter goes a long way. Consider the Hot Buttered Rum and its single pat of

RECIPE CONTINUES

butter. By contrast, the traditional gardenia mix recipe calls for an equal amount of honey and butter. For our purposes, it's both too fatty and not sweet enough.

Instead, let's make a traditional honey syrup but with melted butter replacing the water. Small measures of cinnamon and vanilla syrups, along with allspice dram, add spice to the honey, and the extra liquid they provide hydrates the powdered compound emulsifier. This new ratio of ingredients builds a gardenia mix with less tongue-coating fat. It pours like a 2:1 cane syrup.

The syrup will solidify in the refrigerator but can be returned to service with gentle heating. If you're using it periodically behind the bar, it can be left in a hot water bath. For more sporadic home use, just reheat briefly in the microwave.

**57.5 grams butter**

**250 grams honey**

**26 milliliters cassia cinnamon bark syrup** (see page 65)

**13 milliliters St. Elizabeth Allspice Dram**

**13 milliliters vanilla-sandalwood syrup** (see page 163)

**2 grams compound emulsifier** (Ticaloid 210 S)

- Melt the butter on indirect heat, such as in a microwave.
- Heat the honey in a saucepan until it starts to bubble and break down into a thin liquid. Stir in the cinnamon syrup, allspice dram, and vanilla-sandalwood syrup. Remove the mixture from heat and add the compound emulsifier powder. Blend vigorously with a whisk or hand blender until the powder is dissolved into the syrup-honey mixture.
- Slowly add the fully melted butter to the emulsified syrup and stir until uniform with a whisk or hand blender. Makes 12 ounces.

# Sugar Adjusting

If a drink is out of balance, a common reason is that the sweetener used was not made at the precise level of sweetness the recipe called for. If it's a three-ingredient Whiskey Sour, adding a bit more sugar or acid can fix it; in a multifaceted tropical drink with a long list of ingredients, an issue with any one of them will have a cascading effect.

Syrups are a primary sweetener for mixed drinks. When making a syrup with sugar and water, you know the proportions of both, so you know the sweetness of the resulting syrup (in a standard syrup for bar use, it's half sugar and half water). But when creating flavored syrups with fruit juice, the juice itself contains both sugar and water, so replacing the water with juice won't produce the same sweetness. To handle this more precisely, we can measure the sweetness of the juice, then add the amount of sugar (or water) needed to bring the syrup up (or down) to a desired sweetness. We call this process sugar adjusting.

Brix is the percentage of sucrose, by weight, in a solution. (The unit of measurement is named in honor of Adolf Ferdinand Wenceslaus Brix (1798–1870), who did related work in engineering.) If there are 50 grams of sugar in a solution weighing 100 grams, that solution would be 50 degrees Brix (°Bx). In the bar world, this is generally truncated to just "50 Brix."

## MEASUREMENT

A solution's sucrose content can be measured using a device called a refractometer, which takes advantage of the fact that light entering a fluid will bend, or refract, differently depending on the amount of solids dissolved in it.

It won't tell you what type of solid it is, though, which means that the device works only when your solution has just one thing in it. In our case, we're looking for sucrose. If the liquid has sugar and salt, for example, you won't be able to tell the amount of each. Since we're concerned with syrups and juices, which will mostly contain sucrose, the measurements will work for our purposes.

There are many types of refractometers—analog and digital, and of varying precisions. Refer to the Tools section on page 29 for more guidance, but know that for cocktailing purposes, a digital refractometer with a range of 0 to 85 degrees Brix is most practical.

To adjust the sweetness of a liquid, first we measure the sugar already in the liquid, then we use a simple calculation to determine the amount of extra sugar needed to turn the liquid into a syrup at a desired higher level of sweetness.

This process from Existing Conditions also has a connection to the famed Tommy's Margarita (for a discussion of this drink, see page 69). When Julio Bermejo and company cut agave nectar with water to make a syrup, bringing agave nectar from its usual 65 to 80 degrees Brix down to a syrup-standard 50 degrees Brix, they were sugar adjusting. Sugar adjusting helped make the Tommy's Margarita one of the most widely enjoyed drinks of all time.

## RAISING SWEETNESS

Don't be afraid. These are the only formulas in this book.

$$\text{SUGAR TO ADD, IN GRAMS} = \frac{\text{Weight, in grams} \times (\text{Desired Brix} - \text{Measured Brix})}{(100 - \text{Desired Brix})}$$

Let's say we want to turn pineapple juice into a syrup. First, we weigh the juice. In the following example, it will be 500 grams. Then we measure it in the refractometer, and see that it is at 14.3 Brix. To become a regular simple syrup, we need to get that up to 50 Brix, which would be our final Brix.

$$\text{SUGAR TO ADD, IN GRAMS} = \frac{500 \times (50 - 14.3)}{50}$$

Performing the calculation yields 357. To make this juice into 50 Brix syrup, we'd need to add 357 grams of sugar.

Now that we have the calculation, we implement it by placing the pineapple juice in a blender, blending it on low, and adding the sugar to it until it dissolves. Finishing the pineapple syrup with a touch of citric acid will preserve the bite of the fruit over time; 3 grams of citric acid per liter of syrup will do.

## LOWERING SWEETNESS

There are occasions when you want the final product to be lower in sweetness rather than higher. This can happen when using the vacuum sealer technique (see page 142), which can result in a sweeter syrup that needs further adjusting.

To lower sweetness, we use the same formula for raising sweetness, but with a different denominator. Since we can't remove sugar, we'll be adding water instead.

$$\text{WATER TO ADD, IN GRAMS} = \frac{\text{Weight, in grams} \times (\text{Desired Brix} - \text{Measured Brix})}{(0 - \text{Desired Brix})}$$

The Bird of Paradise (page 199), for example, uses the vacuum sealer technique. Let's say the syrup comes in at 60 Brix but the recipe calls for 50 Brix. If it weighs 500 grams, our formula would be:

$$\text{WATER TO ADD, IN GRAMS} = \frac{500 \times (50 - 60)}{-50}$$

The result is 100. We would add 100 grams of water.

## EXAMPLE SWEETNESS LEVELS

### Simple Syrup (50 Brix)

**Equal parts, by weight, of sugar and water—50% sugar**

Making this syrup in the blender is the best approach. The power of a blender is more than sufficient to dissolve the sugar, and unlike making syrup in a saucepan, the quantity of water you put in is the same as you get out.

### Cane or Demerara Syrup (66 Brix)

**2 parts sugar to 1 part water, by weight—66% sugar**

Richer syrups are useful in crushed ice drinks, due to the reduced water volume in the syrup itself. A little more power is needed to effectively dissolve the sucrose into solution, so stovetop heat is preferred. To ensure an accurate 66 Brix, after the mixture is at a simmer, immediately kill the heat. Then pulse blend with a hand blender to finish dissolving the sugar into the hot water.

### Juices (7 to 20 Brix)

Fruit juices may taste sweet, but as you can see by their range of Brix measurements, even the sweetest among them need help to reach syrup territory.

### Sodas (10 to 13 Brix)

In order to hold carbonation effectively, sodas have to remain within a tight range of sugar content—perhaps you could call it "the sweet spot." If the sugar content is too high, the soda starts to go flat. Staying within this range guarantees a crisp, bubbly soda. (See the Kingston Zing, page 87, for a cocktail along these lines.)

## BECOMING WELL-ADJUSTED

The cocktail recipes that follow showcase the possibilities of precise sugar calibration. Each comes with a new syrup or two to add to your repertoire.

We've estimated the amount of each ingredient in these syrups and have done the calculations for you, so you can skip the refractometer and math for these recipes. If the estimates work for you, by all means, leave the driving to us. But if you want to take sugar adjusting all the way, you now have the tools to determine your own measurements for each specific batch.

If you plan to make larger quantities of syrups, their useful lives can be extended by adding 0.5 gram potassium sorbate (available from sources like Modernist Pantry) per liter of finished syrup. This preservative, which inhibits the growth of yeast and mold, is common in the wine world.

# Derby Daiquiri

*Courtesy of the Order of Rums Royal*

The Kentucky Derby and its Mint Julep so definitively established the expectation of a big horse race involving an official drink that the Florida Derby, founded in 1952, required its own.

The trade organization Rums of Puerto Rico sponsored the "Order of Rums Royal" cocktail competition at Miami Beach's Eden Roc Hotel on November 10, 1958. Seventy entries, including Mai-Kai head bartender Mariano Licudine's Derby Daiquiri, were judged. It's not entirely clear what happened at the competition: Several local columnists reported they would be among the judges, voicing some concern that seventy samples were about sixty-eight too many, but they did not write of the result, perhaps being physically unable.

Nevertheless, Licudine's drink was proclaimed the official drink of the Florida Derby in February 1959, and began appearing in ads from Rums of Puerto Rico the next month, and for a decade or so thereafter.

Licudine took the standard Daiquiri and added the state's most famous product, orange juice. But as we've seen throughout this book, orange juice can be the downfall of many a drink. The Daiquiri must provide a sharp hit of acidity, derived from an exacting proportion of components. Orange juice, with more water and less acid than lime, is too weak to provide sourness but not sweet enough to balance the lime. One solution might be to replace both orange and lime with orange acid adjusted to lime, but that would lose the flavors unique to lime, and complementing these two fruits is the whole point of the Derby Daiquiri. Instead of combining the juices, we'll combine orange with sugar, concentrating its flavor in a syrup and doing away with excess water through sugar adjusting (see page 185).

The original Derby Daiquiri was flash-blended, but to accommodate the way our recipe is put together, it should be shaken for aeration and controlled dilution. Flashing this recipe would aerate the cocktail, but, even with a small amount of ice, the results would be far more watery and full of ice shards than should be the case with a Daiquiri at its zenith.

The addition of orange citrate bitters adds bright orange peel and vanilla. To honor the drink's legacy with Rums of Puerto Rico, we've chosen to showcase Don Q Gold, a delicious exemplar of the style.

The recipe stands up to experimentation with different types of orange—try it with Cara Caras or mandarins. But steadfast Valencia oranges are always a safe bet in this Derby.

**5 drops salt solution** (see page 27)

**6 drops Bittermens Orange Cream Citrate Bitters**

**½ ounce strained lime juice**

**¾ ounce orange syrup** (see below)

**2 ounces Don Q Gold Rum**

- Combine all the ingredients in a shaker with 1 medium ice cube and 2 small ice cubes. Shake and strain into a chilled coupe (6 ounces).

---

## Orange Syrup, 50 Brix

This gorgeous syrup can be used in many cocktail applications. Try it in a Whiskey Collins.

**250 grams strained orange juice**

**190 grams white sugar** (estimated)

**1 gram citric acid**

- Place the orange juice in a blender and set to low speed. Slowly add the sugar, followed by the citric acid. Continue to blend until the sugar is fully dissolved. Bottle and refrigerate. It will keep in the refrigerator for 1 week. Makes 12 ounces.

RECIPE CONTINUES

## Frozen Derby Daiquiri

As mentioned earlier, the Derby Daiquiri originated as a flash-blended drink. At some point, probably the early 1970s, the Mai-Kai added a number of frozen fruit Daiquiris to its menu, and the Derby Daiquiri followed in taking this form. Here's our version.

In frozen applications, orange has a more prominent role, so acid adjusting is needed. Lime zest provides the aromatics of the lime that were lost to this process. Denizen White's more aggressive presence can stand up to the slush, but the imbiber should be sitting down.

**5 drops salt solution** (see page 27)

**1½ tablespoons white sugar**

**¾ ounce orange juice, acid adjusted to lime** (see page 176)

**2 ounces Denizen Aged White Rum**

**¼ teaspoon xanthan gum**

**Channeled lime twist, for garnish**

**Orange slice, for garnish**

- Combine all the ingredients, except the xanthan gum, in a blender. Dry blend (without ice). Once the sugar is fully dissolved, slowly add the gum while continuing to blend. Add 170 grams of crushed ice while continuing to blend. Pour into a large, chilled coupe (10 ounces).
- Garnish with a channeled lime twist and an orange slice.

# From Dusk till Dawn

*Extending seasonal fruit*

Turning fresh juice into syrups is a time-honored method of extending the span of seasonal fruit, and sugar-adjusted syrups preserve not just their existence but their flavor balance.

Freshly squeezed blood orange juice is a luxury that complements many spirits. However, the juice can only last a few days in the fridge, whereas a syrup made from blood orange can last at least a month longer. The height of the blood orange's season is the winter, but the citrus makes for beautiful long drinks suited for warmer weather. Extending its shelf life will allow blood orange to gambol in the springtime.

From Dusk till Dawn is inspired by the Cadillac Margarita. The Cadillac Margarita nomenclature has been applied to a series of Margarita variations, but the general idea, as evidenced by the name and exemplified by its use at Spago in the late 1980s, is premiumization. In Spago's case that meant applying the then-new Patrón Tequila and fancier-than-triple sec Grand Marnier.

In our case, we will deploy two contrasting orange flavors: heady, wooded Grand Marnier and juicy, fresh blood orange syrup. Instead of the now-ubiquitous Patrón, Siete Leguas Reposado is our call for a premium Tequila. Its beautiful balance between minerality and wood earns it a place in this reinterpretation of the "high-end" Cadillac Margarita.

Trader Vic's Pinky Gonzalez, essentially a Tequila Mai Tai, also resembles this drink, though here the blood orange syrup takes on orgeat's role. Oddly enough, while the Pinky Gonzalez is not pink, the From Dusk till Dawn is break-of-day fuchsia.

**5 drops salt solution**
(see page 27)

**¾ ounce strained lime juice**

**¾ ounce blood orange syrup**
(see page 193)

**½ ounce Grand Marnier**

**2 ounces Siete Leguas Reposado Tequila**

- Combine all the ingredients in a shaker with 1 medium ice cube. Shake and strain into an Old Fashioned glass (12 ounces) with a large ice cube.

## Blood Orange Syrup, 50 Brix

You might also try this syrup in other Tequila concoctions or a Gin Sour.

**250 grams strained blood orange juice**
**193 grams white sugar** (estimated)
**1.5 grams citric acid**

- Place the blood orange juice in a blender and set to low speed. Slowly add the sugar, followed by the citric acid. Continue to blend until the sugar is fully dissolved. Bottle and refrigerate. It will keep in the refrigerator for 1 week. Makes 12 ounces.

# Pineapple Princess

*Milk washing and gum syrup*

The Pineapple Daiquiri is currently enjoying a reconsideration by craft bartenders, but versions have been around for a long time. Trader Vic himself offered a rendition he called the Rhum Cosmo, named after his San Francisco bar's location on Cosmo Place—a pioneering appearance of the word *Cosmo* on cocktail menus more than seventy years ago.

But San Francisco had a lust for pineapple much earlier than that. In the 1870s, the local cocktail cause célèbre was Pisco Punch, a concoction that definitely featured Peruvian brandy and pineapple gum syrup and may also have employed cocaine. Such were Pisco Punch's effects that it was said the drink would "make a gnat fight an elephant." (We like to think that luscious pineapple was the cause.)

Precise recipes aside, it's evident that while juice syrups have always been rarer than fresh juice in cocktails, pineapple was being consumed in that fashion fairly early on. So how to set about strengthening the Pineapple Daiquiri with a syrup backbone?

Like our forebears in "Baghdad by the Bay" (as San Francisco was known), we want our pineapple syrup made with acacia gum, an emulsifier and thickening agent that enhances the rich texture already found within pineapple. It also preserves the foam of the pineapple better in a shaken drink—and isn't half the enjoyment of a good Pineapple Daiquiri in the creamy head found on top?

Another inspiring pineapple drink is chronicled by Charles H. Baker Jr., who reported on *leche preparada piña* (pineapple milk) endemic to San Salvador. Brewed from fresh pineapple, milk, vanilla, sugar, and either brandy or rum, the "truly delicious beverage" is credited by Baker with inducing "chronic invalids to take up their—and other—beds and walk." (Yep, definitely the pineapple!)

Adding milk directly to a Pineapple Daiquiri did not appeal, but milk washing seemed like an excellent way to extract additional notes from the complex bouquet of pineapple. This technique can be done in a few ways, but at Existing Conditions the practice was to mix whole milk and a spirit and then add citric acid to break the mix into curds and whey. Once broken, the liquid could either be strained through a coffee filter or spun in the centrifuge, removing the curdled solids but leaving whey proteins in the liquid. The whey provides a creamy texture and, when shaken, a frothiness similar to that provided by heavier egg whites.

A final flourish is oolong infused into one of our rums. A splash of pineapple in iced tea never fails to create an alluring combination of tannic complexity and juicy refreshment, and the pairing works just as well in this more layered drink. We have assembled a proud potation worthy of a Pineapple Princess.

RECIPE CONTINUES

**5 drops salt solution** (see page 27)

**5 drops vanilla extract**

**½ ounce strained lime juice**

**1 ounce pineapple gum syrup** (see page 197)

**½ ounce Appleton Estate 12 Year Old Rum**

**2 ounces milk-washed oolong Barbancourt 5 Star Rhum** (see below)

**Pansy, for garnish**

- Combine all the ingredients in a shaker with 1 medium ice cube and 2 small ice cubes. Shake and strain into a chilled coupe (6 ounces). Garnish with a pansy.

---

## Milk-Washed Oolong Barbancourt 5 Star Rhum

This technique uses citric acid solution to break the solids in the spirit and milk mixture. It strips some tannins from whichever spirit it encounters. Dave Arnold uses this technique to remove the bitter elements from strong tea infusions. The idea is to overinfuse the tea, achieving a strong flavor suited for cocktails, and then use milk washing to reduce the harshness of tannins, while also providing texture.

In this example, milk washing softens the edges of the intense oolong infusion, leaving a clean balance of tea and rum.

**8 grams Rishi Ruby Oolong tea**

**250 milliliters Barbancourt 5 Star Rhum**

**62 milliliters whole milk** (room temperature)

**5 milliliters 15% citric acid solution** (see below)

- Mix the tea and rum in a container and let it sit for 3 hours at room temperature.
- Strain the mixture into a new container. Add the milk. Whisk gently, then let sit for another 15 minutes.
- Add the citric acid solution, gently stirring to incorporate, until the milk begins to break. Let the mixture sit until a layer of clear liquid forms on top.
- If a centrifuge is available, spin the mixture in the centrifuge for 5 minutes. Alternatively, pour the mixture through a basket coffee filter. The yield will be less with the latter method. Makes about 8 ounces.

## Citric Acid Solution (15%)

**15 grams citric acid**

**85 grams water**

- Mix the ingredients together and bottle. Makes about 2 ounces.

## GUM SYRUPS

You can find acacia gum, also known as gum arabic, at online purveyors such as Modernist Pantry.

This process will work with water or juice. For traditional gum syrup, use water as the base. For pineapple gum syrup, use pineapple juice. Or try other juices.

### Gum Syrup, 50 Brix

*Water-based gum syrup needs more acacia gum than juice-based gum syrup, since the solids in citrus or pineapple juice also add texture.*

**250 grams water**

**40 grams acacia gum**

**250 grams white sugar**

- Place the water in a blender and set to low speed. Slowly add the acacia gum. Blend at a higher speed until the gum is fully dissolved (indicated by the formation of a small head). Return blender to low speed, slowly adding the sugar. Continue to blend until the sugar is fully dissolved.
- Bottle and refrigerate. It will keep for 2 weeks in the refrigerator. Makes 14 ounces.

### Pineapple Gum Syrup, 50 Brix

*By estimating the degrees Brix of your juice, we can provide a recipe to follow like any other.*

**250 grams strained pineapple juice**

**25 grams acacia gum**

**179 grams white sugar**

**1 gram citric acid**

- Place the pineapple juice in a blender and set to low speed. Slowly add the acacia gum. Blend at higher speed until the gum is fully dissolved (indicated by the formation of a small head). Return blender to low speed, slowly adding the sugar, followed by the citric acid. Continue to blend until the sugar is fully dissolved.
- Bottle and refrigerate. It will keep for 2 weeks in the refrigerator. Makes 12 ounces.

### Calculating Flavored Gum Syrup with Any Juice

- Measure the degrees Brix and mass of the juice, as described on page 185.
- Measure an amount of acacia gum equal to ⅒ the mass of the juice.
- Calculate the appropriate amount of sugar to add using the sugar-adjusting formula for raising sweetness on page 186.
- Place the juice in a blender and set to low speed. Slowly add the acacia gum. Blend at a higher speed until the gum is fully dissolved (indicated by the formation of a small head). Return blender to low speed, slowly adding the sugar. Continue to blend until the sugar is fully dissolved.
- Measure 3 grams of citric acid per liter of syrup, then add to the blender.
- Bottle and refrigerate. It will keep for 2 weeks in the refrigerator.

# Pisco Punch

We can't tease you without providing a spec for the drink that made pineapple gum famous. In this version, the tendency of both absinthe and makrut lime tincture to slightly numb the tongue hints at one (and only one) of the effects of the cocaine-fortified wine that may have been in the original. El Floridita included an anisette rinse in its Pisco Punch, so there is a historical basis for the addition. But the amounts of the numbing elements are minute enough not to distract from the drink's pineapple focal point.

**2 sprays Vieux Pontarlier Absinthe**

**5 drops salt solution** (see page 27)

**1 dash makrut lime leaf tincture** (see herb tincture, page 121)

**¼ ounce strained lemon juice**

**½ ounce strained lime juice**

**¾ ounce pineapple gum syrup** (see page 197)

**2 ounces Macchu Pisco**

- Rinse a chilled coupe (6 ounces) with 2 sprays of Vieux Pontarlier Absinthe from an atomizer. Combine all the ingredients in a shaker with 1 medium ice cube and 2 small ice cubes. Shake and strain into the coupe glass.

# Bird of Paradise

*Fruit and cream*

Here's another drink documented in *The Gentleman's Companion* by Charles H. Baker Jr. He discovered it at the Stranger's Club in Panama City, Panama, which catered to international trade through a certain canal. Think of it as a Gin Fizz with raspberry syrup.

The raspberry gives this bird its plumage. But an appropriate raspberry syrup is hard to find. Commercial versions vary wildly in quality, and making it at home can result in a consistency too close to jam or, worse, water. It's a brilliant drink with a tricky ingredient. Sugar adjusting sounds right for the job, but how do you adjust whole fruit?

Using a vacuum sealer to bag all the ingredients allows you to cold process this syrup, avoiding the changes to flavor characteristics that would come with doing it in a saucepan. We want fresh fruit, not jam.

The less broken up the raspberries are, the better. Whole raspberries will turn the sugar into a rich syrup without contributing much extra water.

For our Bird of Paradise, the raspberry syrup is backed with raspberry eau-de-vie from St. George. The syrup brings fresh juice but the eau-de-vie contributes other aspects of the fruit, an aromatic shadow in the background. Cream, that age-old partner of the berry, plays the sweet role in this drink. To linger in the moment, we'll add soda, Ramos Fizz style.

For the gin base, you stand at a crossroads. The recommended choice is Old Raj Red Label, with its classical London Dry botanicals plus an extra hit of saffron, to really kick the raspberry into gear. But for a different experience, try Mahón Xoriguer, heralding hearty black pepper notes in an unaged brandy base, which enhances the drink's eau-de-vie aspect.

**5 drops salt solution** (see page 27)

**¾ ounce strained lemon juice**

**¾ ounce raspberry syrup** (see page 201)

**¾ ounce cream syrup** (see page 201)

**½ ounce St. George Raspberry Brandy**

**1½ ounces Cadenhead's Old Raj Red Label Gin or Mahón Xoriguer Gin**

**1½ ounces soda water**

**Raspberries, for garnish**

**Pineapple leaf, for garnish**

- Combine all the ingredients in a mixing tin with 8 ounces of crushed ice. Flash blend for 5 seconds and pour unstrained into a chilled Zombie glass (16 ounces) with 8 ounces of crushed ice.
- Garnish with raspberries on a pick stuck through a pineapple leaf. Serve with a straw.

RECIPE CONTINUES

## WHOLE FRUIT SYRUPS

This method can be adapted to other fruits such as blackberries or blueberries. The force of the vacuum sealer will cold process the fruit and sugar into a syrup. The technique produces a clean fruit flavor.

It's possible for the vacuum sealer process to result in a syrup higher than the 50 Brix the drink requires. In that case, water instead of sugar is added to reduce sweetness. (See the section on sugar adjusting, starting on page 185, for more on degrees Brix and proper measuring for sweetness.)

### Raspberry Syrup, 50 Brix

**250 grams whole raspberries**

**250 grams white sugar**

**59 grams water**

**2.25 grams citric acid**

- Place the whole raspberries and white sugar in a bag and seal it with a vacuum sealer. Let the bag sit in the refrigerator for 24 hours. Alternatively, to expedite the process of breaking down the sugar, you can put the bag in a hot water bath at 125°F for 6 hours, then refrigerate for another 12 hours.
- When the sugar has broken down to syrup, finely strain off the syrup from the berries. Combine with the water and citric acid.
- Bottle and refrigerate. It will keep for 2 weeks in the refrigerator. Makes around 10 ounces.

### Cream Syrup, 50 Brix

This was a staple of Existing Conditions, where it formed the basis of the bar's unique Grasshopper, Eggnog, White Russian, and all things creamy. With its slight citric tang, it resembles sour cream frosting.

This is a thick mixture. At the bar, it was dispensed from syrup pumps. If you're planning many Birds of Paradise, consider combining the raspberry and cream syrups into one bottle for easier pouring.

**250 grams heavy cream**

**250 grams white sugar**

**14 milliliters 15% citric acid solution** (see page 196)

- Place the cream in a blender set to low speed. Slowly add the sugar followed by the citric acid solution. Continue to blend until the sugar is fully dissolved.
- Bottle and refrigerate. It will keep for 1 week in the refrigerator. If it separates over time, it can be stirred together again. Makes 1 pint.

# Languid Belle

*Soda fountain foundation*

Around 1937, Donn Beach whipped up a drink that, even in his varied oeuvre, stands out as a bit unusual. He called it the Caribbean Punch, despite the fact that this did not distinguish it from all his other drinks that were also inspired by some form of punch from the Caribbean. Rather, its focus on sarsaparilla grounded it in the soda fountains of his youth.

In *The Oxford Companion to American Food and Drink,* contributor Ruth Tobias notes that sarsaparilla "may evoke images of languid belles and parched cowboys," but despite its antique, romantic image, it's not completely relegated to the past. Today's root beer and birch beer are from the same lineage, although bottlings of properly old-fashioned sarsaparilla can be hard to come by. Instead, let's make our own sarsaparilla syrup.

In the Caribbean Punch, there were several sweeteners at work whose flavor we want to preserve, but we don't want our version to be too saccharine. This is where sugar adjusting can truly shine, as we can make our syrup at any level of sweetness. In this case we'll aim for 25 Brix, half as sweet as the usual 1:1 syrup. When it's diluted with ice and cut with soda water, it will resemble the degrees Brix of bottled soda but with much more flavor. (See page 185 for a discussion on sugar adjusting.)

Embracing the soda fountain aesthetic, the Languid Belle combines three different syrups, just as soda jerks would add a little bit of this and that to formulate their latest offerings.

With its strong barrel tannins, Barbancourt goes remarkably well with root beer–like flavors. Panamá-Pacific is on hand to dry out the host of other ingredients.

**5 drops salt solution** (see page 27)

**6 drops almond extract**

**3 dashes Angostura aromatic bitters**

**¾ ounce strained lime juice**

**½ teaspoon grenadine** (see page 68)

**1 teaspoon ginger syrup** (see page 83)

**1½ ounces sarsaparilla syrup** (see below)

**1 teaspoon St. George Absinthe Verte**

**½ ounce Panamá-Pacific 9 Year Rum**

**2 ounces Barbancourt 5 Star Rhum**

**2 ounces soda water**

**Mint leaf, for garnish**

**Cherry, for garnish**

- Combine all the ingredients in a mixing tin with 8 ounces of crushed ice. Flash blend for 5 seconds and pour unstrained into a chilled, stemmed Pilsner glass (16 ounces) with 4 ounces of crushed ice and 2 small ice cubes.
- Garnish with a mint leaf speared to a cherry. Serve with a straw.

## Sarsaparilla Syrup, 25 Brix

After reading *Fix the Pumps,* Darcy O'Neil's 2009 examination of soda-fountain techniques, bartender Jim Kearns found himself inspired to introduce a sarsaparilla highball (made with rye whiskey) to the menu of his bar, The Happiest Hour, in Manhattan. Most of today's root beers are overwhelmed by vanilla and missing natural plant flavors, but his syrup recipe, from which this recipe is adapted, went back to basics with sarsaparilla bark, wintergreen oil, and a bit of vanilla. "It was the best of both worlds," Jim said. "The contemporary root beer syrup combined with the old-school sarsaparilla syrup."

Once you've experienced the Languid Belle, follow Jim's lead and try this syrup in a rye highball.

**3 vanilla beans**

**1 milliliter food-grade wintergreen oil** (for example, LorAnn)

**18 grams sarsaparilla bark**

**227 grams white sugar**

**454 grams water**

- Scrape the vanilla beans from their pods and place the paste into a saucepan. Add the remaining ingredients and vanilla stalks.
- Bring the pan to a simmer. Cover and turn heat to low. Let it sit covered on low heat for 15 minutes, then remove from heat. Let the mixture rest for 24 hours in the refrigerator.
- Fine strain, bottle, and refrigerate. It will keep for 2 weeks in the refrigerator. Makes 18 ounces.

# Navy Grog

*Rum and Coca-Cola, but not like that*

Both Donn Beach and Trader Vic had versions of a drink called the Navy Grog. The Trader formed his around a "grog concentrate," and while he published many recipes in his lifetime, this ingredient was never revealed. As the years went by without even the suggestion of a leak, the drink achieved mythic status due to its unavailability to the home bartender. Below is our attempt to conjure a simulacrum, based on the known evidence.

Instead of revealing the Navy Grog recipe, for those who wanted to re-create it at home, Vic offered a bottled grog concentrate at retail. While his company does continue to sell many premade mixes, the Navy Grog mix has been available only intermittently in recent years. However, we've sampled vintage bottles in the hands of truly dedicated collectors. The report: Among the variety of spices in the mix, the most prominent is allspice, among an abundance of high-fructose corn syrup.

Meanwhile, in another corner of the galaxy, a fan recipe posted to an online forum attempted to rekindle the version of grog concentrate found at the defunct Honolulu Restaurant of Alexandria, Virginia. The Honolulu, a local hangout keeping the midcentury tropical dream alive until its closing in 2004, was run by David and Anna Chan. David had worked for many years as a bartender at Trader Vic's in Washington, DC, during its heyday.

The central conceit of this online reinterpretation of Chan's version of Vic's syrup was its basis in Coca-Cola. This makes sense due to commonalities in flavor, but it's hard to miss the irony of using a top-secret blend of spices and water in re-creating another top-secret blend of spices and water.

In adding our own level of reimagination onto this syrup, Coke was swapped out for Mexican Coke, due to its reliance on sugarcane instead of corn syrup. The syrup now goes like this: take Coke, add allspice, sweeten to syrup level—and you're done. There's already a lot going on in Coke. (For more thoughts on Coca-Cola, see the Bay of Pigs on page 133.)

The rum blend for this Navy Grog is based on the rums specified in the recipe from Trader Vic's 1972 *Bartender's Guide*. In addition to his commercially produced mix, Vic calls for equal portions of 86 proof Demerara, dark Jamaican, and light Puerto Rican rums. These rums are included here, except for a switch of Barbancourt White for the latter, due to its affinity with grapefruit.

RECIPE CONTINUES

**1 lime wedge**

**5 drops salt solution** (see page 27)

**3 dashes Angostura aromatic bitters**

**1 ounce grapefruit juice, acid adjusted to lemon** (see page 178)

**¾ ounce grog concentrate syrup** (see below)

**1 teaspoon St. Elizabeth Allspice Dram**

**¾ ounce Hamilton Demerara 86 Rum**

**¾ ounce Appleton Estate 12 Year Old Rum**

**¾ ounce Barbancourt White Rhum**

**Grapefruit slice, for garnish**

**Mint sprig, for garnish**

**Rock candy swizzle, optional**

- Squeeze a lime wedge to remove the juice, and place the spent wedge in a double Old Fashioned glass (16 ounces).
- Combine all the ingredients in a mixing tin with 8 ounces of crushed ice. Flash blend for 5 seconds and pour unstrained into the glass with 4 ounces of crushed ice.
- Garnish with a grapefruit slice, mint, and optionally, a rock candy swizzle. Serve with a straw.

---

## Grog Concentrate Syrup, 66 Brix

**355 grams Mexican Coca-Cola**

**21 grams allspice**

**572 grams white sugar**

- Stir the Coca-Cola to partially decarbonate it. Break the allspice into smaller pieces using a mortar and pestle or a spice grinder.
- Toast the allspice in a saucepan over medium heat until aromatic. Add the cola and sugar. Bring the mixture to a simmer, stirring occasionally, then cover and reduce heat to low. After 15 minutes, remove from heat. Transfer to a container and refrigerate for 12 to 24 hours. Strain, bottle, and refrigerate. It will keep for 4 weeks in the refrigerator. Makes 24 ounces.

# Preserving Citrus

Fresh juice was the first and loudest rallying cry of the craft cocktail revolution, and with good reason. Fresh juice adds much to the dimensions of a drink. The bite, the aroma, the primeval juiciness of it. The return of fresh juice also meant a restoration of the forgotten library of drinks that high-fructose corn syrup sour mixes beat into oblivion; drinks like the Jack Rose, Sidecar, and Daiquiri.

Today, fresh juice has been adopted in every kind of bar program. No longer the sole domain of high-end cocktail bars, you'll find citrus being squeezed at burger joints, music festivals, even the airport. Freshly squeezed juice has made its triumphant return—and that's the way it should be.

But in our rediscovery of juice, there has also been loss. While nineteenth-century cocktail tomes called for juice, they also called for cordials, liqueurs, and syrups that preserved the flavors of fruits out of season or from distant climes. Just as current craft bars often substitute standardized simple syrup where a fuller palette of sweeteners might once have been employed, there's a tendency to use fresh juice whenever fruit flavor is needed, ignoring other routes to the delicious destination.

Preserved citrus has a different profile from fresh, adding another approach to your box of tools. Oxidation and the addition of oils change the character of the juices. You could think of preserved juice versus fresh as sherry versus wine. Both start the same, but the different preparations inform the flavor profiles and how they can be used in recipes. Preserving is also a great way to take advantage of citrus that might otherwise be thrown away.

This section explores several techniques of preserving citrus, transforming the fruit in your kitchen in order to transform it in your cocktails.

## PUNCH SYRUPS

In contemporary American English, "sherbet" is a type of fruit-flavored ice cream. In British English, it's candy in powdered form. In nineteenth-century bar manuals, sherbet meant a fruit-flavored syrup. In fact, the Persian *sharbat,* from which we get the word (as well as *sorbet* in French and *sorbetto* in Italian), means a drink of water and sugar. It should be no surprise that "syrup" comes from the same source.

Citrus syrups were extensively used in the punches that took seventeenth-century England by storm; for this reason, we'll use the new term "punch syrup" instead of sherbet, to make it clear we're not talking about ice cream or candy.

In a classic punch, oleosaccharum is a crucial component. Citrus peel is left to combine with sugar through a bit of muddling and a lot of time. The oils, the "oleo" part of this ostentatious Latinate ingredient, are drawn out by the sugar (you guessed it, "saccharum"), resulting in a thick, oily syrup packed with citrus flavor. (See David Wondrich's essential *Punch* for an extensive lowdown.)

Sherbet, or punch syrup in our parlance, is oleosaccharum plus the fruit's juice.

While punch syrup can be seen as a step in creating bowls of punch, it's also ready for use in any cocktail that needs an extra lift of citrus. We'll get into punch syrups in the Hearthside Punch, but first, let's learn the foundational art of oleo.

## Oleosaccharum Template, 50 Brix

*In 2013, Jim Kearns developed the bar program for Play, a restaurant and bar in the basement of New York's Museum of Sex. "It was a fantastic example of the right bar in the wrong place. It just failed spectacularly—because we didn't have Malibu and pineapple," he told us. "There was a lot of free time since we weren't busy, ever. So I started playing around with syrups and production." Encouraged by Chef Ben Roche, he began to experiment with the kitchen's vacuum sealer. "It was an expedited means of producing very complex prep, and I began making oleos in that manner." Around the same time and across the continent, Jeffrey Morgenthaler was pioneering a vacuum oleo process at Portland bar Clyde Common, which you can read about in his* Bar Book.

*Later, Jim founded his bar The Happiest Hour on the idea of complex syrups prepared in advance, freeing bartenders to produce cocktails at a higher volume while still delivering high-quality, layered flavors.*

*This template is based on the cold-processed vacuum syrup technique Jim developed.*

**250 grams citrus peel**

**250 grams white sugar**

- Cut the citrus peels with a knife to retain the oil in the peels. (While faster to use, a peeler expresses oils from the peel when cutting into the fruit, and we want the oils to stay where they are, so a knife is preferred.)
- Place the peels and sugar in a bag and seal it with a vacuum sealer.
- Let the bag sit in the refrigerator for 48 hours. Alternatively, to expedite the process of breaking down the sugar, you can put the bag in a hot water bath at 125°F for 12 hours, then refrigerate for another 12 hours.
- Once the sugar has dissolved completely, remove and discard the peels. Store in a sealable container and refrigerate. It will keep for 1 week in the refrigerator. Makes around 8 ounces.

## Ginger Oleosaccharum, 50 Brix

*Here's a useful recipe for ginger oleo, which features in the Piña Brava (page 77) and Incantation (page 248). Yes, ginger contains oil, too.*

**250 grams ginger, thinly sliced**

**250 grams white sugar**

- Cut the ginger into thin slices, preferably with a mandolin. Place the ginger and sugar in a bag and seal it with a vacuum sealer.
- Let the bag sit in the refrigerator for 24 hours. Alternatively, to expedite the process of breaking down the sugar, you can put the bag in a hot water bath at 125°F for 6 hours, then refrigerate for another 12 hours.
- Remove and discard the ginger slices. Store in a sealable container and refrigerate. It will keep for 1 week in the refrigerator. Makes 8 ounces.

# Hearthside Punch

*Tea with lemon*

Cognac punch was a staple of celebrations in the eighteenth century, and lemon sherbet was the rock that punch was built upon.

The winter holidays seem more festive with a Cognac punch in hand. Perhaps the fruity brandy recalls warmer days. There are countless recipes for punches made with brandy; here's an amalgamation of some of the best ideas. In particular, tea is an evergreen punch constituent. Its tannins, similar to those found in the oak barrels in which spirits are aged, impart gravitas in the same way.

Water is a vital part of punch, as punch should be more dilute and easier to sip than a cocktail. Once it's been poured over ice, a cup of this beverage should be roughly the strength of wine.

This drink can be mixed à la minute, or it can be batched ahead of time and bottled. To serve four people, multiply the recipe by five. Depending on your group, it will make for a memorable holiday season or one magical evening.

**5 drops salt solution** (see page 27)

**½ ounce strained lemon juice**

**½ ounce lemon punch syrup** (see page 211)

**¾ ounce black tea syrup** (see page 211)

**½ teaspoon Pierre Ferrand Dry Curaçao**

**½ ounce Smith & Cross Traditional Jamaica Rum**

**2 ounces Rémy Martin 1738 Accord Royal Cognac**

**1¼ ounces water**

**Grated nutmeg, for garnish**

- Add all the ingredients to a mixing glass and stir without ice. If not serving immediately, bottle and refrigerate.
- To serve, pour into a punch glass (8 to 10 ounces) filled with cracked ice.
- Dust with grated nutmeg.

RECIPE CONTINUES

### Lemon Punch Syrup, 55 Brix

This punch syrup combines lemon oleo with lemon juice and a bit more sugar to balance the acidity of the juice. This acidity fades with time, which is why citric acid is added to stabilize the tartness. To balance the acid, lemon and lime punch syrups are slightly higher in sugar content than the standard 50 Brix.

**250 grams strained lemon juice**

**125 grams lemon oleosaccharum** (see template on page 208)

**250 grams white sugar**

**11 grams citric acid**

- Combine the juice and oleosaccharum in a blender and run at low speed. Slowly add the sugar, followed by the citric acid. Blend until the sugar is fully dissolved.
- Bottle and refrigerate for at least 24 hours and up to 2 weeks. Makes 16 ounces.

### Black Tea Syrup, 50 Brix

In a punch, tea adds an extra layer of flavor not unlike bitters in an individual cocktail. Here the tea is made into a syrup to provide bold tannins in an easily incorporated ingredient.

**250 grams water**

**3 grams Assam breakfast tea** (for example, Ghograjan Tea Estate)

**250 grams turbinado sugar**

- Combine the water and tea in a nonreactive container and leave in a refrigerator for 12 to 24 hours. Strain the liquid into a blender. Blend on low, slowly adding the sugar. Once covered, increase the speed and blend until the sugar is fully dissolved.
- Bottle and refrigerate. It will keep for 2 weeks in the refrigerator. Makes 16 ounces.

# Pimm's Tropicale

*London—New Orleans—Rio de Janeiro*

James Pimm operated a series of successful oyster bars in London starting in 1823. Pimm, or perhaps one of his successors in the business, concocted a spiced gin liqueur sold as an aid to digestion. That concoction, Pimm's No. 1 Cup, became surprisingly popular, in large part due to the rise of the similarly named Pimm's Cup cocktail—Pimm's liqueur and lemon soda or ginger ale, lavishly topped with mint, cucumber, citrus, apple, or strawberries—which even now remains a summertime favorite across Britain.

The Pimm's Cup somehow found its way to New Orleans by the 1940s, where it has been unashamedly embraced. It's de rigueur at the bar of the Napoleon House, a Gallophilic grog shop where the Brit favorite is a free-poured medley of Pimm's, lemonade, and 7Up—never the same way twice, yet always a refreshing diversion from humid French Quarter afternoons.

Craft bar interpretations of the Pimm's Cup cocktail differ; those focusing on the ginger ale might turn it into a buck, those entranced by the garnish might turn it into sangria. In his 1951 book *The South American Gentleman's Companion,* Charles H. Baker Jr. describes a party in Rio at which the Pimm's Cup cocktail is denigrated and dismissed until a brave defender suggests an adaptation more befitting their tropical latitude. The secret ingredients: a splash of (only sort of tropical) lime cordial and a (downright English) extra pony of gin.

As much as we admire the lateral thinking exhibited by Baker's co-celebrant, we opt to draw our inspiration from the libation the Napoleon House has been dutifully doling out all these years, supercharging it with a combination of juices and punch syrups in place of the lemonade.

In addition to its gin-based Pimm's No. 1, the distiller once sold a full range of different base spirits with their proprietary spice mix. In the 1930s, Pimm's No. 4, with Caribbean rum, was introduced. Its memory is an inspiration here. However, the Pimm's Tropicale also works with the more traditional gin. Just substitute Tanqueray for Chairman's Reserve.

You can juice a cucumber by grating it with a cheese grater, gathering the bits in a nut milk bag, and squeezing.

**5 drops salt solution** (see page 27)

**⅛ ounce strained lemon juice**

**⅛ ounce strained lime juice**

**¼ ounce cucumber juice**

**¼ ounce lemon punch syrup** (see page 211)

**½ ounce lime punch syrup** (see below)

**½ ounce Chairman's Reserve Rum**

**1½ ounces Pimm's No. 1**

**2 ounces soda water**

**Borage or mint sprig, for garnish**

**Cucumber wedge, for garnish**

- Combine all the ingredients, except the soda water, in a shaker with 1 medium ice cube. Shake briefly. Add the soda water to the shaker. Strain into a chilled Collins glass (15 ounces) filled with small ice cubes.
- Garnish with borage and a cucumber wedge. Mint will suffice if borage is not available.

---

## Lime Punch Syrup, 55 Brix

**250 grams strained lime juice**

**125 grams lime oleosaccharum** (see template on page 208)

**250 grams white sugar**

**3.75 grams malic acid**

**7.25 grams citric acid**

- Combine the juice and oleosaccharum in a blender and run at low speed. Slowly add the sugar, followed by the acids. Blend until the sugar is fully dissolved.
- Bottle and refrigerate for at least 24 hours and up to 2 weeks. Makes 16 ounces.

# Puesta del Sol

*Beyond the Spritz*

As the craft cocktail revival gained steam, Audrey Saunders's Pegu Club was its boiler room. Its menus were developed particularly to introduce a new generation to the possibilities of mixed drinks. Pegu Club became a drinking academy for the ages, easing the vodka and soda crowd into unimagined pleasures like Calvados, Chartreuse, pisco, and rye.

Audrey was always cognizant of her role as envoy, conducting these experiences into the lives of her guests. When Pegu opened in 2005, the cocktail most guests were prepared to request was the Cosmopolitan. The bar needed to provide the next step for such imbibers; it created several "Cosmo killers" to entice and enlighten the neophyte. Two such drinks were the Intro to Aperol, created by Audrey herself, and the Aperol Sunset, created by Pegu Club bartender Jasper Milne-Soffer.

Both are lively and light, showcasing the citrusy aperitivo Aperol. The drinks, delicious in their own right, also served as a gateway to bitter drinks, as the Intro name suggests.

"When Aperol finally became available in the US market, I created the Intro to Aperol to introduce it to the American palate," Audrey told us. "While I really like Aperol, I was never a fan of the Spritz. From my personal perspective, I find the sugar lingers on my palate even after being carbonated and diluted. I always felt that its high Brix, low ABV profile needed the support of an acid. Campari's strong, bitter profile was an acquired taste for many at that time. But Aperol was softer and more approachable, a gentle bitter." She combined it with gin, lemon juice, simple syrup, and Angostura bitters—shaken, up, with a flamed orange twist—and palates were thoroughly introduced.

Jasper conceived a Margarita riff—Tequila, Aperol, lemon juice, grapefruit syrup, and Demerara syrup—which became the Aperol Sunset. "Since Aperol has a much lower ABV than Cointreau, he needed to integrate other flavors that would support it and help it shine," Audrey said. "He subbed lemon for lime, as lime would have *locked* with the Tequila and stepped on the Aperol. Grapefruit syrup instead of grapefruit juice provided a muted, restrained brightness, keeping the grapefruit from becoming too assertive."

After considering the lessons of these two Pegu Club drinks, as well as the similarly themed Cuzco by Julie Reiner, we saw the opportunity for another bitter tropical drink outside of the Jungle Bird lineage.

In the Puesta del Sol, the more deeply rhubarb-flavored Select aperitivo meets the hearty Uruapan Charanda rum. Select, halfway in bitterness between Campari and Aperol, features several

RECIPE CONTINUES

unusual notes, including juniper berries and the aforementioned rhubarb. The complex layers of the Uruapan, blended from both cane juice and molasses, balance the salacious juiciness of the grapefruit punch syrup.

All together, it could be your Intro to Select.

**5 drops salt solution** (see page 27)

**¾ ounce strained lemon juice**

**¾ ounce grapefruit punch syrup** (see below)

**¾ ounce Select Aperitivo**

**1½ ounces Uruapan Charanda Blanco Rum**

- Combine all the ingredients in a shaker with 1 medium ice cube and 2 small ice cubes. Shake and strain into a large, chilled coupe (10 ounces).

---

## Grapefruit Punch Syrup, 50 Brix

The variety of grapefruit chosen will impact the flavor. The drier white grapefruit is always preferred, but pink will work, too. Try to avoid sweeter varieties, which tend to be redder, as they lose their grapefruit flavor in the deluge of sucrose. Unlike lemon and lime punch syrups, the grapefruit is a standard 50 Brix, as the underlying fruit doesn't have as much acid.

Try this versatile ingredient in a Daiquiri, swizzle, or highball.

**250 grams strained grapefruit juice**

**63 grams grapefruit oleosaccharum** (see template on page 208)

**173 grams white sugar**

**3 grams citric acid**

- Combine the juice and oleosaccharum in a blender and run at low speed. Slowly add the sugar, followed by the citric acid. Blend until the sugar is fully dissolved.
- Bottle and refrigerate for at least 24 hours and up to 2 weeks. Makes 12 ounces.

## CORDIALS

Another method of preserving citrus is turning juice into a cordial. In a cordial, the pectin and pith are removed (a process known as clarifying) and sugar is added.

Whereas oleosaccharum is made through a cold process, cordials are made with heat. Heated juices become bitter because of the reaction of pulp and pith to the increased temperature, which is why the juice must be clarified first. The clarified juice is then cooked with the peel to add back the oils and flavors they possess.

A cordial many bartenders will be familiar with is Rose's Lime Cordial, also known as Rose's Lime Juice, which was the first commercially produced fruit concentrate, patented by Scottish ship chandler Lauchlan Rose in 1867. In that year, the Merchant Shipping Act required all British ships to carry lime juice, for the prevention of scurvy. Rose's method preserved limes for long journeys with sugar rather than alcohol. In addition to this naval use, the ingredient found a place behind the bar, even where fresh juice was available, as bartenders could use it to layer citrus flavors. Not many sweeteners in the classic cocktail era had both acidity and sweetness, but cordials delivered both through lime peel flavor and citrus acidity. As a clarified product, it could also hop into a variety of stirred drinks.

Today, the Rose's product available in the United States is based on artificial flavors and corn syrup, but we can use a similar method to Lauchlan Rose's original to re-create a standout ingredient for bar use.

Getting lime juice to go clear has been a difficult process for bartenders; Rose patented his process for a reason. A recent technique using agar-agar, a seaweed-derived jelly, has some adherents. This turns juice into a gel, which can be squeezed through cheesecloth. However, it's easy for the results to still be cloudy and the agar-agar strips flavor away. We prefer a different approach derived from the practice at Existing Conditions: wine fining agents, an enzyme, and a centrifuge.

Wine fining agents are used in the production of wine to bind with unwanted materials to make them easier to remove; it serves the same purpose here. The enzyme pectin depolymerase breaks down the pectin in fruit. A centrifuge separates the chemically changed components mechanically.

Without the use of a centrifuge, given time the layers will still separate out. Once you see a clear top layer of juice, skim it off, while being careful not to disturb the separation. You will recover only about half as much clarified juice this way, but it's a method to experiment with before investing in a kitchen centrifuge.

Clarifying does require some equipment. The ingredients are used in very small doses, which need to be measured with a micropipette (about $50). The most affordable home centrifuge is the Spinzall ($700). Although the centrifuge makes things faster and easier, you can get by with just the wine fining agents, enzyme, and patience.

### Clarified Juice Template

*This is the method that was used at Existing Conditions. The juice must be at room temperature for the wine fining agents and enzyme to work properly. Measure the small amounts of ingredients with your micropipette to be sure of exacting precision. This template works with all citrus.*

*Note that not all wine fining agents are suitable for vegans, so check the labels. These products are available from Modernist Pantry, including vegan versions.*

**1 liter fresh citrus juice, room temperature**

**4 milliliters Pectinex Ultra SP-L**

**8 milliliters Kieselsol**

**4 milliliters chitosan solution**

- Combine the juice, Pectinex Ultra SP-L and 4 milliliters of the Kieselsol in a nonreactive container; mix and let rest for 15 minutes. Add the chitosan solution; mix and let rest for 15 minutes. Add the remaining 4 milliliters Kieselsol; mix and let rest for 15 minutes.
- Spin in a centrifuge for 5 minutes or let the juice sit for at least 1 hour. Gently pour the clear juice into a separate container, being careful not to disturb the sediment (some juice will be lost in order to avoid the inclusion of sediment).
- Use within 12 hours in a cocktail or up to 1 week in a cordial. Makes 1 liter.

# Rangoon Gimlet

*Lush lime*

The British Empire left a complicated legacy for the world. It also left a number of iconic drinks, like the Gin and Tonic, Pink Gin, Gimlet, and Pegu Club.

The Rangoon Gimlet is an amalgamation of these colonialist cocktails. In midcentury tropical bars of Los Angeles, like the China Trader and the Tiki-Ti, the Rangoon was a standard gin option. It was served frozen at the China Trader, while the Tiki-Ti flash-blended it on crushed ice. (The frozen recipe from the China Trader's Tony Ramos is available in Jeff Berry's *Taboo Table.*)

In our version, the drink undergoes a transformation in the opposite direction to that of the Slushy Dog (page 103), exploring how nuances can be unveiled by converting it to shaken form. Lime cordial is the key.

The drink is a cross between a Pink Gin and a traditional Gimlet, served up. The heavy hit of Angostura, from the Pink Gin, cooperates with the lime cordial from the Gimlet. The cleaner flavor of the clarified juice is a stronger platform for the bitters while the oily texture of the cordial brings body to the drink.

After this recipe had been created, we inevitably found an analogue in the pages of Baker's *South American Gentleman's Companion,* the Bin-'n'-Gitters. It takes a similar compounding approach but with a much higher heaping of colonialism in the unbelievable personage of Commander J. K. L. Ponsonby-Foulcques, the drink's inventor. (At Milk & Honey, Sasha Petraske offered this drink as a swizzle with fresh lime and a float of bitters.)

You have a choice of gins depending on what you want to emphasize. Old Raj, which adds saffron to the traditional London Dry profile, brings another layer of spice on top of the Angostura. Plymouth brings out the citrus. On a particularly hot day, the drink can be served on cracked ice in a tumbler; Plymouth works best in this serve.

Unusually among the drinks in this book, a spent lime wedge is shaken in the tin. This adds one more layer of lime, contrasting fresh oils with the preserved ones.

**1 lime wedge**

**5 drops salt solution** (see page 27)

**4 to 5 dashes Angostura aromatic bitters**

**¾ ounce lime cordial** (see page 221)

**2 ounces Cadenhead's Old Raj Blue Label Gin or Plymouth Navy Strength Gin**

**Channeled lime twist, for garnish**

RECIPE CONTINUES

- Squeeze a lime wedge to remove the juice, discard the juice, and place the spent wedge at the bottom of a shaker. Add the remaining ingredients to the shaker with 1 medium cube and 2 small cubes. Shake and strain into a chilled Nick and Nora glass (5 ounces).
- Garnish with a channeled lime twist.

---

## Lime Cordial, 55 Brix

This syrup is a great way to recycle older lime juice. If you squeezed a bunch of lime juice for bar service or a cocktail party, this cordial can turn those leftovers into something exceptionally delicious. The addition of citric and malic acid will restore the older lime juice back to its full tartness. Like lime punch syrup, this cordial is slightly higher in Brix as a balance to the higher acid.

**250 grams clarified lime juice**
(see template on page 218)

**250 grams white sugar**

**12.5 grams lime peel**

**2.5 grams malic acid**

**5 grams citric acid**

- Combine the clarified juice, sugar, and lime peel in a saucepan. Bring to a simmer, stirring occasionally. Once at a simmer, cover and reduce heat to low. After 15 minutes, remove from heat and let it sit for 6 hours.
- Strain the syrup and add the acids, stirring until fully integrated. Bottle and refrigerate. It will keep for 2 weeks in the refrigerator. Makes 16 ounces.

RECIPE CONTINUES

# Classic Gimlet

Without easy access to proper cordials, most craft bars have turned to making the Gimlet in the style of a sour. A true Gimlet, with a silky, stirred texture and the spirit prominently in the foreground, is more akin to a Martini than a Daiquiri. Lime cordial tames the gin and provides a bang of citrus flavor but stops well short of limeade.

The jasmine and high citrus tones of Fords Gin harmonize with the lime cordial. But if you want something more classically assertive, Beefeater is the way to go.

The drink is presented here on the rocks but can also be served up. The extra water from being served on the rocks balances out the acidity of the lime and lime cordial, so if you do serve it up, make sure that it is properly diluted beforehand.

It is possible to compose this cocktail with freshly squeezed lime juice instead of clarified. While the clarified juice is a touch cleaner in flavor, regular juice still presents a beautiful counterpoint to the cordial. As long as you carry lime cordial in your luggage, this classic will be within reach anywhere you roam.

**5 drops salt solution** (see page 27)

**1 teaspoon lime juice, preferably clarified** (see template on page 218)

**½ ounce lime cordial** (see page 221)

**2 ounces Fords Gin or Beefeater Gin**

**Channeled lime twist, for garnish**

- Combine all the ingredients in a mixing glass filled with small ice cubes. Stir and strain into a chilled goblet (10 ounces) with 1 medium ice cube.
- Garnish with a channeled lime twist.

# Bourbon Special

*Ginger beer à la minute*

At Existing Conditions, clarified cordials worked much like syrups at a soda fountain. Lime cordial was added to water, spirits, and other modifiers to produce a range of carbonated drinks. This suggested that the cordial technique could also be used to bring other soda flavors to drinks that are otherwise difficult to replicate à la minute in the craft cocktail manner.

Ginger beer is a great example. The usual solution is that of the Sasha Petraske school, incorporating ginger syrup and fresh citrus. In this book, El Diablo (page 81) takes this approach. It works well in many recipes. But others need more than just spice and acidity, as certain ginger beers and ginger ales have more shades of light and shadow that need to be addressed.

An à la minute ginger beer made from lime cordial, ginger syrup, lime juice, and soda water brings the unique tang of ginger beer to cocktails, with the citrus oils offering depth that juice alone would not. The combined sweet-acidic burst of lime cordial is crucial to this drink; it could not be replicated with lime juice and simple syrup.

The original Bourbon Special was another whiskey-forward creation gracing the menus of Steve Crane's Kon-Tiki chain. It's a tropical take on the classic Rickey, which started out as a whiskey cocktail before morphing into a gin drink. As its story goes, circa 1883, lobbyist Joe Rickey wanted a cooling drink to suit the punishing Washington, DC, summers, so he called for his booze to be cut with fresh lemon and soda water (but no sugar, in a foreshadowing of Hemingway's preferences). His choice of lemon over lime has been disregarded by bartenders ever since, and the Rickey has become synonymous with lime-based drinks even though highballs more typically pair whiskey with lemon.

The Kon-Tiki's Bourbon Special uses ginger beer in place of the Rickey's soda water, and then adds a touch of falernum for complexity and a needed balancing of sweetness. In the Western Sour, the Kon-Tiki's other whiskey and lime drink, those key ingredients don't quite interlock because the highly acid lime diminishes the effects of the whiskey's oak aging. (This problem is addressed in our version of the Western Sour, on page 177.) But in the Bourbon Special, that diminishment is actually what you want: The lime cordial cuts through the heavy oak aging of the whiskey, while still preserving the spirit's fruitier notes.

RECIPE CONTINUES

**5 drops salt solution** (see page 27)

**2 dashes Angostura aromatic bitters**

**½ ounce strained lime juice**

**1 teaspoon falernum** (see page 232)

**⅜ ounce ginger syrup** (see page 83)

**⅜ ounce lime cordial** (see page 221)

**1¾ ounces Elijah Craig bourbon**

**3 ounces soda water**

- Combine all the ingredients, except the soda water, in a shaker with 1 medium ice cube. Shake, add the soda water, and strain into a chilled Collins glass (15 ounces) filled with small ice cubes.

# Só Danço Samba

*New flavor possibilities*

Bossa nova albums are known for taking jazz standards in unexpected directions. The Só Danço Samba (named after the João Gilberto and Stan Getz collaboration, translated as "I only dance samba") does this for the highball.

In the two previous recipes, we've seen how the cordial technique can replicate and build upon old-style cordials and sodas. The current drink needs pineapple and makrut lime leaf, which is outside the traditional pantheon of flavor combinations. Lime cordial is the map to the treasure.

Makrut lime leaf tincture is the hero of the drink, working alongside a small measure of lime cordial to conjure a tropical soda that heightens the rest of the ingredients. Big-flavored mixers, used in small quantities, allow the drink to be served diluted in the refreshing highball style.

The same highball method from the Kingston Zing (page 87) is used here, building the drink in the glass with a highly chilled spirit from the freezer—a technique at the basis of highball culture in Japan.

**5 drops salt solution** (see page 27)

**6 drops Bittermens Winter Melon Bitters**

**½ teaspoon makrut lime leaf tincture** (see herb tincture, page 121)

**⅜ ounce pineapple juice, acid adjusted to lime** (see page 180)

**½ ounce lime cordial** (see page 221)

**2 ounces Novo Fogo Silver Cachaça** (freezer temperature)

**Soda water**

- Combine all the ingredients, except the cachaça and soda water, in a shaker. Whisk with a milk frother (or, if not available, stir until uniform) and set aside.
- Fill a chilled highball glass (12 ounces) with small ice cubes. Add the cachaça, then add the soda until the glass is ¾ full.
- Pour the contents of the shaker into the glass while holding the glass at a 45-degree angle. Top with more soda until full. Agitate the mixture with a single brisk dip of a bar spoon.
- Serve with a straw.

# Improved Rum Cocktail

*More precious than gold*

The cordial technique can be applied to fruits other than lime, as illustrated by the Beachcomber Negroni (page 149), which adapts the cordial approach via the grapefruit-based Don's Mix. Another common ingredient in midcentury tropical drinks is passionfruit, with the flavor administered in many ways.

Passionfruit liqueurs are readily available, but they're a mixed bag. They can be clear or cloudy, sweet or dry, neutral or assertive. Their main function isn't to deliver accurate passionfruit flavor in a range of applications but to offer shelf-stable convenience compared to passionfruit puree. By making a clarified passionfruit cordial we can open up the flavor for reliable use in stirred drinks.

In the late nineteenth century, several drinks that underwent changes to their recipes garnered the qualifier "Improved." The Improved Whiskey Cocktail and the Improved Gin Cocktail were at the forefront, though the Improved Rum Cocktail had to wait an extra century or so for our attention. (For another take on this idea, see the Romero, page 129.)

The improvements that those drinks saw were an extra splash of imported liqueur, such as maraschino, curaçao, or absinthe. In the Improved Rum Cocktail, established tropical flavors from the canon are all present but delivered in unusual ways. Fruit is present without juice, through clarified passionfruit cordial as the sweetener. The structure is inspired by the original 1937 version of the Beachcomber's Gold, with its strong anise and almond notes ricocheting off Jamaican rums, plus Donn Beach's later Waikīkī version, which incorporates the aforementioned passionfruit.

The Improved Rum Cocktail presents high-quality rum the same way the original Improved Whiskey Cocktail can highlight a well-made whiskey. The right blend for the drink is funky, but not so funky that all the layers can't be perceived. The three rums chosen here create a similar profile to a pot-stilled, aged rum as it would have been known in the Jerry Thomas era.

RECIPE CONTINUES

**5 drops salt solution** (see page 27)

**3 dashes orange bitters** (see page 62)

**⅜ ounce passionfruit cordial** (see below)

**¼ teaspoon St. George Absinthe Verte**

**½ teaspoon Tempus Fugit Crème de Noyaux**

**½ ounce Coruba Rum**

**½ ounce Two James Doctor Bird Jamaica Rum**

**1 ounce Chairman's Reserve Legacy Rum**

**Lime twist, for garnish**

- Combine the ingredients in an Old Fashioned glass (12 ounces). Stir with a large ice cube until chilled.
- Garnish with a lime twist.

---

## Passionfruit Cordial, 50 Brix

Unlike our other cordials, this recipe requires clarifying a puree instead of juice. We recommend Boiron passionfruit puree as the starting point. The puree must be fully thawed, at room temperature, when applying the wine fining agents and enzyme.

**250 grams clarified passionfruit puree** (see template on page 218)

**25 grams acacia gum**

**183 grams white sugar**

**3.5 grams citric acid**

- Place the clarified puree in a blender and set to low speed. Slowly add the acacia gum. Blend until the gum is fully dissolved (indicated by the formation of a small head). Continue to blend, slowly adding the sugar, followed by the citric acid. Blend until the sugar has fully dissolved.
- Bottle and refrigerate. It will keep for 2 weeks in the refrigerator. Makes 10 ounces.

## LIQUEURS

Liqueurs are a staple of innumerable cocktail recipes, including throughout this book. While we make great use of many creatively composed commercial liqueurs, sometimes there's a flavor profile not available on the market. This chapter outlines two opportunities to make your own liqueurs.

Sometimes, citrus needs a little more than just sugar to unlock the flavors within. At the same time, a cocktail may need a jolt of citrus with a bit of alcoholic kick. Liqueurs boost alcohol volume while drying out the build of a sour-style drink.

Homemade liqueurs are sweetened infusions of alcohol. The art of a good infusion is knowing what proof is needed in the base spirit to get the job done. An example of this process is the sorrel-infused rum in the Jump Up, Jamaica (page 167), which starts with an 80 proof rum because hibiscus flowers steep easily in alcohol. For other ingredients, a higher proof liquor may be necessary, either to be sure the extraction occurs sufficiently or to reduce the time needed.

The following recipes modify existing distillates with flavors and sugar, creating new liqueurs, which wonderfully preserve the essence of citrus.

# Bronze Swizzle

*Falernum, wormwood, bitters*

In the earliest decades of the previous century, many travelers to the Caribbean had a particular item on their agenda: to sample the Green Swizzle. The cocktail, known across the region's English-speaking islands, was praised in travelogue after travelogue—rarely, though, with any hint to its contents.

A more insightful mention comes from a letter to the editor of *The Sun* of New York, in the days when newspapers covered new and popular cocktails like liquid celebrities. A reader from New Jersey, signing himself "Jerseyman," had on more than one occasion trumpeted the mixological achievements of his state, especially as they sprung from locally produced spirits like applejack. Proving that trans-Hudson smack talk is eternal, an exasperated reply from a New Yorker identified as "Swizzle Stick" was published on October 26, 1903:

> What do we care about pear trees and peach trees, or how many there are of them in bloom? Let "Jerseyman" tell us something about the green swizzle, and see if he can make it with applejack. It is made with a swizzle stick. I'll give him that pointer to start with, and if "Jerseyman" has ever twirled one between his palms I need say no more. If he has not, he has something still to live for. . . . The sailor does not pass the Isle of Sombrero [the northernmost island of the Lesser Antilles] on his equatorial journey before the smell of the ripening swizzle stick greets his nostrils. Then comes the aromatic Falernum. . . . Then there is wormwood bitters, as noble a product of the soil as was ever brewed. These were all mixed together in some inexplicable way, well iced and swizzled, and needed only a dash of Angostura on the top to give it color, and there is your green swizzle.

Thus, we received a toehold on the formula: falernum, wormwood, and Angostura. Falernum, a celebrated product of Barbados, has passed through many stages. It may have originated as a punch of rum, ginger, lime, almond, and clove or allspice. Later it was a prepackaged liqueur of those ingredients. Today, that tradition is continued in brands such as John D. Taylor's Velvet Falernum, still produced in Barbados, but the craft cocktail world has also embraced a gamut of nonalcoholic syrup versions.

In our green-gold Bronze Swizzle we'll conjure verdancy with rolling waves of lime, delivered by falernum, punch syrup, and fresh juice. Wormwood comes courtesy of the Bësk liqueur, a potable wormwood bitters with layers of dill, grapefruit, and juniper. The result isn't quite green, but it's a potent flavor combination that brings freshness to the swizzle style.

RECIPE CONTINUES

**5 drops salt solution** (see page 27)

**2 dashes Angostura aromatic bitters**

**½ ounce strained lime juice**

**½ teaspoon Demerara syrup**

**½ ounce lime punch syrup** (see page 213)

**½ ounce falernum** (see below)

**1 ounce Letherbee Bësk Liqueur**

**1½ ounces La Favorite Rhum Agricole Vieux or Clément VSOP Rhum Agricole Vieux**

**Grated nutmeg, for garnish**

**Grated cassia cinnamon, for garnish**

**Cinnamon stick, for garnish**

**Channeled lime twist, for garnish**

- Combine all the ingredients in a mixing tin with 8 ounces of crushed ice. Flash blend for 5 seconds and pour unstrained into a chilled Collins glass (15 ounces) or metal swizzle cup with 8 ounces of crushed ice.
- Dust with grated nutmeg and cassia cinnamon. Garnish with a long cinnamon stick and a channeled lime twist. Serve with a straw.

---

## Falernum

This ingredient has several steps and many ingredients. Stick with it and you'll be among the top falernum producers on your block (excepting neighbors of R. L. Seale & Co. Ltd. of Saint Philip, Barbados).

**0.75 gram star anise**

**0.75 gram mace**

**1 gram nutmeg, grated**

**1.5 grams cloves**

**13 grams lime peel**

**28 grams ginger, thinly sliced**

**30 milliliters Diamond Reserve 151 Rum or Hamilton Demerara 151 Rum**

**125 milliliters Wray & Nephew Overproof Rum**

**0.6 milliliter almond extract** (measure 600 microliters with micropipette)

**15 milliliters strained lemon juice**

**50 milliliters strained lime juice**

**265 milliliters cane syrup, 66 Brix** (see page 52)

**830 milliliters gum syrup, 50 Brix** (estimated amount; see page 197)

- Grind the star anise, mace, nutmeg, and cloves using a mortar and pestle or a spice grinder.
- Combine the lime peel, ginger, and rums in a blender. Blend on high speed until the ginger is liquefied and the lime peel is thoroughly diced.
- Combine the spices and the mixture from the blender in a bag and seal it with a vacuum sealer. Place it in a water bath at 125°F for 12 hours or in the refrigerator for 24 hours.
- Fine strain the mixture, pressing on the solids to maximize extraction, then add the almond extract, juices, and syrup. This should yield about 830 milliliters of liquid. Combine the mixture with an equal amount of gum syrup.
- Bottle and refrigerate. It will keep for 6 months in the refrigerator. Makes 55 ounces.

# Scarlet Fog

*Cherry, not sherry*

In Trader Vic's *Bartender's Guide* of 1947, nestled among the 1,500 recipes, is the Fog Cutter, an unusual shaken drink with rum, gin, brandy, lemon juice, orange juice, orgeat, and—uniquely within the tropical canon—a cream sherry float. Despite it being difficult to balance and dependent on good floating technique, the drink has remained fantastically popular.

Yet there is another Fog Cutter roaming the wild, where the same split base is augmented with sour mix, deprived of orgeat, flash-blended, and topped with a float of cherry liqueur in lieu of sherry. The drink appears in Ted Haigh's *Vintage Spirits and Forgotten Cocktails* with the recipe and commentary provided by Tony Ramos, a legendary bartender who worked spots in the Los Angeles area including Madame Wu's Garden, the China Trader, and Don the Beachcomber's Hollywood flagship. Tony posits that the drink wasn't originally Vic's at all, but the signature beverage at a Hollywood steakhouse called Edna Earle's Fog Cutters (which, at the very least, existed). A similar Fog Cutter is prominent at the Tiki-Ti, which their menu claims was their most popular drink before the advent of the Ray's Mistake.

Did Tony create the oddball cherry version or preserve its legacy? And why cherry instead of sherry—perhaps the result of someone shouting out ingredients in a noisy bar? We may never know, but it served as the point of entry for this iteration, which puts the distinction front and center.

The two sweeteners in Tony's drink are sour mix and the cherry liqueur float. We could have tapped punch syrup or cordial to stand in for sour mix, but the intensity of cherry flavor we sought wasn't likely to come from a commercial cherry liqueur. So we'll lean on our house-blended red fassionola for cherry, incorporating lime through fresh juice and lemon through limoncello (which brings the booze we lost with the liqueur). With these three flavor powerhouses, we've managed to regulate dilution enough to slip in splashes of fresh orange juice (à la Vic) and invigorating soda (à la the Ti). As the convoluted fog disperses, a delightful vista is revealed.

"Fog cutter" is an early Americanism, traced to at least 1833, for an early morning tipple, akin to "eye opener" or, indeed, "cocktail" itself.

RECIPE CONTINUES

**5 drops salt solution** (see page 27)

**2 dashes Peychaud's Bitters**

**¾ ounce strained lime juice**

**¾ ounce strained orange juice**

**¾ ounce red fassionola** (see page 244)

**¼ ounce Beefeater Gin**

**½ ounce limoncello** (see below)

**½ ounce Scarlet Ibis Trinidad Rum**

**½ ounce Hamilton Demerara 86 Rum**

**¾ ounce Hine Rare VSOP Cognac**

**¾ ounce soda water**

**Cherries, for garnish**

**Bamboo leaf, for garnish**

- Combine all the ingredients in a mixing tin with 8 ounces of crushed ice. Flash blend for 5 seconds and pour unstrained into a chilled Collins glass (15 ounces) with 4 ounces of crushed ice.
- Garnish with 3 cherries speared to a bamboo leaf.

---

## Limoncello

This liqueur utilizes a very high-proof spirit (95 to 96 percent ABV) in order to minimize the infusion time and capture as many essential oils as possible before the more bitter, pithy flavors are extracted. This recipe makes for an intense limoncello with very clean flavors.

**16 grams lemon zest**

**250 milliliters 192 proof neutral spirit** (such as Lvov Spirytus or 190 proof Everclear)

**100 grams white sugar**

**125 grams water**

- Combine the lemon zest and 165 milliliters of the alcohol in a nonreactive container. Stir and let infuse for 15 minutes. Strain the alcohol into a second container, retaining the lemon zest. In the first container, combine the lemon zest and the remaining 85 milliliters of alcohol. Stir and let infuse for 5 minutes. Strain the alcohol into the second container and add the sugar. Whisk with a milk frother until the sugar is fully dissolved. Add the water and whisk briefly.
- Bottle and store away from direct sunlight. It does not need to be refrigerated and can be used in cocktails right away. Makes about 12 ounces.

# RESTORATION

Throughout this book, we've made clear our esteem for the classic drinks of the tropical canon and the bar minds that made them possible. While the entire book is focused on the restoration of classics, in this final section we pay respect to a group of the most influential midcentury tropical bartenders—investigating both their greatest hits and album cuts deserving of rediscovery. These recipes leverage many of the ingredients we've discussed throughout the book and provide exquisite opportunities to fully assert the techniques you've learned along the way.

As has been demonstrated in the preceding pages, it's much harder to "restore" a classic than to create a drink from scratch. A restored drink must be true to its original nature and its original inventor, while clearly showing the benefits of the changes made to it.

We're not claiming that the recipes that follow are the originals, merely our interpretations. No long-held bar secrets are to be revealed. Our understanding of these drinks comes from analyzing the printed evidence and our experiences in those bars that still remain. We intend our versions of these classics, well known and less so, to honor the artistic and industrious contributions of their originators.

# RAY BUHEN and the Tiki-Ti

*Where the 1960s never ended*

For us, the most significant aspect of Jeff Berry's *Sippin' Safari* isn't the many recipes he doggedly deciphered, or the detailing of larger-than-life figures like Vic and Donn, as crucial as those prominent elements are. We delight the most in Jeff's careful chronicling of the adventures of the actual bartenders doing the work at those famous bars; people who were relied upon every minute of every shift for turning out the profit-making elixirs, but who remained anonymous to the larger public. In *Sippin' Safari,* we come to know these men and their key contributions.

Ray Buhen (1909–1999) was one of the original four bartenders at Don the Beachcomber when it opened on McCadden Place in Hollywood in 1934. After putting in countless hours of sweat for Donn, Ray hopped around the Los Angeles cocktail scene of the 1950s, selling his serious skills as a free agent at venues such as the Seven Seas, the Dresden, and the Luau. Finally, in 1961, he opened a room of his own: the Tiki-Ti.

Unlike many of the places Ray worked, which were vast bar palaces with live entertainment and dance floors, the Tiki-Ti is a cozy neighborhood spot that just so happens to carry the torch for midcentury tropical drinks. A devoted community developed around it, and there's no doubt that this sense of family allowed it to survive the rise and fall of "Polynesian Pop" into the present day, stewarded after Ray's death by son Mike Sr. and grandsons Mike Jr. and Mark.

Because the bar is run much as it always has been, the Ti is a rare opportunity not only to enjoy midcentury tropicals made right, but to study their making. The Tiki-Ti's eighty-strong drink menu, which offers only the barest hints of what the drinks entail, is a cocktail time machine with the dials spinning wildly. The only way to grok these drinks is to order and find out.

But because the bar has survived the decades, the menu is like an Antarctic ice core sample, revealing what cocktails were like in different eras. It's a timeline that starts with the classics derived from Ray's experience with Donn and continues on to incorporate new trends. The Ti's menu is probably the only place on Earth to feature Donn's Penang from the 1930s next to the disco-era Swamp Water. Despite this wide range of drinks, the Ti heroically manages to have a consistent house style with a recognizable palette of favored flavors.

Following are our interpretations of two of the Tiki-Ti's most popular and historic drinks.

# Ray's Mystique (à la Ray's Mistake)

*Mistakes were made*

A "lost" ingredient of the ancient cocktail world is the syrup known as fassionola. Its Sphinx-like riddle continues to confound bartenders. Was its flavor passionfruit, as the name sort of suggests? Was it a medley of tropical fruit, as in many of its current reimaginings? How do we interpret older recipes that call for it? And since fassionola seems to have come in gold, red, and green, what was the difference?

Syrups made from a composite of different flavors are a mainstay of the Don the Beachcomber oeuvre, but before that they figured prominently in the toolbox of soda fountains. The 1897 *Standard Manual of Soda and Other Beverages* reports seven variations on what was known as Ambrosia Syrup, which contained combinations of citrus, berry, and vanilla. Ambrosia, of course, was a sustenance of the ancient Greek gods, as was nectar, which also found itself interpreted as a soda syrup. In Cincinnati and New Orleans, nectar is known as an almond and vanilla matchup, but sometimes in the historical record the "nectar" appellation ends up on "ambrosia"-like fruit syrups. (In Greek mythology, too, the names were often swapped around.)

Fassionola is in that tradition: another glamorous name applied to a combination of fruit and sugar, for the glorification of our beverages. It appears in Donn Beach drinks from the 1930s like the Pi Yi and Cobra's Fang, and in the Pat O'Brien Hurricane of the 1940s, which was itself based on a Ronrico recipe that explicitly included passionfruit syrup.

The San Diego–based Jonathan English Company was and is the most well-known purveyor of fassionola. It claims its recipe dates to 1914, although the company formed in the '50s, was dissolved in 1984, and revived under new ownership in the subsequent decade. Jonathan English still produces its varicolored varieties, and while they are not generally available at retail, to serve our mission and you, our thirsty readers, we tracked down some bottles for a serious sampling session.

While sharing commonalities, each of the English bottlings of fassionola is distinct in its taste. The gold combines pineapple, vanilla, and passionfruit. Red has a cherry-strawberry-raspberry flavor. Green is heavy on lime, but also exhibits guava and passionfruit. While many modern adaptations of recipes calling for fassionola substitute passionfruit syrup, the English products have more dimensionality, which suggested their application to new drinks.

So, what does this have to do with the Tiki-Ti? Well, possibly nothing.

RECIPE CONTINUES

The Ti keeps its secrets close, which includes the majority of its ingredients. We don't know that they use Jonathan English or any other fassionola in their drinks. But they are certainly aware of those products and their flavors, as well as their heritage with Don the Beachcomber. It certainly seems possible that the Buhens could have been inspired by these flavor combinations when creating their cocktails.

In any event the flavors we found in the gold and red fassionola syrups kickstarted a discovery process that led to the two recipes in this section. The gold inspired our homage to Ray's Mistake, while the red conjures the Toro, Toro, Olé! As for green, we need to hang on to *something* for a rainy day.

Ray's Mistake is the marquee cocktail at the Tiki-Ti, which comes complete with its own legend: In 1968, founding bartender Ray Buhen put the wrong ingredient into a drink he was mixing, but the customer preferred it that way. Since then, the Ray's Mistake has been one of the Ti's crown jewels and its recipe is accordingly guarded.

However, in early 2020, the Ti released its most detailed menu to date—and, for the first time, with drink descriptions! Therein, the Mistake is said to contain "passion, lime, gin, dark Jamaican rum float, and our secret flavoring which has a hint of vanilla." Passionfruit and vanilla recalled elements of the gold fassionola. Could a quasi-Mistake be assembled from the idea of fassionola and the list of flavors from the menu?

Instead of concocting a gold fassionola just for this drink, we'll build it from elements we already know. Let's stick with the sturdy passionfruit puree featured throughout the book, as it is the best delivery for that flavor. We can pull in vanilla-sandalwood syrup and pineapple gum syrup, which are also already in your repertoire. All together, this combination is a craft reinterpretation of gold fassionola, forming the basis of our heavily researched homage to Ray Buhen's serendipitous masterpiece. What the master formed in one blithe moment, the rest of us are still trying to fathom.

**5 drops salt solution** (see page 27)

**6 drops Bittermens Orange Cream Citrate Bitters**

**¼ ounce passionfruit puree**

**¾ ounce strained lime juice**

**¼ ounce vanilla-sandalwood syrup** (see page 163)

**¾ ounce pineapple gum syrup** (see page 197)

**1½ ounces Fords Gin**

**1½ ounces soda water**

**½ ounce Coruba Rum**

**Pineapple wedge, for garnish**

**Cherry, for garnish**

- Combine all the ingredients, except the Coruba, in a mixing tin with 8 ounces of crushed ice. Flash blend for 5 seconds and pour unstrained into a chilled Collins glass (15 ounces) with 4 ounces of crushed ice. Float the Coruba.
- Garnish with a pineapple wedge and a cherry. Serve with a straw.

# Toro, Toro, Olé! (à la Blood and Sand)

*Spice, smoke, and no sand*

When Spanish novelist Vicente Blasco Ibáñez's 1908 fictive contemplation of bullfighting, *Sangre y arena* (*Blood and Sand*), was adapted by Hollywood into a 1922 vehicle for Rudolph Valentino, it was honored with a cocktail bearing its name. The Blood and Sand—an up drink with equal parts Scotch whisky, Cherry Heering, sweet vermouth, and orange juice—is an unusual tipple with no particular aura of *duende*, but it's been a staple of the craft cocktail revival as one of a precious few Scotch cocktails.

The film was remade in 1941 with Tyrone Power, but it took longer for the drink to get a second look. In the 1970s, Ray Buhen updated it for the Tiki-Ti by replacing Scotch with Tequila, adding lime, and flash blending it. This balanced the acid and water content, while preserving the smoky, hearty flavor—a huge step forward for the drink. At the Ti, the Blood and Sand is revered enough to merit its own special ritual. Whenever it's ordered, the bartender lets a wind-up toy bull totter along the bar as the whole room chants, "*Toro! Toro!*"

For this refresh, Cherry Heering suggested red fassionola's cherry-oriented delights, providing the way into this drink's interpretation. To add back a bit of tangible *torero*, we considered the Mexican tradition of pairing Tequila with Sangrita, a side shot that is sometimes savory and tomato-based, but can also be a citrus and chile combo. Echoing the chile's spice are Bénédictine's herbaceous honey notes.

Don your *traje de luces* and prepare to engage with this raging *toro*.

**5 drops salt solution** (see page 27)

**1 dash pasilla chile tincture** (see below)

**3 dashes Peychaud's Bitters**

**¼ ounce passionfruit puree**

**½ ounce strained lime juice**

**¾ ounce strained orange juice**

**½ ounce red fassionola** (see page 244)

**½ ounce Bénédictine**

**½ ounce Pelotón de la Muerte Espadín Mezcal**

**1½ ounces Pueblo Viejo Reposado Tequila**

**Pineapple wedge, for garnish**

**Cherry, for garnish**

RECIPE CONTINUES

- Combine all the ingredients in a mixing tin with 8 ounces of crushed ice. Flash blend for 5 seconds and pour unstrained into a chilled red wine glass (14 ounces) with 4 ounces of crushed ice and 3 small ice cubes.
- Garnish with a pineapple wedge and a cherry. Serve with a straw.

## Red Fassionola, 66 Brix

This interpretation goes full force on the cherry flavor, utilizing the flavorful syrup found in the jars of Luxardo cherries. The often-discarded syrup has a gorgeous character, dark and intense. Combine it with the brightness of grenadine, and you've made a red fassionola that lives up to the legend. (For the drinks in this book, the best way to make fresh grenadine is with actual pomegranates, as explained in the recipe for grenadine on page 68.)

Commingling the two also strikes a desirable sugar content. Equal parts of the viscous 70 (or higher) degrees Brix cherry syrup and the standardized 50 degrees Brix grenadine results in a solution in the 60–66 Brix range, similar to a rich Demerara syrup and perfect for tropical cocktails.

**250 milliliters grenadine** (see page 68)

**250 milliliters Luxardo cherry syrup** (from the jar)

**1 long peel of lemon, oil expressed**

- Combine the grenadine, cherry syrup, and oils expressed from the lemon peel in a nonreactive container. Mix thoroughly.
- Bottle and refrigerate. It will keep for 2 weeks in the refrigerator. Makes 500 milliliters.

## Pasilla Chile Tincture

Pasilla chiles have both smoke and capsaicin in their profile.

**8 grams dried pasilla chiles**

**250 milliliters 151 proof neutral spirit** (such as Devil Spring Vodka or Diamond 151 Rum)

- Break up the chiles into small pieces. Add the spirit and broken chiles to a nonreactive container. Let the mixture steep for 24 hours, then fine strain and bottle. Does not need to be refrigerated. Makes 8 ounces.

# MARIANO LICUDINE and the Mai-Kai

*Rum, citrus, and a show*

Like the Tiki-Ti in Los Angeles, the Mai-Kai in Oakland Park, Florida, was built on the skills of a Don the Beachcomber alumnus. Mariano Licudine (1907–1980) was headhunted from his role at the Chicago outpost of Don the Beachcomber by the Thornton brothers, developers who imagined their own tropical getaway on US Highway 1. Opened in 1956, the Mai-Kai stands today as the most elaborate, fantastical bar-restaurant in the country, with seating for 600 among tapa cloth, intricate carvings, a garden with a waterfall, and a bar within a shipwreck.

Mariano was a key part of the Mai-Kai's identity, often featured in newspaper profiles and advertising. His genius for cocktails was what it was all about, and he delivered. Like Ray Buhen, he developed drinks by starting with the Donn canon, and as at the Tiki-Ti, the menu grew and grew. At present time, it contains 52 drinks, most of which were developed by Mariano during his long tenure.

Since there are no remaining Don the Beachcomber locations today, and as the menu has remained relatively stable since Mariano's retirement, the Mai-Kai is an important case study into the nature of midcentury tropical cocktails.

However, as this book has repeatedly noted, as ingredients disappear over time, it's necessary to recast old recipes in order to make them at all. Through its longevity, the Mai-Kai has faced this issue with its own menu. "We've had to become masters of re-creating our own recipes," the Mai-Kai's longtime manager, Kern Mattei, told us. "We're always trying to make sure that our menu will have the same drinks without a taste difference, even though it has a new rum or a new syrup." All the more reason to study how they've expertly updated their own recipes for changing times.

One significant difference between the Mai-Kai's offerings and their Donn antecedents is the size of the portions. The Mai-Kai, which offers a nightly Polynesian-themed floor show with dancers, drummers, and fire jugglers, prefers to serve one extra-large drink to last through the whole show, rather than disrupting it with another round of orders. This requires the drinks to withstand the dilution that would occur during a feature-length performance, which may be why it's the only bar left to put serious effort into ice shells and other time-release techniques.

# Rum Drum (à la Barrel O'Rum)

*Savor the layers of flavor*

Of Donn Beach's many creations, his Rum Barrel ranks as one of the most widely imitated across the diaspora of bars trying to replicate his aesthetic. Imitators tended to simplify Donn's formulation of multiple rums, juices, and sweeteners in ways prioritizing efficiency (with few iterations that stand out in a world of limitless rum punch variations). But in our opinion the Rum Barrel never really ranked among the best of Donn's work to begin with.

At the Mai-Kai, Mariano Licudine made a brilliant, deceptively simple modification: He discarded all sweeteners save honey and passionfruit syrup, which also conveys tartness. Suddenly, layers of citrus were unveiled and the drink made sense.

The changing availability of rums over the decades has made the Mai-Kai's Rum Barrel (served under the more playful moniker Barrel O'Rum) a moving target. While Jamaican rums never disappeared en masse, workarounds had to be found whenever a particular brand was discontinued. Drinks that might have called for Dagger in the 1950s turned to Appleton Punch in the '70s, and finally Kohala Bay in the '90s (all distilled by Wray & Nephew in Jamaica). When Kohala Bay was removed from the market in 2016, the Mai-Kai began creating its own blend from several commercially available Jamaicans, and we will, too.

The Rum Barrel should be easy-drinking while still revealing layers—not an easy task to accomplish with any drink, but here the key is how the blend of rums interacts with the blend of citrus. Worthy Park and Coruba bring complementing characteristics of Jamaican rum that are now hard to find in a single distillation, while the 151 Demerara totes additional firepower.

As in the Full Fathom Five (page 181), backing orange with calamansi amplifies the signature tang of Florida citrus. Note that Angostura bitters are an especially important part of the package; make sure you heave in three proper dashes.

Due to the popularity of the Rum Barrel, there are many barrel-shaped ceramic mugs on the market, but most are oversized for our version of the drink. We suggest a 16-ounce beer mug, which can also be found in barrel motifs.

**5 drops salt solution**
(see page 27)

**3 dashes Angostura aromatic bitters**

**¼ ounce strained calamansi juice**

**¼ ounce passionfruit puree**

**¼ ounce strained lime juice**

**½ ounce strained orange juice**

**½ ounce strained grapefruit juice**

**½ teaspoon Demerara syrup**

**½ ounce honey syrup, 66 Brix**
(see page 44)

**1 teaspoon St. Elizabeth Allspice Dram**

**½ ounce Hamilton Demerara 151 Rum**

**1 ounce Coruba Rum**

**1 ounce Worthy Park Estate 109 Dark Rum**

**Lime wedge, for garnish**

- Combine all the ingredients in a mixing tin with 8 ounces of crushed ice. Flash blend for 5 seconds and pour unstrained into a mug (16 ounces) with 8 ounces of crushed ice and 3 small ice cubes.
- Garnish with a lime wedge.

# Incantation (à la Black Magic)

*Coffee enchantment*

In proper dining tradition, the Mai-Kai presents a list of after-dinner drinks, including the Kona Coffee Grog, set ablaze tableside like Café Brûlot à la Broward County. But, since its inception, the Mai-Kai has made more innovative use of coffee in Mariano Licudine's mixture of fresh brew, rum, and citrus—the Black Magic. On the Mai-Kai's immense menu, it stands out for its special bite.

In the 1930s, Donn Beach developed the Jamoca, which Jeff Berry in *Sippin' Safari* termed an "early experiment" with coffee in a tropical drink, but it's in the Black Magic that coffee found its role within the tropical palette. Unlike the Black Russian, where coffee liqueur provides sweetness, or the Irish Coffee, where it acts as the acid, in Mariano's Black Magic coffee works in concert with an array of tropical juices. After all, coffee is itself a tropical fruit.

While the Mai-Kai uses hot-brewed coffee that has cooled, for our tribute we'll be calling upon cold-brewed concentrate. Slow extraction manages the acidity, so the coffee won't overwhelm the juices in the mix—as the Mai-Kai menu puts it, "smooth but forthright."

The biggest mystery surrounding the Black Magic is not the coffee but its sweetener. Jim "Hurricane" Hayward, writing on his website, The Atomic Grog, has reported that the Black Magic employs an element known only as No. 7 syrup. Black Magic fans have spun many theories as to its makeup, and to this day we do not know with absolute certainty, but we have learned (thanks to Berry's second edition of *Sippin' Safari*) that Don the Beachcomber used the label No. 7 for his ginger syrup. Knowing that Mariano was working in the Donn tradition, we think it more likely than not that the rhizome plays a role in the Black Magic. For our Incantation—as delicate as its inspiration—our standard ginger syrup is too intense. With the drink's honey and coffee, our more floral ginger oleo harmonizes perfectly.

The structure of this drink has commonalities with our Rum Barrel homage, outlining the house style of the marvelous Mai-Kai. The blend of rums is similar, with a few adjustments to correlate with coffee.

RECIPE CONTINUES

**5 drops salt solution** (see page 27)

**3 dashes Angostura aromatic bitters**

**½ ounce strained lime juice**

**½ ounce strained orange juice**

**¾ ounce strained grapefruit juice**

**¼ ounce ginger oleosaccharum** (see page 208)

**½ ounce honey syrup, 66 Brix** (see page 44)

**½ ounce cold-brewed coffee concentrate** (see below)

**1 teaspoon St. Elizabeth Allspice Dram**

**¼ ounce Hamilton Demerara 151 Rum**

**½ ounce El Dorado 15 Year Rum**

**¾ ounce Panamá-Pacific 9 Year Rum**

**¾ ounce Coruba Rum**

**¾ ounce Appleton Estate 8 Year Old Rum**

**Channeled lemon twist, for garnish**

- Combine all the ingredients in a mixing tin with 12 ounces of crushed ice. Flash blend for 5 seconds and pour unstrained into a chilled snifter (22 ounces) with 8 ounces of crushed ice and 3 small ice cubes.
- Garnish with a channeled lemon twist. Serve with a straw.

---

## Cold-Brewed Coffee Concentrate

There are many great bottled concentrates on the market, but this recipe will also do the trick. The subtleties of a single-origin coffee will be lost to the extraction of the cold brew method, so choose a workaday coffee instead. This recipe was adapted from one Jeffrey Morgenthaler developed for Stumptown Coffee.

**113 grams ground coffee**

**500 grams water**

- Combine the coffee and 250 grams of the water in a nonreactive container. Let the mixture rest for 30 minutes. Add the remaining water, cover, and refrigerate for 24 hours.
- Strain through a fine mesh strainer, then again through a basket coffee filter, to remove the oils. Bottle and refrigerate. Will keep for 1 week in the refrigerator. Makes 8 ounces.

# HARRY YEE and the Hilton Hawaiian Village

*Hawaiian originals*

By the 1950s, mainland Americans were far more knowledgeable about the vision of Polynesia manufactured in venues like Don the Beachcomber, Trader Vic's, and the Kon-Tiki than they were about actual Polynesian locales. Hawai'i was not, in actuality, one vast tropical bar, to the consternation of many mainland tourists.

Harry Yee (1918–2022) was among the Hawaiian bartenders to confront this issue early on. As he told journalist Rick Carroll in the *Honolulu Advertiser* of December 28, 1983: "When tourists came in, they said, 'Give me a Hawaiian drink.' . . . We didn't have any Hawaiian drinks. . . . There were no such things as exotic drinks. We had Planter's Punch, Singapore Slings, Zombies, Grasshoppers, and Pink Ladies, that was it. . . . So, we started thinking, 'Gee, we better start making something for the tourists—something catchy, not too strong, nice to sip.' "

Harry turned that crisis into opportunity, rolling out a series of original drinks over his long career at the Hilton Hawaiian Village and other iconic Honolulu destinations (including the Oceania, a 2,000-seat floating restaurant). Harry is credited with drinks like the Tropical Itch, Chimp in Orbit, Hawaiian Eye, Tapa Punch, Diamond Head, Hukilau, and many more. He was also a pioneer in "statement garnishes"—the first to popularize vanda orchids floating atop a drink, as well as paper umbrellas (as seen in the Tapa Punch), and even a miniature back scratcher for the Tropical Itch. His most famous and influential creation, of course, is the Blue Hawaii.

Working all on his own, outside of the traditions and influence of Donn, Vic, and the mainland band of bar consultants, Harry Yee designed the first truly Hawaiian cocktails, which are still enjoyed today, all over the globe.

# Blue Leilani (à la Blue Hawaii)

*Yee's blue heaven*

In 1929, the French surrealist Paul Éluard wrote, *"La terre est bleue comme une orange"*—the Earth is blue like an orange. He might have been off about the planet as a whole, but about that little bit of paradise known as the Blue Hawaii—Harry Yee's cocktail that's blue by sight, orange by taste—it's strangely prescient.

As a rule, comestibles aren't blue, so those that are prove particularly arresting. The world of drinking is suffused with aquamarine-tinted drinks, which have a reputation for leaning on their visual appeal rather than true gustatory justification. Which is why we want to rescue the Blue Hawaii from those who would do it wrong.

The liqueur curaçao, made from dried peels of the bitter orange, is naturally clear. In the first half of the last century, a fad developed for recasting it in various unnatural hues like green, red, and especially blue, which spirits producer Lucas Bols offered by 1912 as *"crème de ciel"*—cream of the sky. There are four pages of blue curaçao drinks in the *Café Royal Cocktail Book* of 1937, though *The Savoy Cocktail Book* of 1930 hedges its bets by specifying both orange-flavored Cointreau and blue-colored vegetable dye. A notable ancestor to the trend is the liqueur Parfait Amour with its indigo tone and vanilla-citrus finish.

If we contemplate the white sand beaches of Waikīkī slipping into the famously blue Pacific, can we fault the urge to invite a bit of blue into a resort cocktail? To be sure, the Blue Hawaii was built to the requirements of a resort—fast execution by the bartender, slow sipping by the guest—but Harry's bespoke spec is fruit-forward and multilayered, with vodka letting the notes of pineapple, lemon, and orange lap gently over each other.

Harry named his late-'50s drink for a song from the 1937 musical film *Waikiki Wedding*. Bing Crosby, the film's star, released "Blue Hawaii" as the B side of "Sweet Leilani." Leilani is a popular Hawaiian name, literally meaning "heavenly garland of flowers," but figuratively meaning "heavenly child," as children were carried on their parents' shoulders like a lei. The combination of the two tracks inspired the name of our version of this drink. Of course, the return of the song "Blue Hawaii" in the 1961 Elvis movie of the same name certainly helped to bring attention to the cocktail.

RECIPE CONTINUES

As its popularity grew, the Blue Hawaii drew imitators. A particularly vexatious one, going by the almost identical name Blue Hawaiian, was simply a Piña Colada over-sweetened with blue curaçao. As a result of this muddying of the cerulean waters, even in these enlightened times bar-goers are likely to receive a Blue Hawaiian when ordering a Blue Hawaii.

Our offering, the Blue Leilani, is a bridge over those troubled waters, connecting the coconut of the Blue Hawaiian to the original Blue Hawaii's multifaceted fruits.

This is made possible by fat washing: mixing a lipid in its liquid state into a liquor and then cooling it to a solid for removal. Fat washing captured the imagination of the drinking public thanks to Don Lee's Benton's Old Fashioned, served at PDT in 2007, which brought together two traditional Southern foodways by infusing bacon into bourbon. But it also works with vegetable fat.

Coconut oil's melting point around room temperature is particularly convenient for the process, and it's perfect for our purposes. Because fat washing removes some dominant notes from the spirit, we can start with something less neutral than vodka. We turn to Plymouth Gin, trusting that the oil will remove much of the juniper bite while leaving some citrus notes to linger beneath the coconut, an elixir worthy of Yee's fruit-layering masterpiece.

**5 drops salt solution** (see page 27)

**½ ounce strained lemon juice**

**1½ ounces strained pineapple juice**

**1 teaspoon cane syrup** (see page 52)

**½ ounce lime punch syrup** (see page 213)

**½ ounce Giffard Blue Curaçao**

**¾ ounce Denizen Aged White Rum**

**¾ ounce coconut oil–washed Plymouth Gin** (see below)

**Pineapple wedge, for garnish**

**Pineapple leaves, for garnish**

**Orchid, for garnish**

- Combine all the ingredients in a mixing tin with 8 ounces of crushed ice. Flash blend for 5 seconds and pour unstrained into a chilled Hurricane glass (15 ounces) with 4 ounces of crushed ice.
- Garnish with a pineapple wedge, pineapple leaves, and an orchid.

## Coconut Oil–Washed Plymouth Gin

Don't rush your concoction into the freezer. Don Lee has emphasized that room-temperature resting is a crucial step in wresting the most flavor from this combination.

Also, be sure to use unrefined virgin coconut oil; it must taste like coconut. There are some coconut oil products that have their flavor refined out.

This method is a great alternative to artificially flavored coconut liqueurs, and can be adapted to a number of spirits. Try it with a favorite lightly aged rum or blended Scotch.

**250 milliliters unrefined virgin coconut oil**

**1 liter Plymouth Gin**

- Place the coconut oil in a microwave-safe container and heat in the microwave until melted.
- Combine the oil with the gin in a nonreactive container. Allow the mixture to sit at room temperature for at least 4 hours.
- Freeze the mix for several hours until solidified.
- Strain off the spirit from the solid coconut oil, then pour through a coffee filter or cheesecloth to extract all solids. Strain and bottle. Does not need to be refrigerated. Makes 32 ounces.

# Frozen Banana Daiquiri

*Top banana*

It's hard to imagine that there was ever a world without the Banana Daiquiri, but someone, sometime, had to invent it. The earliest someone with a documented claim on that distinction is one Don Ramon, who, according to the September 19, 1946, edition of the *Miami News,* won first prize for his Banana Daiquiri at a cocktail competition held during the Wine and Food Society of New York's "A Tasting of Cooling Rum Drinks for Summer" event at the Hotel Pierre on June 27, 1946.

Harry Yee has also claimed to have been the first to put a banana in a Daiquiri, in the 1950s. It's perfectly plausible that Harry made this development without knowledge of Ramon's antecedent, and certainly it's his Banana Daiquiri that was introduced to generations of holiday-makers, cementing the drink in the tropical canon.

The Banana Daiquiri is an important milestone because it's perhaps the first drink placing bananas in a sour, rather than creamy, context. Before that, there was the Banana Cow (see our discussion along with the Banshee, page 45). Trader Vic was an enormous and lifelong proponent of this massively milky mixture, which spent the 1930s as the house specialty at Trad'r Sam in San Francisco. It was pitched mostly as a stomach tonic for the hung over.

In contrast to the complexities of the Blue Hawaii, the Banana Daiquiri offers simple pleasures. It's a whole fruit Daiquiri that's different because the banana is a different kind of fruit, and the rest of the drink just needs to clear its path. In this drink, banana is both a flavor and textural element, which is why adding banana liqueur to a Frozen Daiquiri isn't a practicable shortcut.

Freezing the banana, as is done with strawberries in the Frozen Strawberry Daiquiri (page 95), also won't work, as it causes the flavor to become too candied. Ripeness, even over-ripeness, is key: rescue a banana in its final moments of edibility.

Instead, use the freezer for your rum. This helps the temperature drop faster in the blender, causing less dilution. The delights of the Frozen Banana Daiquiri deserve to be in concentrated form.

**5 drops salt solution** (see page 27)

**60 grams unrefrigerated very ripe or even overripe banana** (about ½ a typical banana)

**1 tablespoon sugar mix** (see page 94)

**½ ounce strained lime juice**

**2 ounces Flor de Caña 4 Year Old Rum** (freezer temperature)

**¼ teaspoon xanthan gum**

**Banana chip, for garnish**

**Lime zest, for garnish**

- Combine all the ingredients, except the xanthan gum, in a blender. Dry blend (without ice). Once the sugar is fully dissolved, slowly add the gum while continuing to blend. Add 170 grams of crushed ice while continuing to blend. Pour unstrained into a large, chilled coupe (10 ounces).
- Garnish with a banana chip and lime zest.

# VICTOR BERGERON and Trader Vic's

*The Colossus that strode from Oakland*

Donn Beach and Trader Vic cast long shadows over this whole book, but let's shine one more candle on them before we drift into the night.

Victor Jules Bergeron Jr. (1902–1984) ran fast and far with tropical drinks, turning a cultural practice into a global commercial phenomenon. As his empire spread from nation to nation, his versions of tropical drinks became the most well known, the "default" of how we think of the category, based on their ubiquity but also their dependable quality. Witness the Mai Tai.

Many of those drinks were directly inspired by Cuban traditions as exemplified by Constantino Ribalaigua Vert, or the intricate work of Donn Beach. Yet the Trader Vic versions survived, as did the empire, in a much-reduced capacity in the United States but continuing in London, Munich, and Tokyo, plus a twenty-first-century burst of building in the Middle East.

In addition, Vic contributed many discoveries of his own. He prominently included spirits then unusual to the American palate, like pisco and Tequila. He embraced citrus beyond the lime and incorporated traditional bar syrups, like orgeat, into tropical drinks.

On the other hand, Vic's drinks were structured in line with the classics. He knew his cocktail history and drew inspiration from nineteenth-century drinks manuals even as he advocated moving beyond them. Was the Mai Tai rooted in Donn's Q.B. Cooler, El Floridita's Daiquiri No. 2, or the Knickerbocker à la Jerry Thomas? Why not all three?

Vic's encyclopedic bar knowledge, again and again deployed to sculpt enduring recipes, continues to invigorate tropical bartenders today.

# Yacht Rock (à la Tortuga)

*The beer was empty and our tongues were tired*

The Tortuga is one of Trader Vic's most baroque creations, sporting a lineup of hearty spirits that take it into Zombie territory. While it may have been devised to compete with some of the especially strong Beachcomber offerings, its roots are, as with many Vic drinks, back in Old Havana.

Constantino Ribalaigua Vert's Floridita Cocktail is a Daiquiri variation with crème de cacao, curaçao, grenadine, and sweet vermouth—one of the few classics to borrow the confectionery pairing of citrus and chocolate. Vic supercharged this formula in the Tortuga, adding 151 proof Demerara rum and 123 proof Cuban rum, while also turning the up drink into a tall one over crushed ice.

The Yacht Rock is to the Tortuga as that drink was to the Floridita—a tribute that steps things up. To focus on the chocolate and orange medley at the heart, sweet vermouth has been bisected into two ingredients: Campari amaro and vermouth de Chambéry. Campari bolsters the citrus while the vermouth's vanilla tones enhance the chocolate.

Seeing Campari, vermouth, and rum under the same roof sent our thoughts to the Negroni format, specifically the Kingston Negroni by the charming and talented Joaquín Simó, and we let those pleasant memories direct our rum selection.

The Yacht Rock is a rare tropical drink incorporating bitterness yet not based on the Jungle Bird. (Not to brag, but we even have another one in this unusual category; see the Puesta del Sol on page 214.) Vic included drinks with amari in his publications (such as Fernet Branca in the Don't Give Up the Ship from his 1947 *Bartender's Guide*), so Campari would not be out of character for him.

If you find yourself sailing around any of the islands named Tortuga in the Caribbean, Pacific, or Gulf of Mexico, load up Steely Dan and Gerald Rafferty on the LP changer and give this drink a try.

RECIPE CONTINUES

**5 drops salt solution** (see page 27)

**3 dashes Dave Arnold's chocolate bitters** (see page 46)

**½ ounce strained lime juice**

**½ ounce strained orange juice**

**½ ounce Tempus Fugit Crème de Cacao**

**½ ounce Comoz Blanc Vermouth de Chambéry**

**¾ ounce Campari**

**¾ ounce Smith & Cross Traditional Jamaica Rum**

**¾ ounce Coruba Rum**

**Lime, for garnish**

**Orange peels, for garnish**

**Grated dark chocolate, for garnish**

- Combine all the ingredients in a mixing tin with 8 ounces of crushed ice. Flash blend for 5 seconds and pour unstrained into a double Old Fashioned glass (16 ounces) with 8 ounces of crushed ice.
- Garnish with a lime boat with orange peel sails and grated dark chocolate. Serve with a straw.

# Red Sky at Night (à la Port Light)

*Manifesting mirth in Midwestern mariners*

While both Trader Vic and Donn Beach prized their original recipes as trade secrets, Vic let at least a little information trickle out in his series of bar guides, and amidst the fervor over the Mai Tai (page 71), many Trader Vic–derived drinks became centerpieces on the menus of his imitators. Though most of those bars have long since closed, intensive research efforts by cultural historians like Jeff Berry have recovered records that provide a rare glimpse into how bartenders reinterpreted these drinks even in the midst of their initial popularity.

The ambitious Kahiki Supper Club opened in Columbus, Ohio, in 1961 in a towering A-frame building reminiscent of a war canoe. Inside was a fantastical conception of a South Seas village, with bars and dining tables under thatched roof huts, approached by a bridge over a moat, and leading to a fireplace in the mouth of a stone Moai statue three stories high.

The Port Light, a Trader Vic staple, also became a signature for the Kahiki, albeit with modifications. The two Port Lights shared bourbon, passionfruit, and lemon. Where Vic goes all-in on texturizing the drink with honey and egg white, the Kahiki version lets grenadine provide extra viscosity. Our Red Sky at Night adopts a spicy rye backbone to knit together both conceptions.

The Minoan (page 160) and Winter in L.A. (page 49) are flash-blended with egg white, but neither is poured over crushed ice like the Red Sky at Night. Here, Vic's combination of egg white and honey foments a huge head of foam to disseminate the drink's aromatics.

At Trader Vic's, the Port Light was served in red glassware in the shape of a ship's lantern from the Imperial Glass Company of Bellaire, Ohio (a couple of hours down the road from the Kahiki). A complementary green glass was used for the Scotch-based Starboard Light. If you have that vintage glassware, now is your time, but please note that Imperial Glass tumblers do not currently meet the requirements under international law for navigation lights on a seagoing vessel.

RECIPE CONTINUES

**5 drops salt solution**
(see page 27)

**2 dashes Angostura aromatic bitters**

**½ ounce passionfruit puree**

**¾ ounce strained lemon juice**

**½ ounce egg white**

**½ ounce grenadine**
(see page 68)

**½ ounce honey syrup, 66 Brix**
(see page 44)

**2 ounces Rittenhouse Rye**

- Combine all the ingredients in a mixing tin. Flash blend without ice for 5 seconds. Add 8 ounces of crushed ice to the tin and flash blend for 5 seconds. Pour unstrained into a ship's lantern tumbler or a Collins glass (15 ounces) with 4 ounces of crushed ice.
- Serve with a straw.

# DONN BEACH and Don the Beachcomber

*The lion in winter where it's always summer*

Ernest Raymond Beaumont Gantt (1907–1989), variously known as Don Beach-Comber, Donn Beachcomber, and ultimately Donn Beach, was an enigmatic fellow who kicked off just about everything detailed in the pages of this book.

While his rival Trader Vic tracked the ideals exemplified by the Cuban Daiquiri, Donn experimented with heavier spices and layered rums from far and wide. There were never as many Don the Beachcomber locations as Vic amassed in his dominion, and after World War II, Donn made a tactical retreat to Honolulu.

He spent most of his latter days there, building the International Market Place, which featured an open-air shopping district and several restaurants in addition to the Waikīkī headquarters of his eponymous bar. Donn rests still in Honolulu, interred at the National Memorial Cemetery of the Pacific, appropriately known as the Punchbowl Cemetery due to its location within an extinct volcanic crater.

Donn's Hawaiian years found our artist as restless as ever. Donn was not satisfied with merely reproducing old work, so for the Waikīkī implementation of Don the Beachcomber, he adjusted and rethought his classic drinks from years gone by. Many of the changes embraced ingredients associated with the islands, bringing a bit of real Polynesia into the famed Polynesian fantasia.

# Donn's Demon (à la Zombie '56)

*The wraith of Waikīkī*

The Zombie unveiled by Donn in 1934 is the standard most people swear by, but its formulation was not known until Jeff Berry revealed his extensive research in *Sippin' Safari,* released in 2007. Before that, the only published recipes purporting to be a Don the Beachcomber Zombie were to be found in Louis Spievak's 1950 cookbook *Barbecue Chef* and a 1956 issue of men's magazine *Cabaret Quarterly.*

All three are distinct. The 1934 original is deep in mythic lore, and sports the mysterious Don's Mix absent from the others. (See page 149 for a discussion of the Mix.) The streamlined spec from 1950 performs well for passionfruit fanatics. But the 1956 iteration has found less love. As it's from Donn's later years, and specific to his Waikīkī bar, investigating it is a method of fathoming the progress of his craft.

Like most of Donn's 1934 lineup, the original Zombie is based on the rich, pungent, spicy Planter's Punch as served in its homeland of Jamaica. By the 1950s, Donn had refocused the drink on the tropical juices that had become popular with consumers. (At the International Market Place, Donn installed a fresh pineapple juice stand.) The 1956 Zombie exhibits signature touches of Donn's, such as falernum spice, the combo of absinthe and bitters, and the zing of grapefruit. But it adds more layers of fruit, suggesting that Donn recognized that guests visiting Hawai'i would expect a different style of Zombie.

As Donn's spec includes a maraschino and grapefruit pairing, integral to the Hemingway Daiquiri (page 58), we will apply the same solution: grapefruit punch syrup instead of juice. With grapefruit now a sweet rather than tart element, the role of the other juices can also be reconsidered. Pineapple becomes tart through acid adjusting. This balances the punch syrup but also enhances the fresh pineapple flavor.

By reversing the roles of these fruits, the 1956 spec comes into focus. Grapefruit perfumes the drink and pineapple adds lovely layers of texture. The Zombie rises again.

RECIPE CONTINUES

**5 drops salt solution** (see page 27)

**3 dashes Angostura aromatic bitters**

**1 ounce pineapple juice, acid adjusted to lime** (see page 180)

**½ teaspoon red fassionola** (see page 244)

**¼ ounce falernum** (see page 232)

**¾ ounce grapefruit punch syrup** (see page 216)

**½ teaspoon St. George Absinthe Verte**

**¼ ounce Luxardo Maraschino**

**½ ounce Coruba Rum**

**½ ounce Two James Doctor Bird Jamaica Rum**

**1 ounce Chairman's Reserve Rum**

**1 ounce Hamilton Demerara 151 Rum**

**Pineapple slice, for garnish**

**Pineapple leaves, for garnish**

**Orchid, for garnish**

- Combine all the ingredients in a mixing tin with 8 ounces of crushed ice. Flash blend for 5 seconds and pour unstrained into a chilled Zombie glass (16 ounces) with 8 ounces of crushed ice and 3 small ice cubes.
- Garnish with a pineapple slice, pineapple leaves, and an orchid.

# Doctor Funkenstein (à la Doctor Funk)

*Funkentelechy*

Dr. Bernhard Funk, from the town of Neubrandenburg in the north European duchy of Mecklenburg-Strelitz, stepped off a steamer in the Samoan capital of Apia in 1879.

"Because Apia was 'the nexus that joined Samoa to a foreign world', the small port-side community was also a cesspool of introduced disease," Leilani Burgoyne explains in her 2007 paper, "Going 'Troppo' in the South Pacific: Dr. Bernhard Funk of Samoa, 1844–1911." "The arrival of a fully qualified medical practitioner and surgeon who was prepared to live and work in Apia was therefore greeted by local residents as a long-awaited blessing.... Funk was an anomaly in that he was a non-missionary qualified doctor and was also willing to treat both settlers and the indigenous Samoans alike."

Whatever Dr. Funk's talent for medicine, his enduring fame owes at least as much to his prescription of absinthe. "Herr Funk was better known in the [Tahitian social club] Cercle Bougainville than Charcot or Lister or Darwin," Frederick O'Brien wrote in *Mystic Isles of the South Seas,* his 1921 romantic portrait of the region. "I had been introduced to a Doctor Funk by Count Polonsky, who told me it was made of a portion of absinthe, a dash of grenadine—a syrup of the pomegranate fruit—the juice of two limes, and half a pint of siphon water.... It would restore self-respect and interest in one's surroundings when even Tahiti rum failed." The thought was profound enough to have continued from his previous volume, *White Shadows in the South Seas,* where O'Brien noted that the concoction offered "an imparting of courage to live to men worn out by doing nothing."

A fellow traveler in the tropics, Donn Beach took up Dr. Funk's recipe and added it to his own repertoire, first fortifying it with dark Jamaican rum and continuing to make a number of refinements over the years. Other bars put their own spin on it too: The Tiki-Ti converted the base to gin and Trader Vic's rebalanced the citrus. Our version imagines how Donn might have approached its reconfiguration for his bar at the International Market Place in Waikīkī, with a reinvigoration of tropical fruit like many of Donn's other drinks of that period. Their bouquet buffs the absinthe while a lighter yet assertive mix of rums, we hope, restores your interest in your surroundings.

Since the 1970s, there's been no way to escape the fact that the word "funk" has been completely captured by the efforts of George Clinton and his bands Parliament and Funkadelic. It's now a core term for describing characteristics of music—and rum as well. In addition to his aural innovations, Clinton is a yarn-spinner, with his songs and albums parading a colossal list of dramatis personae, many developed with and portrayed by artist Pedro Bell, including Sir Nose d'Voidoffunk, Rumpofsteelskin, and Clinton alter ego Doctor Funkenstein. (Which means this drink may be the first to receive its nomenclature from the complex lineage of Bernhard Funk, Donn Beach, Mary Wollstonecraft Shelley, and George Clinton.)

Among Clinton's many brilliant coinages is "funkentelechy," combining the funk with entelechy, the complete realization and final form of a concept. Here, accordingly, we draw the curtain on our shared tropical drink journey. May everything you do be funky from now on.

**5 drops salt solution** (see page 27)

**¼ ounce passionfruit puree**

**¼ ounce guava puree**

**½ ounce strained lemon juice**

**½ ounce strained lime juice**

**½ ounce cane syrup** (see page 52)

**½ ounce grenadine** (see page 68)

**⅜ ounce Vieux Pontarlier Absinthe**

**1 ounce Denizen Merchant's Reserve Rum**

**1 ounce Barbancourt 5 Star Rhum**

**Mint sprig, for garnish**

**Cherry, for garnish**

**Channeled orange slice, for garnish**

- Combine all the ingredients in a mixing tin with 8 ounces of crushed ice. Flash blend for 5 seconds and pour unstrained into a chilled, stemmed Pilsner glass (16 ounces) with 4 ounces of crushed ice.
- Garnish with mint and cherry speared to a channeled orange slice. Serve with a straw.

# ACKNOWLEDGMENTS

Our first readers—Martin Doudoroff, Kayla Ferguson, Avery Glasser, Annene Kaye, H James Lucas, David Nir, and Marilyn Schaffer—strengthened and shaped this volume.

We gained many insights from interviews with Dave Arnold, Jeff Berry, Richard Boccato, Rick Carroll, Dale DeGroff, Meaghan Dorman, Jim Kearns, Kern Mattei, Julie Reiner, and Audrey Saunders.

The book would be but a shadow without the supreme talents of illustrator Pearl Shen and photographer Nico Schinco. Designer Raphael Geroni magically materialized our vision. The paintings of Emilio Sanchez inspired the cover.

We are beholden to Meaghan Dorman of Dear Irving on Hudson, St. John Frizell of Gage & Tollner and the Sunken Harbor Club, Bryan Schneider of Chez Zou, and Will Wyatt of Mister Paradise for offering the spaces where our photographs were elegantly staged. The photos included glassware from the collections of Edward Cercone, Adam Demerath, Adam Kolesar, and Don Schaffer.

The world-class palates of the team at the Sunken Harbor Club played a pivotal role in refining the recipes. Our gratitude goes to Chelsea Leigh Barrett, Stephen Bielawski, Jimmy Colon, Adam Demerath, Clayton Hughes, André Morales, and Dan Olivo.

Eve Bergeron, Tom Felt, Kerry Hucul, François Monti, Frederick H. Smith, Linda Walker, David Wondrich, and the staff of the New York Public Library research desk patiently answered our questions and assisted in finding historical material.

Our agent Stacey Glick, of Dystel, Goderich & Bourret, introduced us to Ann Treistman and her team at Countryman Press, including art director Allison Chi, copyeditor Diane Durrett, marketing manager Devorah Backman, and publicist Rhina C. Garcia—all of whom worked tirelessly to bring this volume to you.

We are grateful to them all for their contributions.

If you meet these folks, buy them a drink.

# BIBLIOGRAPHY


"'Banana Daiquiri' Wins First Prize." *Miami Daily News*. September 19, 1946, p. 14-A.

Arnold, Dave. *Liquid Intelligence: The Art and Science of the Perfect Cocktail*. New York: W. W. Norton, 2014.

Baker, Charles H., Jr. *The Gentleman's Companion*. New York: Crown, 1946.

———. *The South American Gentleman's Companion*. New York: Crown, 1951.

Beebe, Lucius. "Among the Epicures of Hollywood." *New York Herald Tribune*, March 22, 1936, E3.

———. *The Stork Club Bar Book*. New York: Rinehart, 1946.

Belgiorno, Maria Rosaria. *Behind Distillation: A Research Born After the Discovery in Cyprus of 2000 B.C. Alembics*. Nicosia, Cyprus: De Strobel, 2017.

Bergeron, Victor J. *Trader Vic's Book of Food and Drink*. Garden City, NY: Doubleday, 1946.

———. *Bartender's Guide by Trader Vic*. Garden City, NY: Doubleday, 1947.

———. *Trader Vic's Bartender's Guide, Revised*. Garden City, NY: Doubleday, 1972.

Berry, Jeff. *Beachbum Berry Remixed: A Gallery of Tiki Drinks*. San Jose, CA: Club Tiki, 2010.

———. *Beachbum Berry's Potions of the Caribbean*. New York: Cocktail Kingdom, 2014.

———. *Beachbum Berry's Sippin' Safari*. New York: Cocktail Kingdom, 2017.

Bitner, Arnold. *Scrounging the Islands with the Legendary Don the Beachcomber*. Lincoln, NE: iUniverse, 2007.

Boccato, Richard. *The Cold War (or How I Learned to Stop Worrying and Love the Ice)*. Unpublished manuscript, 2013.

Brillat-Savarin, Jean Anthelme. *The Physiology of Taste, or Meditations on Transcendental Gastronomy*. Translated by M. F. K. Fisher. New York: Alfred A. Knopf, 2009.

Burgoyne, Leilani. "Going 'Troppo' in the South Pacific: Dr. Bernhard Funk of Samoa 1844–1911." University of Auckland, Dept. of German and Slavonic Studies, 2007.

Carroll, Rick. "When your drink means more than a wet whistle." *The Honolulu Advertiser*, December 28, 1983, p. D1.

DeGroff, Dale. *The Craft of the Cocktail*. New York: Clarkson Potter, 2002.

———. *The New Craft of the Cocktail*. New York: Clarkson Potter, 2020.

Edmunds, Lowell. *Martini, Straight Up*. Baltimore: Johns Hopkins University Press, 1998.

Felt, Tom. *Glassware by Dunbar: Reprint of the 1938 Catalog of the Dunbar Glass Corporation*. Weston, WV: West Virginia Museum of American Glass, 2011.

Fougner, G. Selmer. "Along the Wine Trail: Explaining the High Cost of American Whisky—Requested Cocktail Recipes." *New York Sun*, April 14, 1934, p. 6.

Grimes, William. *Straight Up or On the Rocks: A Cultural History of American Drink*. New York: Simon & Schuster, 1993.

Guild, Caroline. *Rainbow in Tahiti*. Garden City, NY: Doubleday, 1948.

Haigh, Ted. *Vintage Spirits and Forgotten Cocktails: From the Alamagoozlum to the Zombie and Beyond.* Beverly, MA: Quarry, 2009.

Hahn, Fritz. "Rock-a-Hula Baby While You Still Can." *Washington Post,* February 13, 2004, p. 6.

Hiss, A. Emil. *The Standard Manual of Soda and Other Beverages.* Chicago: G. P. Engelhard, 1897.

Jha, D. N. (ed.). *Drink of Immortality: Essays on Distillation and Alcohol Use in Ancient India.* New Delhi: Manohar, 2020.

Laszlo, Pierre. *Citrus: A History.* Chicago: University of Chicago Press, 2007.

Mayabb, James. *International Cocktail Specialties: From Madison Avenue to Malaya.* New York: Hearthside, 1962.

McGee, Harold. "Just Add Water." *The New York Times,* July 28, 2010, p. D1.

Mencken, H. L., Raven I. McDavid, Jr. (ed.). *The American Language: An Inquiry into the Development of English in the United States (abridged ed.).* New York: Alfred A. Knopf, 1963.

Myrick, George F. *Incredible Virgin Island Adventure: A True Story,* 2008.

O'Brien, Frederick. *Mystic Isles of the South Seas.* New York: Century, 1921.

———. *White Shadows in the South Seas.* New York: Century, 1919.

O'Neil, Darcy. *Fix the Pumps: The History and Recipes of the Soda Fountain.* Ontario, Canada: Art of Drink, 2009.

Regan, Gary. *The Joy of Mixology.* New York: Clarkson Potter, 2003.

Regan, Gary, and Mardee H. Regan. *New Classic Cocktails.* New York: Macmillan, 1997.

Saucier, Ted. *Bottoms Up.* New York: Greystone, 1951.

Saunders, Audrey. "The Daiquiri Dossier: Pegu Perspective." *The Rum Reader,* September 24, 2018, https://www.rumreader.com/the-daiquiri-dossier-pegu-perspective/.

Schaffer, Ben. "The Local: How Dale DeGroff's Epochal Blackbird Revitalized Cocktail Culture." *The Rum Reader,* July 28, 2020, https://www.rumreader.com/the-local-how-dale-degroffs-epochal-blackbird-revitalized-cocktail-culture/.

Schumann, Charles. *Tropical Bar Book.* New York: Stewart, Tabori & Chang, 1989.

Sinesky, Alice. Transcript of interviews with Donn Beach. Honolulu: The Watumull Foundation Oral History Project, 1987.

Smith, Andrew F. (ed.). *The Oxford Companion to American Food and Drink.* Oxford: Oxford University Press, 2007.

Swizzle Stick [pseud.]. Letter, "The Green Swizzle of the Tropics." *New York Sun,* October 26, 1903, p. 4.

Talon, Manuel, Marco Caruso, and Fred G. Gmitter. *The Genus Citrus.* Duxford, United Kingdom: Woodhead, 2020.

Thomas, Jerry. *How to Mix Drinks, or the Bon-Vivant's Companion.* New York: Dick and Fitzgerald, 1862.

Weatherman, Hazel M. *Colored Glassware of the Depression Era 2.* Ozark, MO: Weatherman Glassbooks, 1974.

Winchell, Walter. "On Broadway." *New York Daily Mirror,* July 25, 1940, p. 10.

Wondrich, David. *Imbibe! From Absinthe Cocktail to Whiskey Smash, a Salute in Stories and Drinks to "Professor" Jerry Thomas, Pioneer of the American Bar.* New York: Perigee, 2007.

———. *Punch: The Delights (and Dangers) of the Flowing Bowl.* New York: Perigee, 2010.

Wondrich, David, and Noah Rothbaum (ed.). *The Oxford Companion to Spirits and Cocktails.* New York: Oxford University Press, 2021.

Wu, G., J. Terol, V. Ibanez, et al. "Genomics of the Origin and Evolution of Citrus." *Nature* 554, no. 7692, 2018, pp. 311–16.

# RECIPE INDEXES

The recipes in this book are grouped under the main techniques they exemplify, so that following them in order adds up to a class in cocktail creation. However, we also cross-reference recipes and ingredients to allow nonlinear discovery.

In addition to an alphabetical index, here are two other ways to slice up our offerings: by the drinks' preparation (shaken, stirred, flash-blended, and so forth), and by the menu categories once commonly used to distinguish cocktails by type, strength, and position during a meal—in this case inspired by the Don the Beachcomber's Dagger Bar in Honolulu, which demarcated drinks by time of day. *Italics* indicate illustrations.

## Alphabetical

## By Preparation

### BATCHED



### BUILT



### FLASH-BLENDED

## FROZEN



## HIGHBALL



## SHAKEN



## SLUSHY



## STIRRED

# By Menu Category

### HIGHBALLS AND LONG COOLERS



### BEFORE SUNDOWN



### AFTER SUNDOWN



### MUCH LATER

## APERITIFS



## DIGESTIFS



## DESSERT

# INDEX

*Italics* indicate illustrations.

Printed in Canada

For information about permission to reproduce selections from this book, write to Permissions, Countryman Press, 500 Fifth Avenue, New York, NY 10110

For information about special discounts for bulk purchases, please contact W. W. Norton Special Sales at specialsales@wwnorton.com or 800-233-4830

Manufacturing by TC Transcontinental
Book design by Raphael Geroni

Countryman Press
www.countrymanpress.com

An imprint of W. W. Norton & Company, Inc.
500 Fifth Avenue, New York, NY 10110
www.wwnorton.com

978-1-68268-715-4

10 9 8 7 6 5 4 3 2 1